THE END OF
NOSTALGIA

THE END OF NOSTALGIA

Mexico Confronts the Challenges of Global Competition

DIANA VILLIERS NEGROPONTE
editor

BROOKINGS INSTITUTION PRESS
Washington, D.C.

Copyright © 2013
THE BROOKINGS INSTITUTION
1775 Massachusetts Avenue, N.W., Washington, D. C. 20036
www.brookings.edu

Library of Congress Cataloging-in-Publication data
The end of nostalgia : Mexico confronts the challenges of global competition / Diana Villiers Negroponte, editor.
    pages   cm
    Includes bibliographical references and index.
    Summary: "Explores how Mexico, in transition from one-party rule to liberal democracy, can develop the institutional and cultural underpinnings needed to meet the challenges of global economic competition. Examines in particular education, energy, domestic politics, regional trade and investment, public security, and relations with the United States"— Provided by publisher.
    ISBN 978-0-8157-2494-0 (pbk. : alk. paper)
    1. Mexico—Economic policy—21st century. 2. Mexico—Economic conditions—21st century. 3. Mexico—Politics and government—21st century. 4. Globalization—Mexico. I. Negroponte, Diana Villiers.
    HC135.E553 2013
    330.972—dc23   2013013784

9 8 7 6 5 4 3 2 1

Printed on acid-free paper

Typeset in Minion

Composition by R. Lynn Rivenbark
Macon, Georgia

Printed by R. R. Donnelley
Harrisonburg, Virginia

Contents

Acknowledgments

Many individuals have supported this project since Arturo Franco brought the idea for it to Brookings in August 2011. While each of the authors bears responsibility for the contents of his or her chapter, we would like to thank Mauricio Cárdenas for supporting the initial project and Rafael Rangel Sostmann and Kevin Casas-Zamora for guiding the project. Andrew Selee, Robert Pastor, Carla Hills, Karen Antebi, and Karina Ramirez shaped ideas on regional economic issues. Eunises Rosillo, Roberto Arnaud, and Jorge Zendejas provided essential help, and Roberto Valladares collaborated in an important way on the security chapter. We extend our thanks to Michael Walton, Irene Mia, José Carlos Rodriguez Pueblita, and Katherine M. Tweedie for early feedback on the political and economic chapters. The ITAM and the Asociación Mexicana de Cultura supported the energy chapter, and IMCO, Fundación Cinépolis, and Fundación Televisa provided material and intellectual support to the education chapter. Willem G. Daniel, Carlos Aramayo, Alma Caballero, and Rashide Assad Atala provided invaluable research assistance, and Diana Caicedo played a key administrative role. Thanks also to Liberty Mutual, which supports the Latin America Initiative at Brookings. Finally, I am grateful to Eileen Hughes and Janet Walker, who asked perceptive questions and edited text as part of the strong team at the Brookings Institution Press.

DIANA VILLIERS NEGROPONTE

1

The End of Nostalgia: Mexico Confronts the Challenges of a Global Era

Mexicans are proud of their noble ancestors: the most ancient Olmecs; Zapotec artists; Mayan traders; and Aztec warriors, who created a century-long empire. Later, Spanish conquerors, bringing with them both disease and Catholicism, melded with the indigenous populations to form a complex people whose adherence to a glorious past and whose fierce nationalism have become an integral part of the national discourse. Every school child absorbs tales of conquest, religion, and art derived from Mexico's ancient roots. The oversized national flag, emblazoned with an eagle devouring a serpent, reminds citizens that they are both a conquering and a conquered people.

In the nineteenth and twentieth centuries, the United States presented an existential threat. The Mexican-American War (1846–48) represented the loss of vast tracts of Pacific coast and inland deserts, and it served to remind Mexicans that the outside world was avaricious. Accordingly, for more than a hundred years, relations between Mexico and its northern neighbor were contentious. What Mexico needed was a defensive posture toward the emerging North American giant, whose interference was evident in President Woodrow Wilson's attack on Veracruz (1914) and General Pershing's raid deep into Mexico's heartland (1916). In response, relations with nonaligned countries were preferred precisely because those countries contested U.S. hegemony.

The Mexican Revolution (1910–20) was merciless in its savagery. After ten years of brutality, Mexico's leaders were determined to avoid war. Meantime, the "Great Revolution" provided the justification for an authoritarian government that co-opted the power of the army, peasants, business community, and emerging trade unions. The grand bargain between each constituent group and the Mexican presidency was constructed to provide a means for the respective interests of each group to reach up to the highest authority. However, it was also a means for the president to send his instructions down to the groups. Co-option rather than conflict became an essential feature of the Mexican political system, and patronage was ingrained throughout the nation. Powerful sponsors ensured access to employment, food for the family, and advancement in the political sphere. In exchange, few groups contested presidential mandates. Tacit acceptance of the patronage system formed between the government and the people, assuring citizens of security and moderate economic prosperity. For seventy-one years, the president of the dominant party, the PRI (Partido Revolucionario Institucional [Institutional Revolutionary Party]), appointed his successor and ensured that opposition was never strong enough to threaten the state.

The doubtful legitimacy of the 1988 presidential election began the unraveling of the old regime. The patronage system continued to ensure Mexico's century-long single-party rule, but signs of its demise began to appear. President Ernesto Zedillo recognized the need to dismember the one-party state and, like Mikhail Gorbachev in the Soviet Union, spurred the process of political democratization. In Mexico, this process was viewed as weakness because it resulted in victory for the opposition party, the center-right PAN (Partido Acción Nacional [National Action Party]). However, there appeared to be no stopping Mexico's historic march toward a multi-party system.

The PAN won the presidency in 2000 but struggled to negotiate legislation with a congress that was no longer compliant. The transition of a society from authoritarian rule to a government based on consensus building is necessarily slow, and the tendency to return to the old authoritarian ways remains strong. Political players found the freedom to contest the president through the media as well as in the halls of congress, and the 1998 decision to distribute federal resources to the thirty-one state governors, without demanding commensurate accountability, resulted in the diminution of the president's authority. State governors acquired new powers based on the transfer of federal funds, and a new power equilibrium ensuring greater rights for citizens spread throughout the nation. It also affected foreign relations.

Mexico's history reflects the national pride of its people, a hierarchical state structure that provided security, and a tradition of commercial trading. Mexicans, like the British, are traders. They have always ventured into new waters to find different goods, enriching their churches and homes with jade from

Meso-America, turquoise from the deserts of modern-day Arizona, silk from China, and ivory from the Philippines. In exchange, they exported gold, silver, and foods. Apart from the times of intense internal turmoil during the War of Independence and the Revolution, Mexicans have always looked beyond their nation's borders; thus, their contemporary engagement with the modern world is a phenomenon with ancient roots.

President Miguel de la Madrid's decision to join the General Agreement on Tariffs and Trade (GATT) in 1986 and the pursuit of a free trade agreement with Canada and the United States by his successor, Carlos Salinas de Gortari, opened the economy to new trading opportunities. But was the nation that had protected itself behind high tariff walls ready to engage with international competitive forces? In 1993, this author's speech before an association of engineering companies in Guadalajara on the opportunities presented by the North American Free Trade Agreement (NAFTA) was greeted with significant criticism. The prospects of competitive trade implied a threat, and all the questions from the audience centered on how their businesses might survive. Twenty years later, the same companies have either gone out of business or adapted to the reality of international trade and global competition.

Today, Mexico has become a manufacturing center, with family-owned companies engaging in international trade and acquiring new technologies. Protectionist regulations are being dismantled, and young business leaders learn colloquial English, study at international business schools, and connect easily with foreigners. The young men and women whom I met over two years at a business summit held in the colonial city of Queretaro are not resigned to the new reality; instead, they seek to thrive in a competitive world. Their network is global, including colleagues encountered at school, at professional conferences, and on social media. They interact with foreigners with enthusiasm; they take on new international contracts with excitement.

But the old ways are hard to eradicate. The yearning for the predictability of government contracts, dependence on political patrons, and reliance on family ties have not disappeared. The authors of these chapters therefore agreed on the need to analyze and relate how the old Mexican system is changing. Metamorphosis is not easy; economic and political transformation, in particular, is hard. However, a proud trading people can find confidence in their heritage. I believe that continued democratization and exposure to foreign competition is inevitable, but efforts to put the brakes on that process should not be ruled out. Therefore this volume is also about protest and conflict deep within the Mexican political economy.

In chapter 2, "Piecing Together the Puzzle of Mexico's Growth," Arturo Franco seeks to understand why the lusty 7 percent growth of the 1960s and 1970s has declined to an average of 3 percent growth today. He provides a comprehensive review of the factors that might explain Mexico's lack of competitiveness—rigid labor markets, inadequate infrastructure and access to finance, size of the informal labor sector, high cost of energy, poor education system, and Chinese competition—and asks whether those factors explain Mexico's economic underperformance. Using data from Harvard's Center for International Development, Franco asserts that there is no single constraint to growth that affects the Mexican economy across a broad range of activities. He concludes that Mexico's weak economic growth remains a puzzle.

What is known is that if its economic constraints can be overcome, Mexico has very high growth potential. Franco notes that a BRIC paper drafted in 2005 by Goldman Sachs concluded that Mexico, given its distinctive geopolitical location, ample natural and human resources, and highly competitive characteristics, had the potential to rival Brazil, Russia, India, and China. Mexico's Goldman Sachs Growth Environment Score ranks in the upper third, above Brazil's but below China's. Moreover, according to Harvard's Atlas of Economic Complexity Index, which measures growth potential, Mexico's per capita GDP is expected to increase 3.5 percent a year during the 2013–20 period. In addition, overall GDP is expected to grow by 4.56 percent over the same period. Such growth is essential if Mexico is to meet the expectations of the 2 million citizens who enter the work force each year in search of quality jobs.

In chapter 3, "Unlocking Mexico's Political Gridlock," Franco examines the Mexican legislative agenda. He observes that in the last twenty years, Mexico has moved from a hegemonic party system under the PRI to a political equilibrium in which the three major political parties together account for 90 percent of the votes but none exceeds 42 percent. Since the election of a president from the PAN in 2000, no president has enjoyed a majority in congress, and coalitions must be formed to pass legislation. Historical review suggests that this is feasible during the first three years of a president's six-year term (*sexenio*) but becomes much harder in the second three years—a situation familiar to observers of the U.S. Congress.

Franco asks whether the accusation that the national legislature is a "Siesta Congress" is fair, pointing out that a good number of constitutional reforms requiring two-thirds approval were initiated and passed during President Felipe Calderón's first three years in office. A slight decrease is shown in the last three years, but the number should silence those who claim that a "do-nothing" congress appears during that period. In response to the critique that the bills passed were relatively insignificant with respect to the national interest, Franco notes that in the last ten years Mexico's congress has passed major health care reform, pension reform, judicial reform, and labor reform. It also created a new freedom of information law and a corresponding agency, as well as less significant changes with respect to electoral laws, the energy sector, and the fiscal regime.

However, political reforms that Calderón proposed in 2009—which would have allowed for reelection of legislators, a run-off election for presidential candidates, reduced campaign costs, participation of independent candidates in elections, and an increased voice for the electorate in forming legislation—were blocked by the PRI's intransigence. Franco asks whether the PRI, with an increased number of legislative seats in 2012, will find it advantageous to introduce similar political reforms. If so, how might the PAN and PRD (Partido de la Revolución Democrática [Party of the Democratic Revolution]) now respond?

Duncan Wood, in chapter 4, "Energy Challenges for the Peña Nieto Administration," examines the serious decline in petroleum reserves in Mexico and presents specific solutions to augment energy supplies. Wood diagnoses internal problems within PEMEX (Petróleos Mexicanos), the state-owned petroleum company—political interference, corrupt practices, and lack of accountability—and the role played by STPRM (Sindicato de Trabajadores Petroleros de la República Mexicana), the oil workers' union. Without significant changes to allow opening of the oil industry to private investors, he fears that PEMEX will not be able to take advantage of new exploration in the Gulf of Mexico and the shale fields of northeastern Mexico. Wood analyzes the consequences of developing shale gas and warns that given the high projected cost of developing the fields and the current low market price of gas, it makes little immediate sense to develop Mexico's shale reserves. He also examines Mexico's renewable energy potential, concluding that the long-term outlook for Mexican energy output is extraordinarily positive.

In chapter 5, "Toward a Regional Competitiveness Agenda: U.S.-Mexico Trade and Investment," Christopher Wilson examines the record for Mexican trade and investment and demonstrates that both are strategic drivers of the U.S.-Mexican relationship. Mexico is the United States' second-largest export market, and the United States is by far Mexico's largest export destination. Merchandise trade has quintupled since 1993, and bilateral foreign direct investment holdings have grown sixfold. However, the high growth rate of bilateral trade and investment between 1994 and 2000 has slowed, leading Wilson to ask what more could be done to spur trade and increase regional competitiveness.

With the technological and logistical improvements that define modern manufacturing, labor costs now account for less and less of production costs. The consequences are critical for Mexico: foreign manufacturers are less likely to move their plants abroad in search of low wages and more likely to seek out locations where needed human capital and robust supply chains exist. Therefore the quality of Mexican engineers, the education of its workforce, and its capacity to innovate become critical components of regional trade, investment, and competitiveness.

Wilson favors a strategic regional approach to the Trans-Pacific Partnership (TPP), a nine-nation free trade group that Mexico and Canada joined in 2012. He believes that a joint pivot toward Asia by Mexico, Canada, and the United States to coordinate trade policy and negotiate agreements would benefit all three nations. He also believes that the TPP creates an opportunity to strengthen NAFTA without renegotiating it because the TPP seeks to create common standards and regulations in multiple areas, including financial services and intellectual property, that should facilitate the joint production of North American goods destined for the global market.

In chapter 6, "The Priority of Education in Mexico," Armando Chacón examines both the quantity and quality of education in Mexico, noting its bottom rank in Program for International Student Assessment (PISA) scores for OECD countries. He points out the value added with respect to earnings, health, absorption of new technologies, and parenting skills for every additional year of schooling beyond the sixth grade. Recognizing that all recent presidential candidates have made improved education one of their highest priorities, Chacón examines public policies to reach that goal. He advocates a comprehensive assessment of teachers, their capabilities, and their performance in the classroom, but he recognizes the opposition from both the largest teachers' union, the SNTE (Sindicato Nacional de Trabajadores de la Educación [National Educational Workers Union]), and the CNTE (Coordinadora Nacional de Trabajadores de la Educación [National Coordinator of Educational Workers]). With the arrest of the SNTE's leader in February 2013, the union may become more reasonable and willing to work with the new government. Meantime, Chacón calls for continuing teacher training, with courses and level of training determined both by the needs of specific teachers and by the level and performance of specific schools—a lengthy and costly undertaking. A recent performance measurement, RENAME (Registro Nacional de Alumnos, Maestros, y Escuelas [National Registry of Students, Teachers, and Schools]), provides detailed information on school infrastructure as well as the monitoring of teacher and student performance. Chacón recommends that this information be published so that parents and the public may distinguish schools that add value from those that detract. With the publication of this information, government, civil society, and the business community can coordinate their responses to meet the needs of Mexican students.

The location of schools and the socioeconomic background of both students and teachers make a difference. Programs to improve education must be evaluated against carefully designed criteria in order to develop programs that stretch the value of public funds and achieve more positive results. Meantime, Chacón notes that Peña Nieto's administration has yet to propose a budget that provides the funding needed to implement critical educational reforms.

In chapter 7, "Security Policy and the Crisis of Violence in Mexico," Eduardo Guerrero presents a critical assessment of the current public security situation in Mexico and argues in favor of the process to alter security strategies. Guerrero identifies the weaknesses in President Calderón's efforts to stop drug trafficking and discusses Calderón's shift toward reducing violence and crime, a shift that is accentuated and ongoing under President Peña Nieto. The number of intentional homicides in Mexico has diminished since the fourth quarter of 2011 as a result of four factors: increasing public demand to stop the violence; more effective intervention by the federal and state governments; reduced availability of new recruits; and a shift to a selective law enforcement strategy. However, serious problems still remain, such as the slow pace of implementing reforms to criminal justice procedures; inadequate resources to reform the correction system; and inadequate domestic intelligence capabilities.

Guerrero presents eight recommendations that are tailored to address the main sources and consequences of organized crime–related violence. The goal is to reduce predatory crime, such as extortion and kidnapping; reduce violence throughout Mexico; improve the criminal justice system; and regain control of the prisons. To achieve these goals, Guerrero proposes a combination of short-term measures intended to deliver results in a six-month period, such as imposing a curfew on main roads to ensure public safety, conducting a prison population survey, and separating the marijuana market from the market for more damaging drugs. He also recommends medium-term interventions, intended to deliver results in a two-year period, to strengthen security-related institutions. In order to undertake intensive institution building, Guerrero calls on outsiders with meaningful international experience to help design effective interventions for Mexico.

In chapter 8, "The Mérida Initiative: A Mechanism for Bilateral Cooperation," Diana Villiers Negroponte examines the initiative, the principal mechanism for bilateral relations since its inception in 2007, and asks whether it has now outlived its usefulness. When President Calderón invited the U.S. government to collaborate with the Mexican government at a previously unseen level of integration, the State Department welcomed the opportunity. Since that time, the Mérida Initiative has evolved from being a mechanism for the delivery of sophisticated and custom-made equipment to being a developer of programs that support the training of law enforcement officers and seek to prevent youth from joining gangs. She traces the evolution of the initiative from integrated information sharing and operations to the creation of stand-alone programs such as the twenty-first-century border program. What lies ahead?

After announcing that it will concentrate less on drug interdiction and more on combating violence, the Mexican government is reexamining its security policy. That requires hiring more effective and less corrupt law enforcement officials at the state and municipal levels—an undertaking that President Peña Nieto is best placed to carry out as his party, the PRI, holds nineteen governorships among the thirty-one Mexican states and the Federal District (Mexico City). Under these circumstances, what might the most appropriate U.S role be? The U.S. government's priorities have also evolved: they now focus on strengthening the rule of law within Mexico, which means training investigative police, prosecutors, judges, and prison personnel. Focus is also given to empowering youth by developing alternatives to gang life, such as programs to train young people in IT skills. Given the evolution of policy on each side of the border, should both governments agree that Mérida has run its course? If so, what bilateral mechanism might emerge to ensure ongoing U.S. congressional support and funding?

In chapter 9, "Mexico and the United States: Where Are We and Where Should We Be?" Andrés Rozental demonstrates his deep knowledge of the U.S.-Mexican bilateral relationship, which is based on thirty years of negotiations with the U.S. government on maritime boundaries and fish stocks, nuclear nonproliferation, border issues, and immigration. From the days of a prickly relationship in the 1970s and 1980s, he notes significant improvement in bilateral affairs. However, Rozental stresses the underlying Mexican tension over U.S. failure to address long-standing problems related to immigration, drugs, and the southward shipment of firearms. He regrets that security issues have dominated the bilateral relationship and calls for a more muscular U.S. response on drug consumption and shipment of arms and bulk cash in order to meet what Secretary of State Hillary Clinton has acknowledged is the U.S. "shared responsibility" for the violence in Mexico.

Rozental raises a question asked by many Mexicans today: "Why should Mexico expend so much money and effort on keeping drugs out of the United States when Americans fail to do much about the demand side of the equation?" Should the Peña Nieto government focus more on protecting its citizens from robbery, kidnapping, and extortion instead of keeping drugs away from U.S. consumers?

As Mexico confronts significant challenges from economic competitors in Asia, it is time to "de-securitize" the bilateral agenda and give priority to trade, investment, and climate change. Rozental joins Wilson in advocating a joint North American approach to the Trans-Pacific Partnership and argues that the United States should coordinate with Canada and Mexico in these negotiations as well as in the Trans-Atlantic Trade. Rozental also calls for frequent high-level discussions among the three North American nations to develop common positions on three subjects on the G-20 agenda, namely climate change, food security, and economic development, given their joint interest in these issues.

Finally, recognizing that the hemisphere is not homogeneous, Mexico, with one foot in North America and the other in South America, can act as a bridge. It can help develop assistance programs for the neediest countries in the region and diminish the need of the ALBA socialist countries, such as Venezuela, Ecuador, and Bolivia, to pursue policies that deliberately exclude the United States and Canada.[1]

Note

1. ALBA refers to the Alianza Bolivariana para los Pueblos de Nuestra América (Bolivarian Alliance for the Peoples of Our America).

2

Piecing Together the Puzzle of Mexico's Growth

By the end of the twentieth century, Mexico had convincingly positioned itself as one of the most promising emerging economies in the world. After several episodes of economic instability, marked by high inflation, fiscal excesses, and recurring financial crises, the country, following the economic orthodoxy of the time, experienced an impressive transformation. Moreover, Mexico's entrance into powerful trading blocs and groups that had included only more developed economies was seen as a promising sign. Heading into its first democratic transition in modern history, this geographically privileged, globally integrated, and resource-endowed country seemed set for a prosperous future.

Yet for at least two decades now, Mexico's economic performance has been disappointing. Having achieved average growth rates of almost 7 percent during the 1960s and 1970s, the country has settled recently for rates closer to 2 percent. In addition, both income per capita and total factor productivity have stagnated and remain close to 1980 levels. Consequently, during a period in which countries such as India and Chile almost doubled the size of their economies, Mexico's expanded by less than one-fifth.

The conventional explanation for this lackluster growth is that the country is constrained by a series of flaws that continue to deter its growth. Typically these flaws are said to include, among others, an overly rigid labor market, inadequate infrastructure, limited access to finance, the informal labor market, the high cost of energy, and a poor public education system. Despite some agreement among analysts on a set of reforms that could halt the country's decline, there is no consensus on exactly how and how much each of these flaws actually hurts the economy.

In this context—and with the added impetus of the recent presidential election—it is imperative to review, discuss, and understand Mexico's most pressing challenges, policy options, and reform priorities from an economic growth perspective. Enrique Peña Nieto, sworn in as president in December 2012, campaigned on the explicit promise of tripling Mexico's growth average of the last decade during his six-year term, but is that an achievable goal? The purpose of this chapter is to place the reader in the middle of Mexico's current economic state of affairs and serve as a concise briefing on the growth prospects of a country that looks to its future with both hope and uncertainty.

Growth Matters

The last few years have witnessed a prolific increase in the analysis of Mexico's economic growth and development dynamics. Publications have ranged from in-depth reports produced by leading organizations, such as the World Economic Forum's *Mexico Competitiveness Report* and the World Bank's *No Growth without Equity?* to scholarly articles by leading economists Ricardo Hausmann, James J. Heckman, and Gordon H. Hanson, to more recent publications by Mexico's intellectual "red circle," including best sellers by Carlos Elizondo Mayer-Serra, Héctor Aguilar Camín, Jorge Castañeda, and Luis Rubio. Yet despite their scrutiny of the evidence, the divergence among their conclusions is notable.

One of the recurring themes in this expanding literature is that Mexico's economic performance is rather puzzling.[1] We can find as many explanations for Mexico's low growth as there are variables in almost any comprehensive growth or competitiveness framework: everything and anything seems to be included. Hanson explains it best: "Any discussion of growth and development in Mexico ends up resembling a Diego Rivera mural, overstuffed with historical characters that collide in repeated and unexpected ways. Mexico's underperformance is over-determined."[2] This perplexing situation, in which Mexico's economic performance seems to be overanalyzed and still not clearly understood, provokes a couple of questions.

First, why focus on economic growth? A simple variable that aggregates the total economic activity of a country could be too narrow for relevant discussion and too broad based for any specific or useful recommendation. However,

I believe that zooming in on Mexico's recent growth performance is pertinent, for two reasons. First, while many other variables are used to measure a country's progress, gross domestic product (GDP) growth rates usually have a strong and positive correlation with the most commonly used development indicators, including the quality of a country's health and education systems, its public institutions, and its democracy.[3] Even small differences in growth, when sustained over long periods of time, can make or break a country's development trajectory. As Easterly and many others have argued, while GDP growth is not by itself the "holy grail" of development, it is in many ways a necessary precondition for social advancement and an important phenomenon to study.[4]

Moreover, achieving higher growth rates has never before been as imperative for Mexico as it is today. With almost half of Mexico's comparatively young population of 113 million living in poverty, a combination of glaring inequality, mounting social tensions, and a change in the government's public security strategy has fueled a recent surge in organized crime and violence. To make matters worse, survey respondents continually show dramatically lower levels of trust in government and democratic values, primarily because of politicians' inability to agree on many urgent matters. In recent polls, economic growth has become the main concern of Mexican citizens, overriding security. Growth was a central issue in the country's 2012 presidential election.[5]

Second, Mexico needs to understand why its economic growth has been so weak. The main purpose of this chapter is to summarize and discuss in a coherent way the different pieces of the growth puzzle. It analyzes Mexico's economic history from 1960 to 2011, moving quickly through the different growth and reform stages, and then presents a brief comparative analysis of Mexico's economic performance in order to evaluate why Mexico has not closed its per capita income gap with the world's richest countries. A thorough review of some of the most common explanations for the country's loss of productivity follows, and the chapter concludes with an assessment of Mexico's future growth prospects.

Mexico's Episodes of Economic Growth

During the last fifty years, Mexico's growth trajectory has been volatile, marked by sharply distinct stages (figure 2-1). The many extreme year-on-year variations in Mexico's growth are captured in the famous opening lines of Charles Dickens's a *Tale of Two Cities*: "It was the best of times, it was the worst of times . . . we had everything before us, we had nothing before us . . . in short, the period was so far like the present period, that some of its noisiest authorities insisted on its being received, for good or for evil, in the superlative degree of comparison only."

The "best of times," also known as the Mexican Miracle, was an unprecedented stage of high growth that occurred between 1960 and 1979, when national income grew more than 6.7 percent a year.[6] That level of economic expansion was the result of inward-looking economic policies—such as import substitution, which developed domestic markets—and resulted in significant improvement in productivity, income per capita, and living standards. It was also a result of sound fiscal management and the lack of external shocks over almost two decades.

As a net importer of oil up until the mid-1970s, when large discoveries turned the country into a significant exporter of petroleum products, Mexico was hit by the first oil price shock in 1973 and a subsequent slowdown in overall productivity around 1975; however, it recovered later in the decade as public expenditure on infrastructure in the energy sector boosted aggregate demand. By 1980 various macroeconomic imbalances that had been building since the mid-1970s led to an external debt crisis and sharp declines in GDP growth. The miracle was over.

During the subsequent period, known as the "Lost Decade" of the 1980s, Mexico's macroeconomic performance was hampered by output reduction, inflation, and a distorted exchange rate policy. During the worst of the 1982 crisis, output fell by 3.9 percent, inflation topped 120 percent a year, and the peso depreciated by 90 percent.[7] Real GDP grew by less than 1 percent in 1980–87, while GDP per capita declined sharply and total factor productivity growth turned negative.

Mexico's Great Transformation

In 1982, after having declared a moratorium on servicing one of the largest foreign debts in the developing world at the time, Mexico embarked on an impressive process of trade liberalization, opening of the economy, and macroeconomic stabilization. The depth and breadth of the many changes that took place in both economic and political terms are reminiscent of those depicted in the classic 1944 work *The Great Transformation,* by Austro-Hungarian political economist Karl Polanyi.[8] The government's aim at the outset was to solve three endemic problems: extreme vulnerability to external shocks, double-digit inflation, and current account and fiscal deficits. With

Figure 2-1. *Mexico's Economic Growth History, 1960–2011*

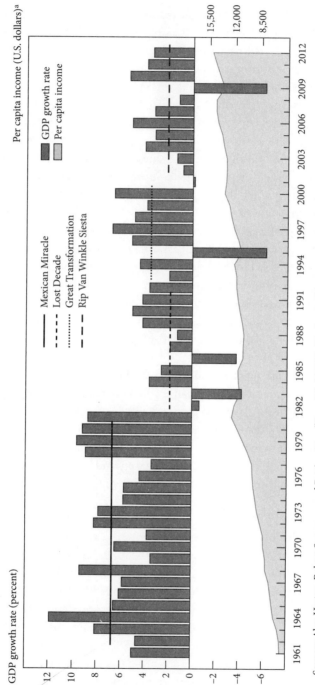

GDP growth rate (percent)

Per capita income (U.S. dollars)[a]

- Mexican Miracle
- Lost Decade
- Great Transformation
- Rip Van Winkle Siesta

GDP growth rate

Per capita income

Sources: Alan Heston, Robert Summers, and Bettina Aten, "Penn World Table Version 7.1" (University of Pennsylvania, Center for International Comparisons of Production, Income, and Prices, 2012) (http://pwt.econ.upenn.edu/), and "World Development Indicators 2012" (Washington: World Bank, 2012) (https://openknowledge.worldbank.org/handle/10986/6014).
a. Income per capita values are in purchasing power parity (2005).

help from the United States through the Baker Plan and with the cooperation of private lenders, the Mexican government was granted access to $12 billion in new financing and was able to implement structural reforms.

This comprehensive program, which included Mexico's entrance into the General Agreement on Tariffs and Trade (GATT), reversed the existing import substitution policy so that foreign competition would drive down prices while simultaneously addressing inflation. Despite these structural reforms, however, prices remained high, suggesting that it was being driven by expectations and not economic fundamentals.[9] According to Lustig, "A sustainable recovery required a turnaround in the flow of net resource transfers: that is, some combination of higher external credits, lower external debt payments, capital repatriation, and higher foreign investment."[10]

In 1988, the government and private companies agreed to the PACTO (Pacto de Solidaridad Económica [Economic Solidarity Pact]), which lowered government-controlled prices, including the minimum wage, the exchange rate, and prices in nationalized industries. It also reduced commercial lending, decreased import tariffs by more than half, and eliminated import licenses. An addendum to the PACTO in 1990 required participants to agree to a projected inflation rate for a market basket of goods. Price increases were subject to negotiation, and wages were set to rise by the projected inflation rate of the basket.[11]

Ultimately, the reforms worked: inflation fell from an average monthly rate of 8.3 percent to an average monthly rate of 1 percent, and economic growth also rebounded, from −4 percent to 2 percent by the end of the 1980s.[12] Mexico's recovery was a result of the expansion of the trade sector, which experienced a 150 percent increase in import volume. During this time Mexico also announced its willingness to participate in a free trade agreement with the United States and Canada, which was expected to continue the policies that had helped the country escape from stagflation. Optimism for Mexico's future was in the air.

Mexico in 1992: Welcome to the Club

By the beginning of the 1990s, it appeared that Mexico had reestablished the preconditions for economic growth.[13] Fiscal and monetary discipline had been attained, and runaway inflation had been brought to a halt. Relative price adjustments, particularly a reduction in real wages, had been achieved, and structural reforms in the public sector and the trade regime were moving ahead. For four years, between 1989 and 1992, the country's GDP growth rate averaged almost 5 percent.

More important, following the policies commonly catalogued under the term "the Washington Consensus," Mexico had established the independence of the central bank and succeeded in privatizing hundreds of state-owned enterprises, including the telecommunications giant Telmex and most of the financial sector.[14] By 1992, the year that the North American Free Trade Agreement (NAFTA) was signed by U.S. president George H. W. Bush, Mexican president Carlos Salinas, and Canadian prime minister Brian Mulroney, the country's economic transformation seemed on track.

NAFTA was a groundbreaking agreement in several aspects: it was the first comprehensive free trade arrangement between advanced countries and a developing economy, and it created the largest free trade area in the world in terms of total GDP and the second largest in terms of total trade volume. The agreement also gave Mexico a head start in entering the coveted U.S. consumer market. As a result, Mexico's trade as a percentage of GDP increased sharply, from about 27 percent of GDP in 1980 to almost 65 percent in 2000.

NAFTA's estimated impact on economic growth was huge and made for a relatively easy sell domestically. The average tariff rate on NAFTA imports was reduced from 12 percent in 1993 to less than 2 percent in 2001, while the rate of effective protection was projected to continue to decline as integration with North American markets continued.[15] In 1992 President Salinas, a Harvard-trained economist, said that "NAFTA will allow sustained recovery of the Mexican growth, and this global change [trade liberalization] is the only way to restore growth, create jobs and meet the needs created by new generations."[16]

Around the same time, Mexico launched a bid to join the Organization for Economic Cooperation and Development (OECD). The country's admission in 1994, which was unusual in that the OECD is primarily a group of rich nations, was recognition by OECD members that Mexico was on the road to success.[17] In its country assessment of Mexico, the Paris-based organization believed that the country's short-term prospects were for continued growth and further deceleration of inflation.[18] Many years before the world's focus began to shift toward emerging economies, creating new groups such as the BRIC and the G-20, Mexico was already part of "the club."

In fact, Mexico's absence from the original Goldman Sachs BRIC report in 2001 was the result of Mexico's membership in the OECD: Goldman Sachs justified Mexico's exclusion on the grounds that the BRICs referred to non-OECD countries. A second BRIC paper, published by Goldman Sachs in 2005, explained that while Mexico and South Korea had the potential to rival Brazil, Russia, India, and China in the future, they were excluded initially because they were already considered to be more developed.[19] In the last few years, due to the popularity of the BRIC acronym, acronyms such as BRIMC and BRIMCK (both of which include Mexico) have become common but less prevalent than BRIC in popular, everyday use.

In short, for a brief period in the early 1990s, Mexico's citizens had good reason to dream about a future of increasing prosperity. The country had managed to recover most of the ground that it lost in the 1982 and 1987 crises, and with the signing of NAFTA and other structural adjustments, it had gone a step beyond. National sentiment at the time was crystallized in the popular expression *"El desarrollo está a la vuelta de la esquina"* ("Development is just around the corner"). Adding to the positive momentum, in his 1992 State of the Nation address President Salinas declared: "Today, Mexican citizens have more confidence in themselves. They know that through hard work and shared efforts they can aspire to a better livelihood. Behind us lie the times of crisis and the bitter memories. Ahead lie the rewards for our struggle, the substantiated hope, and the better future."[20]

The Rip Van Winkle Siesta

A short story by the American author Washington Irving published in 1819, *Rip Van Winkle* is the tale of a man of the same name who sleeps for twenty years and awakens to find that he has a long white beard, that his wife and many of his friends have died, and that the world has greatly changed. An American journalist recently alluded to this popular folktale in referring to Mexico, suggesting that the country has been asleep for the past two decades. Figure 2-1 shows that Mexico achieved a disappointing average growth rate, lower than 3 percent. Moreover, even in years of significant economic expansion, annual growth has not crossed the 7 percent threshold, as it had more than nine times during the miracle years. Finally, the two recessions of the last twenty years, in 1995 and 2009, constituted the two deepest declines in income in more than fifty years.

If a Mexican Van Winkle had begun such an elongated siesta around 1992, a time of great economic promise, upon awakening he might have assumed that he had become rich. Obviously, our friend would have been sadly mistaken. Over the intervening period the country's per capita income showed only moderate increases (figure 2-2). In addition, Mexico's productivity, which had plummeted during the previous decade, has not fully recovered. Our own

Figure 2-2. *Mexico's per Capita Income and Productivity, 1961–2009*[a]

Per capita income (U.S. dollars)   Income per worked hour

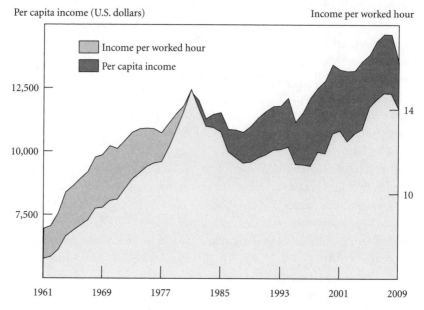

Source: Alan Heston, Robert Summers, and Bettina Aten, "Penn World Table Version 7.1" (University of Pennsylvania, Center for International Comparisons of Production, Income, and Prices, 2012) (http://pwt.econ.upenn.edu/).

a. Purchasing power parity converted GDP per capita and GDP Laspeyres per hour worked by employees at 2005 constant prices.

Van Winkle might then wonder, as many Mexicans have wondered, what happened to the promise of development, the first-mover advantage of NAFTA, the benefits of economic modernization? Where is the better future that every Mexican woman and man had pinned her or his hopes on, two decades ago?

By early 1994, Mexico's self-imposed expectation of achieving developed nation status came to a shattering halt. The country faced, once again, serious macroeconomic imbalances, with a widening current account deficit in the face of strong domestic spending, emerging problems in the financial sector, increasing concerns about the fiscal outlook, and outflows of private capital. The initial response of the authorities to these market pressures was to shift toward increasingly risky financing instruments as other credit channels dried up. However, the plan failed as the country moved into a period of unprecedented turmoil.

Mexico faced tough political and economic challenges in 1994, a national election year. On January 1, a group of peasant rebels—the EZLN (Ejército Zapatista de Liberación Nacional [Zapatista Army of National Liberation])—

took over six towns in the southern Mexican state of Chiapas, one of the poorest states in Mexico, which suffered from job declines in the coffee and oil production sectors. Late in the month of March 1994, Luis Donaldo Colosio, the presidential candidate of the ruling party, the PRI (Partido Revolucionario Institucional [Institutional Revolutionary Party])—who had vowed not to accept any illegal votes and had prepared for a competitive election—was assassinated. In December, the newly elected president, Ernesto Zedillo, devalued the Mexican peso in an attempt to correct a major trade imbalance, causing stocks to drop 16 percent and creating panic among international investors. In what became known as the "tequila crisis," the currency depreciated sharply, output plunged, and inflation rose significantly.

Nevertheless, just one year after the 1994–95 macroeconomic crisis, the outlook was positive once again. Between 1996 and 1999, under the leadership of Zedillo, the country became the fastest-growing economy in Latin America, helped in part by the rebound from the tequila crisis. During his first three years in office, before the PRI lost its majority in congress for the first time, Zedillo produced over fifty constitutional reforms, more than any president in recent history. A more fundamental point, as Giugale and his coauthors observed at the time, was that "[Mexico's] poverty head-counts are again descending and its creative social assistance programs are beginning to bear fruit. Mexicans can also point proudly to the watershed July 2000 elections as another step toward the strengthening of a modern state that is not only economically sound but also forward looking and responsive to its citizens."[21]

President Vicente Fox (2000–06), the PAN (Partido Acción Nacional [National Action Party]) candidate who put an end to the PRI's continuous seventy-year rule, inherited a country filled with newfound hope. Mexico had recently become an investment-grade borrower and a regional leader in terms of financial and commercial integration. Van Winkle was back in his happy dreamland, at least for some months. But after recording a 6.9 percent growth rate in 2000, the economy came dangerously close to a recession, with growth rates of 0.01 percent and 0.75 percent in Fox's first two years in office. By 2006, the average growth rate for his *sexenio* (six-year presidential term) was below 2.5 percent. Fox's economic policies contributed to the decline, which was driven by the Argentinean economic crisis and slower growth throughout the hemisphere.

From the onset in December 2006 of President Felipe Calderón's administration, Mexico's ability to promote economic growth, increase productivity, and lower the poverty rate has remained very limited. The 2008–09 global financial crisis—and more specifically, the U.S. economic downturn that followed—had notably strong negative effects on the Mexican economy, due largely to the strong economic ties between the two countries. Mexico's income, which contracted by 6.6 percent in 2009, the sharpest decline of any Latin American economy, rebounded slightly in 2010 and grew below the 4 percent mark in 2011. The Calderón *sexenio* ended with a less-than-favorable average growth rate of 1.8 percent and without delivering urgently needed structural reforms.

Contextualizing Growth: Has Mexico Underperformed?

In analyzing Mexico's economic history, I have established so far that in recent decades the country has not been capable of reproducing or sustaining the periods of high growth seen in the past. Yet this worrying trend could easily be justified by citing either convergence theory or what some analysts call the new normal of economic growth, a theory of decreasing limits to income generation capacity in the world. So before we jump to any conclusion about Mexico's underperformance, I need to discard a rather unlikely but plausible explanation: that faster growth during recent years simply was not possible.

One way to approach this is to present relevant international comparisons, the premise being that if other countries with similar characteristics achieved significantly better results, then Mexico could have too. In the following section, therefore, Mexico's economic performance is compared with that of three different groups of countries. A second option is to measure Mexico against itself in a slightly different fashion. Rather than using observed outcomes across a time series, Mexico's growth is evaluated against estimates of its theoretical growth potential, given the country's productive capacity, at any given point in time.

Mexico versus the Developed Economies

A series of ten-year growth averages for the United States and Canada, the two developed markets with which Mexico is most tightly integrated, can be seen in figure 2-3. After sustaining a considerable advantage during the miracle years, Mexico's growth average fell behind in the 1980s and only slightly outperformed that of its neighbors during the Van Winkle years. As early as 2002, researchers found evidence that while the speed of convergence of productivity among NAFTA participants accelerated during the post-treaty period, institutional gaps had inhibited the convergence of the income levels of Mexico and its two partners.[22] In other words, while trade liberalization did

Figure 2-3. *Economic Growth: Mexico Compared with NAFTA Partners*

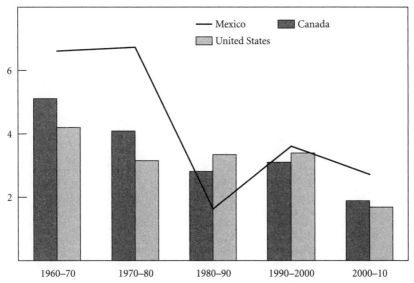

Percent

Source: Alan Heston, Robert Summers, and Bettina Aten, "Penn World Table Version 7.1" (University of Pennsylvania, Center for International Comparisons of Production, Income, and Prices, 2012) (http://pwt.econ.upenn.edu/), calculated from GDP purchasing power parity values (2005).

improve the efficiency of many of Mexico's industrial segments, the country's economy did not benefit proportionally. Moreover, in the last ten years, the decrease in the relative importance of Mexico as a U.S. trading partner exacerbated the inability of Mexico's income level to converge with the income levels of the United States and Canada.[23]

In addition, the OECD Economic Survey for 2011 shows that Mexico has one of the largest GDP per capita gaps with respect to the richest 50 percent of OECD countries, which, according to the report, is due almost entirely to a persistent gap in labor productivity. The fact that Mexico has not been able to close the gap in per capita income between it and most of the world's richest countries is important evidence of Mexico's poor performance.

Mexico versus the Emerging Economies

Emerging and developing economies, as a whole, have arrived at a much safer financial position during the last few decades, with far more manageable debts and greater potential for economic growth. Today, the BRICS economies—

Figure 2-4. *Economic Growth: Mexico Compared with Selected Latin American Economies*

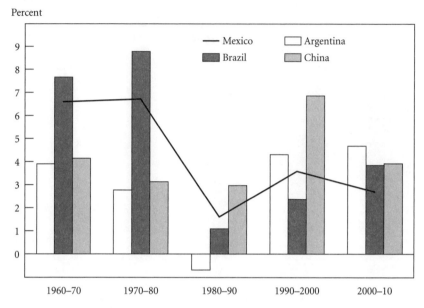

Percent

Source: Alan Heston, Robert Summers, and Bettina Aten, "Penn World Table Version 7.1" (University of Pennsylvania, Center for International Comparisons of Production, Income, and Prices, 2012) (http://pwt.econ.upenn.edu/), calculated from GDP purchasing power parity values (2005).

Brazil, Russia, India, and China, together with the recent addition of South Africa—are widely seen as the emerging leaders of global trade and investment activity. Currently this bloc contributes one-third of the world's growth in GDP. Together with the superstars of the last few decades—Singapore, South Korea, Chile, and, during certain periods, Argentina—they make for an interesting group to compare with Mexico.

Between 1985 and 2008, Mexico managed an annual per capita GDP growth rate of 1.1 percent, lower than all comparison countries except Venezuela (0.8 percent). Given the vigor of its reforms, Mexico seems to have underachieved. As seen in figure 2-4, during the miracle years only Brazil's strong average growth compared with Mexico's. Later, during the Lost Decade, all of these countries were hit by similar external shocks, including jumps in world interest rates, plummeting prices of their primary exports, and a cutoff of foreign lending.

Figure 2-5. *Economic Growth: Mexico Compared with Selected Asian Economies*

Percent

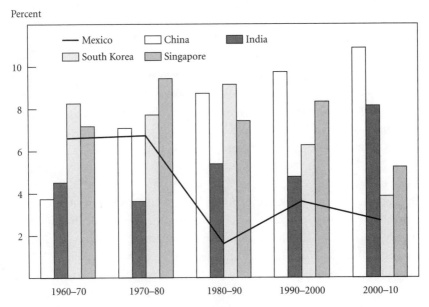

Source: Alan Heston, Robert Summers, and Bettina Aten, "Penn World Table Version 7.1" (University of Pennsylvania, Center for International Comparisons of Production, Income, and Prices, 2012) (http://pwt.econ.upenn.edu/), calculated from GDP purchasing power parity values (2005).

Starting in the 1980s, for instance, Mexico and Chile faced fairly similar macroeconomic conditions, with sizable foreign debts, appreciating real exchange rates, large current account deficits, and weaknesses in the banking system. A similar picture emerges from figure 2-5, which compares Mexico's economic growth with that of selected Asian economies. In comparing Mexico's growth with that of its emerging economy peers, with the exception of Brazil, we find evidence of relative economic underperformance.

Mexico versus Mexico: Economic Growth Gaps

How much should Mexico have grown during the last twenty years? The deficit of a country's economic growth can be measured as the difference between potential output and actual output. Potential output is the amount of economic activity that would be expected if the economy experiences no cyclical fluctuations—no bull or bear markets—and normal conditions for economic development. Figure 2-6 presents two different measures of Mexico's growth against estimates of its theoretical growth potential.

First, following a similar International Monetary Fund exercise from 2005 and updating it for all the Van Winkle years, I have estimated Mexico's potential output using a Hodrick-Prescott filter that smooths out the real business cycle fluctuations in output (panel A).[24] In this way, the country's potential output is shown to develop at a steady rate determined by the raw inputs of labor, capital, and productivity growth. The gap is the difference between the actual GDP line and the potential output line. The general result is that for most of the period 1995–2011 (with the exception of the tequila crisis of 1994 and again in 2008), Mexico had plenty of room to grow.[25]

Second, I used the results of a recent study on Mexico that was developed using Harvard's Atlas of Economic Complexity.[26] Here I estimated the size of the mismatch between Mexico's current level of aggregate output (GDP per capita) and the predicted level of per capita income given its economic complexity (panel B). In simple terms, the results of this report suggest that Mexico began the Van Winkle siesta with a level of income that was already half of what it should have been given the country's productive structure. During the last decade, as seen in figure 2-6, Mexico's per capita income gap has stretched far beyond 50 percent and seems to be widening quickly.

Explaining Mexico's Economic Underperformance

The discussion so far has established through historical and comparative analysis that over the past two decades, GDP growth in Mexico has been disappointing. I now explore some of the factors that have led to Mexico's lackluster performance. Fortunately, there is an extensive literature that has analyzed Mexico's economy in recent years. Instead of adding yet another analysis to this expanding field of study, here I seek to provide a sensible ordering of the different factors used to explain this phenomenon. This section presents a comprehensive review of these explanatory factors, which amount to more than a dozen individual determinants of Mexico's low growth. The intent is to present the principal factors together with evidence for and against each as an explanation of Mexico's economic underperformance.

Business Environment: Infrastructure, Regulation, and Credit

Many researchers have hypothesized that Mexico's business environment is not well developed enough to allow for significant economic growth. The business

Figure 2-6. *Mexico's Estimated Output and GDP per Capita Gaps, 1992–2011*

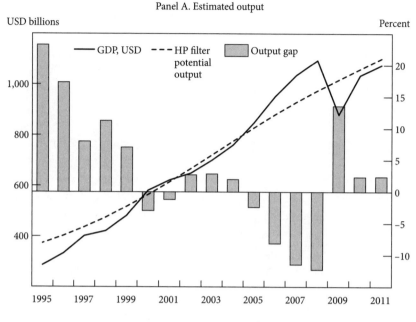

Panel A. Estimated output

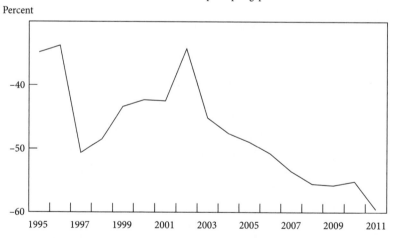

Panel B. GDP per capita gap

Source: Alan Heston, Robert Summers, and Bettina Aten, "Penn World Table Version 7.1" (University of Pennsylvania, Center for International Comparisons of Production, Income, and Prices, 2012) (http://pwt.econ.upenn.edu/); "World Development Indicators 2012" (Washington: World Bank, 2012) (https://openknowledge.worldbank.org/ handle/10986/6014); and calculations by William Daniel, Brookings Institution, 2012. Also Arturo Franco and Ricardo Hausmann, "Mexico's Economic Complexity," working paper (Harvard University, Center for International Development, 2012)

environment is affected by several different components: credit and financial services, infrastructure development, regulation, and competitive markets. While not agreeing on every element, most of the literature that I have reviewed suggests that important opportunities for growth exist in this area.

According to my analysis, the single most common explanation for Mexico's low growth is the underdeveloped state of the country's infrastructure. Undoubtedly, the quality of Mexico's infrastructure has not risen to that of infrastructure in the developed world. For example, telecommunications provision is insufficient. Furthermore, connectivity costs are higher for Mexican companies than for their international competitors, which makes it difficult for companies that rely on information technology to operate profitably. A series of economic studies examining Mexico's growth potential has shown that infrastructure is a major potential obstacle to its development, given that one of the strongest determinants of long-run economic growth is investment in physical capital. Due to uneven economic conditions across different regions in the country, growth rates in those Mexican states that lack significant infrastructure investment are lower than growth rates in other states.[27]

INFRASTRUCTURE. Mexico's infrastructure certainly has developed, but slowly. President Calderón's administration estimated that road modernization under any single previous administration amounted to at most 9,500 kilometers of new roads. For a country whose total land area is almost 2 million square kilometers, investment is certainly lacking. In 2007 Calderón's administration enacted the National Infrastructure Program, the largest national investment program in Mexico's history, designed specifically to modernize Mexico's road, port, and air networks. Between 2007 and 2012, the administration committed almost 5 percent of GDP to investment in the program. The National Infrastructure Program provides substantial funds for public-private partnerships. As investment vehicles, public-private partnerships are especially important because they speed the development of infrastructure projects. Crucially, the partnerships provide legal certainty that the promised infrastructure funds will actually materialize.

Furthermore, if Mexico's growth has been limited by underdeveloped physical infrastructure, the economy should respond strongly to the new infrastructure spending with significant economic growth. Given that infrastructure development takes time to pay off economically, testing the responsiveness of the Mexican economy during the 2007–12 time frame would be unfair. In addition, during that time the world economy went into recession and the U.S. economy suffered a significant downturn. If infrastructure development is in fact Mexico's growth constraint, then economic growth should accelerate as the National Infrastructure Program leads to the modernizing of Mexico's communication and transportation networks.

REGULATION. The numerous government regulations are another constraint on Mexico's business environment. Complying with government regulations increases the costs of production because some employees have to be employed to do something that is not related to the primary business. As negligible as compliance costs may be for a single regulation, compliance costs for numerous regulations become burdensome. The Secretaría de Economía (Ministry of the Economy) compiled an inventory of the more than 23,570 internal rules of the Administración Pública Federal (Federal Public Administration). The Calderón administration committed to reducing the administrative burden of compliance with federal requirements. Reducing the costs of complying with government regulations is expected to save more than 0.4 percent of GDP, which can be used for more productive economic activities.

The direct effects of private monopolies on an economy are well known. Dominant companies that earn profits on top of the normal rate generally do so by forcing customers to pay a higher price, offering less to buy, and providing goods and services of lower quality than they would have to provide under competitive conditions. In Mexico more than one sector faces these monopolistic practices. For instance, for the telecommunications industry alone, the OECD has estimated an annual 1.8 percent of GDP in deadweight loss, or social cost, which has adverse effects on Mexico's economy.[28] Furthermore, other documented cases of excessive market power or disproportional profit margins exist in many industries, from the media to building materials, food and beverages, and financial services.

CREDIT. The provision of credit is central to the process of economic development, and a poorly performing financial sector can represent a significant constraint to growth.[29] Without mechanisms that move savings from lenders to borrowers, a country has poor prospects for taking advantage of productive investment opportunities. Mexico stands out for channeling low levels of private credit to firms, particularly small and medium-size enterprises, and households. Over the period 2001–08, domestic credit to the private sector, as a share of GDP, averaged 18 percent in Mexico. That amount is lower than in other developed countries, which suggests that Mexico's poor economic growth may be the result of its underdeveloped financial markets.

How important, then, are Mexico's credit problems in explaining its growth performance? Citing a survey of 4,000 firms in fifty-four countries during the late 1990s, Thorsten Beck and others reported that the fraction of firms saying that they faced severe obstacles in obtaining finance was highest in Mexico.[30] If access to finance is a serious constraint to economic growth, then, as that constraint relaxes, there should be significant growth. Recent experiments with microfinance institutions have provided a natural case study of this hypothesis.

Two microfinance institutions—NAFIN and Bancomext—granted loans through direct finance and guarantee programs to 154,000 small and medium-size enterprises in 2010, a number that represented a 48 percent increase over the figure for 2009. An additional 32 percent increase followed in 2011. Ultimately, the total loan portfolio increased to around US$30 billion, a significant amount of credit. Yet despite the increase, to date no major economic growth has resulted from the expansion. If credit were tight enough to constrain growth for decades, then even a small increase in credit should produce notable economic benefits.

Human Capital: Labor Markets, Informality, and Education

Another suggested cause of the slowdown in Mexico's growth is perverse labor market incentives. The informal labor sector is composed of workers who are not subject to any government oversight. Typically, the informal labor sector is less efficient because without government benefits and employment protection, workers lack a long-term vested interest in their jobs. Since their benefits tend to be short term, informal workers do not stay in their jobs long enough to develop technical skills or other human capital. Productivity suffers as a result. It has been suggested that this loss of productivity is the cause of Mexico's growth deficit.[31]

The formal sector is expected to be more productive than the informal sector. As a reward for their greater productivity, workers in the formal sector should earn higher wages than their informal counterparts. In response to the higher-wage incentive, Mexican workers should try their hardest to move into the formal sector. Some suggest that Mexico's labor market institutions are structured perversely so that workers in the informal sector lack incentives to move to the formal sector. If Mexico is truly constrained by the informal sector, then wages in the formal sector should be higher than in the informal sector—substantially higher given the size of Mexico's growth deficit.

There is some evidence to suggest that labor market informalities cause a significant wage differential. The tax and regulatory system in Mexico does not apply to the informal sector. Informal workers do not incur any tax or regulation costs. In the formal sector, however, taxes and regulatory costs apply with full force. The discrepancy between the participation costs in the formal and informal sectors could prevent workers from moving from the informal to the formal sector. Some academics suggest that labor productivity would have to rise by 30 to 50 percent as a result of moving to the formal sector in order to increase wages sufficiently to cover the workers' increased tax burden in the formal sector.[32]

The magnitude of the tax wedge certainly suggests that informality is a plausible cause for Mexico's growth deficit. However, more recent studies that look for a wage gap do not find one. Azuara and Marinescu found that workers in the formal and the informal sectors earn approximately the same wages. That suggests that the two sectors are equally productive and that the informal sector is caused by idiosyncratic preferences, not by barriers to entry or similar market distortions.[33] One might therefore conclude that labor market informality is not a plausible cause of Mexico's growth deficit if employers want to have formal employees. Employers benefit from being in the formal sector because, among other reasons, they have access to the financial markets and are therefore not limited to their cash on hand when trying to start a new business or expand current production.

The formal sector comes with a higher tax burden for entrepreneurs as well as for employees. Very productive entrepreneurs earn a high enough return on capital to offset the additional tax burden. It is possible that many Mexican entrepreneurs are not productive enough to offset their tax burden and that consequently the perverse incentives in Mexico's tax regime are the cause of Mexico's low growth.[34] But to attribute Mexico's low growth to unproductive entrepreneurs is to ignore the country's massive growth potential, which entranced commentators up to 1992—and some beyond. A more plausible explanation for the informal labor sector is that it is the result and not the cause of Mexico's low growth.[35] If growth is slow for other reasons, then there are no profits for entrepreneurs to earn by entering the formal sector—not because of their low productivity but because they are operating in an unfortunately slow economy. Bosworth notes that Mexico's large informal sector demonstrates that capital markets do not provide a sufficient return on capital.[36]

Another phenomenon that is frequently cited as a cause for Mexico's persistent lack of growth is the poor schooling and training of workers. Armando Chacón raises this issue in greater detail in chapter 6. Growth can result from additional capital, labor, capital productivity, or labor productivity. It is only

natural to ask whether poor labor productivity may be the cause of low economic growth. Human capital is a key component of labor productivity and
hence of profitable business. In this area Mexico lags behind the developed
world because Mexico's educational system is especially poor and finding
high-quality workers can be difficult.[37]

On the Program for International Student Assessment (PISA), an interna-
tionally administered educational test, Mexican students perform substantially below their OECD counterparts. Performance in critical areas, such as
math and science, is especially lacking. Poor performance in these areas is
detrimental to labor productivity because employees who use math and science most frequently—engineers and scientists—are crucial for economic
growth. Mexico's inadequate educational performance is due to the pervasive
influence of its teachers' unions, particularly the SNTE (Sindicato Nacional de
Trabajadores de la Educación [National Educational Workers Union]), which
allow teachers to produce mediocre results while retaining job security. In an
exhaustive study of teacher wages and union strength, labor economists studying human capital in Mexico determined that performance was low in states
with strong unions. However, in regions with higher teacher wages and low
levels of union strength, students had cognitive outcomes that compared
favorably with those of their OECD peers.[38]

Despite Mexico's poor educational performance, particularly with respect
to math and science, it is not clear that education is the cause of Mexico's
growth deficit. Here Mexico's size works in its favor. Even though its educational system graduates relatively few engineers and technicians, it still graduates 100,000 students every year from science and technology programs. The
number of graduates in these fields exceeds those in countries such as Germany, Canada, the United Kingdom, and Brazil.

Globalization: NAFTA, China, and Diversification

For many years researchers have suggested that a deteriorating competitive
environment and worsening terms of trade could affect Mexico's growth.
Some of the most commonly mentioned adversities in this respect include a
significant loss of competitive advantages in the context of NAFTA; an
increase in international competition in manufacturing, particularly from
China; and Mexico's inability to diversify into new, more dynamic, export
markets.

Mexico's growth exposure to U.S. domestic demand is significant: 82 percent of Mexico's total exports in 2010 went to the United States, and Mexico

is the second-largest importer of U.S. goods, with 12 percent of the total value. Perhaps due to a loss in productivity, Mexican exports to the United States flattened after 2000, with slight recoveries in 2004 and 2010 that were attributable to higher oil prices rather than to increased trade volumes. From the well-known Mexican adage "When the United States sneezes, Mexico catches a cold," it is evident that when the United States grows, Mexico grows, and when the United States slows down, Mexico does not fare well. It should be noted, however, that this correlation in outcomes is only partly due to the strong trade links between the United States and Mexico. Remittances, direct investment, and other noncommercial transfers play an equally important role in the bilateral economic relationship.

Some authors have gone further, suggesting that Mexico has experienced a net loss from NAFTA. While it is clear that Mexico's manufacturing sector has benefited, primarily because of low wages, the agricultural sector has been decimated by unprotected exposure to U.S. and Canadian agricultural subsidies. Audley and others found that unprecedented growth in trade, increasing productivity, and a surge in foreign direct investment led to an increase of 500,000 jobs in Mexican manufacturing from 1994 to 2002.[39] However, according to the authors, the agricultural sector, where almost a fifth of Mexicans still work, lost 1.3 million jobs in the decade after 1994. That could be part of a more general trend of human capital transfers to higher-productivity sectors, a common outcome of market liberalization and industrialization.

In short, Mexico's trade is overly dependent on the U.S. market. That fact, combined with the negative effects of remaining market distortions and the lower dynamism of the world's largest economy, could represent an important constraining piece of Mexico's growth puzzle. However, the opposite could also be argued: without exports to the United States, Mexico could have experienced even lower growth rates over the last decades.

THE RISE OF CHINA. A second explanation for Mexico's decreasing gains from trade is China's rise as a manufacturing power, a potential key threat to Mexico's growth prospects. There is reliable evidence that in 2006, well before the financial crisis, Mexican exports to the United States slowed down dramatically, not only because of the slowing of the U.S. economy but also because of the rising challenge from China and other lower-wage Asian countries. This is particularly problematic given the size of the Chinese economy and its potential to compete with Mexico in the U.S. market.

Moreover, in 2007 Mexico was displaced by China as the second-largest source of U.S. imports, just behind Canada, which remains the largest U.S.

trading partner in both exports and imports. Chinese exports to the United States more than doubled in value during the Van Winkle years. However, Chinese manufacturing is not the likely cause of Mexico's lackluster growth. For instance, while Lopez-Cordova, Micco, and Molina estimated that if trade barriers were completely abolished, U.S. imports from China would increase by 40 percent, they also found that Mexico would see its share of the U.S. market decline by only 2 percent.[40] China's gains would come mostly at the expense of other countries.

Furthermore, an OECD Development Centre–World Economic Forum report shows that for certain industries that are also present in Mexico, China acts as an engine for export growth, allowing exporters to access cheaper intermediate goods.[41] The share of Mexican imports from China rose to almost 15 percent during the last decade, and almost 90 percent of that increase came from inputs for export industries.[42] In other words, while exports to China are mostly commodity products, the country also plays a catalyzing role in global supply chains. That represents complementary, not competitive, activity with respect to Mexico. Finally, Mexican companies like Gruma, Maseca, and Bimbo have made important inroads into the Asian giant's consumer market

EXPORT DIVERSIFICATION AND SOPHISTICATION. In 2011, Mexico had a trade surplus with only three countries: the United States, Guatemala, and, for the first time, Brazil. According to data from Mexico's Central Bank, the share of total exports to the United States decreased from 90 percent in 2000 to 82 percent in 2011, with the biggest increases in export destinations during the last decade being South America (+3.9 percent) and Asia (+2.6 percent). That is quite a modest change, considering that Mexico has signed free trade agreements with more than forty countries and can access a potential market of over 1 billion consumers. Until today, the country remains one of the world's most connected export platforms, reaching over 60 percent of the world's markets. In addition, research has found that approximately 40 percent of Mexican exports is made up of products in which Mexico has lost its comparative advantage. Furthermore, 12 percent of Mexico's manufacturing is devoted to products in which Mexico is in the process of losing that advantage; the remaining 48 percent of manufacturing is devoted to products in which Mexico has maintained its competitive edge. Contrary to what is generally believed, China is not the main threat, because seven other emerging economies, including Taiwan, Thailand, South Korea, Malaysia, and Turkey are more highly ranked as Mexico's toughest competitors in the U.S. manufacturing market.[43] However, by 2015 half of Mexican manufacturing exports will be included in product categories in which Mexico could potentially face a significant displacement in international markets.

This apparent loss of competitiveness and increase in international competition could plausibly explain Mexico's low growth paradox. Yet according to Hausmann and others, Mexico joins other countries "with productive structures that are able to hold vast amounts of productive knowledge, and that can manufacture and export a large number of sophisticated goods."[44] In 2011 the country was ranked in the top twenty economies on measures of economic complexity. In addition, Mexico today is the largest producer of smartphones and the fourth-largest exporter of mobile phones, accounting for 65 percent of Blackberry's worldwide production. It is also the ninth-leading producer and the sixth-leading exporter of motor vehicles in the world. Furthermore, Mexico is the largest recipient of investment in aerospace projects in the world, with over 200 aerospace companies based in Mexico. It is noteworthy that the country's engineers have participated in designing the engine for the Airbus 380, which is the world's largest mass-produced aircraft, with the longest range.

Finally, according to the U.S. Manufacturing-Outsourcing Cost Index, in 2011 Mexico was the most cost-effective country in the world for the offshore production of manufactured goods for the U.S. market.[45] This coincides with the year in which San Luis Potosí, a growing city in Mexico's central region, ranked first as a zone of major economic potential, according to a study by the *Financial Times Intelligence*.[46] Among "Economic Zones of the Future," the city came out at the top in the "economic potential" category, and it ranked third among "Global Free Zones of the Future," after Shanghai and Dubai.[47] On the other hand, the city of Queretaro has also become an important hub for the aerospace industry during the last few years.

Rule of Law: Corruption, Courts, and Crime

The final set of explanatory factors is related to the economic impact of corruption and criminal activities. Evidence suggests that private individuals and businesses change their behavior in order to avoid the consequences of crime. Behavioral disruptions can also cause significant decreases in economic growth. Due to the country's high crime rates, Mexican entrepreneurs are less likely to plan expansionary business ventures.[48] Mexican citizens themselves also change their behavior because of crime rates, and some academics suggest that Mexicans are willing to pay significant monetary costs in order to avoid crime. Whatever the amount of time and money Mexicans spend to

avoid the consequences of crime, those assets are not available for more productive economic activities.

On the other hand, Mexico's war on drugs has created a climate of violence,
and in 2008 *The Economist* suggested that the war on drugs itself might be
responsible for the slowdown in economic growth.[49] Violence and economic
growth are hardly complementary, and many researchers have suggested that the
violent climate may be responsible for the slowdown in Mexico's growth. Mexico's drug problem is undoubtedly serious, and crime has been shown to cause
a decrease in growth. In 2009, the minister of finance, Agustín Carstens, suggested that crime in Mexico cost the Mexican economy 1 percent of GDP each
year, and a recent World Bank report on the economies of crime has corrobo-
rated that estimate.[50] However, there is no conclusive evidence of a causal and
significant impact of Mexico's crime and violence issues on its economic growth.

Many Cartridges but No Smoking Gun

In 2009, in a thorough analysis of the structural factors that may be constraining Mexico's economic growth, Ricardo Hausmann and Bailey Klinger
reached an empirical dead end: low economic growth in Mexico is a puzzle.
Nevertheless, their analysis—which employed some of the most novel growth
diagnostic methodologies devised by Harvard's Center for International Development—was not fruitless, because they managed to discard many hypothe-
ses on cross-cutting binding constraints to growth in the country's economy:

> Given that Mexican investment declined rather than rose at a time when
> access to international finance improved, country risk declined, and
> interest rates declined, it is clear that the binding constraint to growth
> in the country is one of low appropriable returns [not capital con-
> straints]. [Moreover,] the evidence strongly suggests that growth in
> Mexico is not constrained by macroeconomic uncertainty, political
> uncertainty, high or variable taxes, labor market rigidities, or coordina-
> tion failures in the discovery of new productive activities. . . . We found
> no evidence of barriers to entry, an overall poor business climate, or
> microeconomic risks constraining economic growth.[51]

In other words, Hausmann and Klinger did not produce the evidence
required to identify a unique constraint to growth that would affect the Mexican economy across a wide cross-section of activities. Their diagnosis, like
many others, failed to find the primary binding constraint to Mexico's growth.
Instead, they reached an alternative conclusion: that, unlike many other coun-

tries, Mexico may have no particular constraint harming a large cross-section of the economy. This is worth serious consideration.

In a similar fashion, Hanson would end his analysis by stating that while the faulty provision of credit, persistence of informality, control of key input markets by elites, continued ineffectiveness of public education, and vulnerability to adverse external shocks may have a role in explaining Mexico's development trajectory over the last three decades, the relative importance of these factors for the country's growth record is unknown.[52] What is known is that Mexico will continue to have very high growth potential if its growth constraints can be overcome.

A Look into the Future: Once More into the Breach

According to Goldman Sachs, by 2020 emerging economies are expected to account for 75 percent of global growth; China alone should contribute one-third of that, and the other BRIC-like countries should contribute two-thirds. Not surprisingly, Goldman Sachs finally included Mexico in its third BRIC paper in 2005.[53] Goldman Sachs says that eleven countries have substantial potential to join the BRICs as high-growth countries between 2011 and 2050, and it was so impressed by Mexico's potential that it claimed that Mexico and Korea have the potential to become as globally important as the BRICs by 2050. Goldman's optimism about the country is also reflected in its Growth Environment Score: Mexico is globally ranked at 59, which is in the upper-third of all countries and higher than Brazil (95), Russia (81), and India (97) but slightly lower than China (53).[54] However, it ranks significantly higher than Korea (17). Overall, Mexico's growth potential compares strongly with that of the emerging markets.

Similarly, Mexico fares extremely well in the ranking of the 2011 Atlas of Economic Complexity, which classifies countries according to their expected annual per capita growth until 2020. Here, countries are ranked according to the relationship between a country's current level of aggregate output (GDP per capita) and its level of economic complexity. The authors claim that economic complexity is much more predictive of economic growth than other well-known development indicators, such as competitiveness, governance, and education.[55] The list includes 128 countries, with China being the highest and Mauritania the lowest ranked. The leaders in Latin America are Panama (9), Mexico (10), El Salvador (31), Guatemala (35), and Colombia (36). Mexico's relative ranking reflects significant GDP per capita growth, which is expected to average 3.5 percent a year. In addition, Mexico's overall GDP is expected to grow by 4.56 percent over the same period.

In a manner reminiscent of the early 1990s, Mexico seems once again to be ranked among the world's elite with respect to its economic potential.[56] With a distinctive geopolitical location, ample natural and human resources, and highly competitive characteristics, Mexico is frequently mentioned as an attractive investment destination and favorably compared with the high-profile emerging markets of China, India, and Brazil. In this privileged position, the country will most certainly continue to attract large amounts of foreign direct investment, and it will also continue to benefit from its closeness with the United States, while increasing its exports to other regions. Moreover, its strong macroeconomic fundamentals, its young and growing population, and its highly sophisticated productive structure all seem to point to a positive economic outlook.

President Enrique Peña Nieto and his administration have inherited an economy that could grow more, perhaps as much as 6 percent or more a year—and the country urgently needs to grow more. Mexico will have to increase its long-term growth rate by as much as 2 percentage points if it wants to meet the expectations of its citizens, especially in terms of job creation and poverty alleviation. The country requires the creation of at least 1.3 million jobs a year simply to accommodate new labor market entrants. In spite of challenging economic scenarios, particularly with respect to the United States and Europe, today Mexico can and must rally its growth to more than 6 percent on average during the next decade. Yet, as has been the case for almost twenty years, economic potential alone will not be enough. Mexico has been there before.

If one goes back to read these lines in 2018 or to review the country's economic growth record in 2024, how will Peña Nieto's campaign promises read? Will they sound painfully optimistic? Will their accuracy prove to be prophetic? Will Mexico be able to tell of its most successful decade in modern history? Today, as Mexico heads once more unto the breach in its quest for economic growth, it is clear that the most crucial elements for triumph will be political will and resolve. The diagnosis is shared, the necessary corrective measures are known, and the target is clear, but to achieve a stellar economic performance, the country needs the kind of democratic and persuasive leadership that extends above and beyond authority. Today, the Mexican economy has another opportunity to demonstrate to the world—and to itself—that it can be both dynamic and resilient.

Notes

1. For example, Hausmann and Klinger conclude their analysis with "Low growth in Mexico is a puzzle," and Levy and Walton begin theirs with "This volume is concerned with explaining an important puzzle." See R. Hausmann and B. Klinger, "Mexico Growth Diagnostic," in *The Mexico Competitiveness Report 2009*, edited by Ricardo Hausmann and Irene Mia (Geneva: World Economic Forum and Harvard University, 2009) (www.cid.harvard.edu/mexico/docs/MCR_2009.pdf); and Santiago Levy and Michael Walton, "Equity, Competition, and Growth in Mexico: An Overview," in *No Growth without Equity? Inequality, Interests, and Competition in Mexico*, edited by Santiago Levy and Michael Walton (Washington: World Bank, 2009).

2. Gordon Hanson, "Why Isn't Mexico Rich?" *Journal of Economic Literature* 48, no. 4 (2010): 987–1004.

3. See Lant Pritchett, "Understanding Patterns of Economic Growth: Searching for Hills among Plateaus, Mountains, and Plains," *World Bank Economic Review* 14, no. 2 (2000): 221–50.

4. William Easterly, *Elusive Quest for Growth* (MIT Press, 2001).

5. Surveys continually sought to know which issues most concerned the Mexican electorate in the July 2012 presidential election. See "The Mexico Institute's Elections Guide," June 28, 2012 (http://mexicoinstituteonelections.wordpress.com/category/the-polls/).

6. By many accounts, the "Mexican Miracle" began in 1940. I have shortened it for analytical purposes.

7. Organization for Economic Cooperation and Development (OECD), "Economic Surveys: Mexico" (Paris, 1992).

8. *The Great Transformation* analyzes the social and political upheavals that took place in England during the rise of the market economy. Polanyi argues that the modern market economy and the modern nation-state should be understood not as discrete elements but as the single human invention that he calls the "Market Society."

9. OECD, "Economic Surveys: Mexico."

10. Nora Lustig, "Life Is Not Easy: Mexico's Quest for Stability and Growth," *Journal of Economic Perspectives* 15, no. 1 (2001): 85–106.

11. OECD, "Economic Surveys: Mexico," pp. 33–34.

12. Lustig, "Life Is Not Easy."

13. Ibid.

14. Nora Lustig, *Mexico: The Remaking of an Economy* (Brookings, 1998).

15. Ebrima Faal, "GDP Growth, Potential Output, and Output Gaps in Mexico," Working Paper WP/05/93 (Washington: International Monetary Fund, 2005).

16. Statement of President Carlos Salinas (1988–94) in making the official announcement of the NAFTA negotiations.

17. Hanson, "Why Isn't Mexico Rich?"

18. OECD, "Economic Surveys: Mexico," p. 182.

19. Jim O'Neill and others, "How Solid Are the BRICs?" Global Economic Paper 134 (Goldman Sachs, December 1, 2005).

20. Translated by author from *Informe Presidencial* [Presidential Report], 1992 (www.diputados.gob.mx/cedia/sia/re/RE-ISS-09-06-17.pdf).

21. M. Giugale, O. Lafourcade, and V. Nguyen, *Mexico: A Comprehensive Agenda for the New Era* (Washington: World Bank, 2001).

22. See W. Easterly, N. Fiess, and D. Lederman, "NAFTA and Convergence in North America: High Expectations, Big Events, and Little Time," working paper (Washington: World Bank, 2002).

23. See R. Blecker, "The North American Economies after NAFTA: A Critical Appraisal," *International Journal of Political Economy* 33, no. 3 (2005): 19.

24. See Faal, "GDP Growth, Potential Output, and Output Gaps in Mexico."

25. The estimated GDP growth gap averages 2.3 percent over the period, similar to previous results.

26. See S. Bustos, A. Franco, and R. Hausmann, "México: Su Complejidad Económica y el Camino a la Prosperidad [Mexico: Its Economic Complexity and the Path to Prosperity]" (Harvard University, Center for International Development, 2012).

27. Alejandro Díaz-Bautista, "The Role of Telecommunications Infrastructure and Human Capital in Mexico's Economic Growth," paper presented at the Seventy-Seventh Annual Conference of the Western Economic Association, Seattle, Washington, July 1, 2002.

28. *OECD Review of Telecommunication Policy and Regulation in Mexico* (Paris: OECD, 2012) (http://dx.doi.org/10.1787/9789264060111-en).

29. R. Rajan and L. Zingales, "Financial Dependence and Growth," *American Economic Review* 88 (1998): 559–86.

30. Thorsten Beck and others, "Finance, Firm Size, and Growth," Policy Research Working Paper Series 3485 (Washington: World Bank, 2005).

31. J. J. Heckman and others, "Policies to Promote Growth and Economic Efficiency in Mexico," Working Paper Series (Cambridge, Mass.: National Bureau of Economic Research, November 2010).

32. Barry Bosworth, "Productivity Growth in Mexico," background paper prepared for "Mexico: Enhancing Factor Productivity Growth," Report No. 17392-ME (Washington: World Bank, August 1998), p. 30.

33. Oliver Azuara and Ioana Marinescu, "Informality and the Expansion of Social Protection Programs: Evidence from Mexico," unpublished paper, University of Chicago, 2010.

34. Levy and Walton, "Equity, Competition, and Growth in Mexico: An Overview."

35. Heckman and others, "Policies to Promote Growth and Economic Efficiency in Mexico."

36. Bosworth, "Productivity Growth in Mexico."

37. See chapter 6 in this volume.

38. Jesús Álvarez, Vicente Garcia Moreno, and Harry A. Patrinos, "Institutional Effects as Determinants of Learning Outcomes: Exploring State Variations in Mexico," HDN Policy Research Working Paper 4286 (Washington: Human Development Network, World Bank, 2007).

39. John J. Audley and others, "NAFTA's Promise and Reality: Lessons from Mexico for the Hemisphere" (Carnegie Endowment for International Peace, 2004) (www.carnegieendowment.org/files/nafta1.pdf.).

40. Ernesto Lopez-Cordova, Alejandro Micco, and Danielken Molina, "How Sensitive Are Latin American Exports to Chinese Competition in the U.S. Market?" *Economía* 8, no. 2 (Spring 2008).

41. Ángel Alonso Arroba, Rolando Avendaño, and Julio Estrada, "Adapting to the Rise of China: How Can Latin American Companies Succeed?" (OECD Development Centre–World Economic Forum 2009).

42. Ibid.

43. Chiquiar and Ramos-Francia calculate the Spearman coefficient to determine which countries are Mexico's greatest competitors. See D. Chiquiar and M. Ramos-Francia, "Competitiveness and Growth of the Mexican Economy," Working Paper 2009-11 (Mexico, DF: Banco de México, 2009), p. 18.

44. Ricardo Hausmann and others, "The Atlas of Economic Complexity" (Center for International Development, Harvard University, 2011).

45. Alix Partners,"U.S. Manufacturing-Outsourcing Cost Index," 2011 (www.alixpartners.com/en/WhatWeThink/Manufacturing/2011USManufacturingOutsourcingIndex.aspx).

46. *Financial Times Intelligence*, July 12, 2010 (www.fdimagazine.com/news/fullstory.php/aid/3358/Global Free_Zones of_the_Future 2010_11_Winners.html).

47. Ibid.

48. Ariel BenYishay and Sarah Pearlman, "Crime, Informality, and Microenterprise Growth: Evidence from Mexico," working paper (Washington: Millennium Challenge Corporation, 2010).

49. See "No Country for Old Men," *The Economist*, January 24, 2008.

50. See World Bank, "Crime and Violence in Central America: A Development Challenge—Main Report" (Washington, 2011).

51. Hausmann and Klinger, "Mexico Growth Diagnostic."

52. Hanson, "Why Isn't Mexico Rich?"

53. O'Neill and others, "How Solid Are the BRICs?"

54. The Growth Environment Score (GES) is an index that Goldman Sachs calculates every year for around 180 countries.

55. Hausmann and others, "The Atlas of Economic Complexity."

56. Tom Friedman, "How Mexico Got Back in the Game," *New York Times*, February 24, 2013.

ARTURO FRANCO

3

Unlocking Mexico's Political Gridlock

As the Mexican congress approached the end of its final spring session in April 2012, it became clear that the inability of the country's major political parties to reach consensus would continue to deter progress on both the political and the economic front. The prolonged failure of more than a decade to approve so-called structural reforms has created the widespread perception of political gridlock. Mexico's future has been said to be kidnapped inside the legislative palace of San Lázaro. To add insult to injury, a recent article in *The Economist* referred to Mexico's legislature as the do-nothing "Siesta Congress" for having Latin America's most overpaid and underworked lawmakers.[1]

Yet, in stark contrast with the times when almost all of the country's laws came directly from the president's office, a practice that continued until recent decades, Mexico's congress seems to be wide awake. Since the mid-term elections of 1997, when any party's hope of gaining an absolute majority in the lower house was lost forever, presidents Ernesto Zedillo, Vicente Fox, and Felipe Calderón have seen as many as half of their own reform initiatives blocked or delayed by the opposition. Even more telling is the fact that more than 90 percent of the almost 1,000 laws passed by congress during the past *sexenio* (six-year presidential term) originated in the legislative branch, not the executive.

Without any doubt, the country's recent democratization and decentralization of political power have been welcomed as positive developments. After a groundbreaking presidential election in 2000 put an end to seventy years of single-party rule, Mexico's political class seems to be more sensitive to the growing demands of voters. However, opinion polls still do not show any significant increase in citizens' positive perceptions of political responsiveness or government accountability. In spite of marked improvements in the quality of electoral competition since the mid-1980s, the effectiveness of Mexico's incipient democracy is still overshadowed by unions and interest groups.

With a newly elected president and congress, the country is in great need of transformation in many areas. Yet vital reforms in energy, education, fiscal, labor, and competition policy have sunk in congress in the past. In addition, the government is facing increasing public pressure to support a series of daring legislative initiatives intended to improve democratic governance. The proposed changes include allowing reelection of legislators, introducing a run-off election for presidential candidates, reducing campaign costs and public financing of parties, allowing for the participation of independent candidates in elections, and providing mechanisms to increase the say of the Mexican electorate over proposed legislation.

This chapter addresses some of the main concerns about Mexico's political gridlock through several perspectives. It begins by analyzing the recent history and main characteristics of Mexico's political system, particularly with respect to its recent democratization process and the evolving relationship between the executive and congress. It then evaluates the hypothesis of reform paralysis and presents a brief comparative analysis of Mexico's legislative performance in terms of productivity and efficiency. The chapter concludes with an assessment of Mexico's agenda for enhancing governance and accountability through a series of political reforms and changes in the design of the country's institutions.

Mexico's Transition to Democracy

In 2010 Mexico found two good reasons to throw a national fiesta: the country celebrated both the bicentennial of its independence and the hundredth anniversary of the beginning of the Mexican Revolution, a war that ultimately led to the building of the modern Mexican state. To these two historical milestones Mexico could have easily added a third: the ten-year anniversary of a presidential election and political transition that marked the culmination of Mexico's recent democratization process. To help explain the current state of Mexico's political system, I briefly review the key events leading to this extremely important and fairly recent transformation.

For more than seventy years the PRI (Partido Revolucionario Institucional [Institutional Revolutionary Party]) was able to maintain one-party rule and control of the presidency. Peruvian Nobel laureate Mario Vargas Llosa once referred to this political system as "the perfect dictatorship." However, by the end of the 1980s, the PRI's hold on power began to wane. In 1987, when the Pacto de Solidaridad Económica (Economic Solidarity Pact) was signed to confront a deepening economic crisis, some of its internal opponents challenged the PRI by creating a new party, the FDN (Frente Democrático Nacional [National Democratic Front]), which later became the PRD (Partido de la Revolución Democrática [Party of the Democratic Revolution]). The new party was led by Cuahutemoc Cárdenas, the son of former president Lázaro Cárdenas, who had a major role in the establishment of the PRI, and Porfirio Muñoz Ledo. Just one year later, in 1988, the PRI lost the two-thirds majority in congress required to approve amendments and reforms to the Mexican constitution. Before the end of the decade, Baja California became the first state to be ruled by an opposition party, in this case the more conservative PAN (Partido Acción Nacional [National Action Party]).

In 1990 the Instituto Federal Electoral (IFE) (Federal Electoral Institute) was formed, as was the Tribunal Electoral del Poder Judicial de la Federación (TRIFE) (Electoral Tribunal of the Federal Judiciary). An electoral reform in 1993 increased accountability in party financing, and in 1994 the Acuerdo por la Paz, Justicia, y Democracia (Agreement for Peace, Justice, and Democracy) became the basis for future electoral competition. In 1995 an agreement between President Zedillo and the political parties, the Acuerdo Político Nacional (National Political Agreement), led to important changes in the relationship between the executive and the legislature, strengthening of the federal system, and increased participation of the media and citizens in politics. In 1996 Mexico had a second major electoral reform, and in 1997, after stripping the PRI for the first time of its absolute majority in the lower house, the two main opposition parties, PAN and PRD, became firmly established actors in an increasingly open political process. The same year Mexico City held its first elections for head of government and Cuahutemoc Cárdenas (PRD) became the first opposition governor of the Federal District (also known as Mexico City).

In 2000 the PRI lost the presidency to the PAN when President Vicente Fox Quezada was elected. In addition, since 2000 there has been a boom in democratic changes at the local and state levels. Moreover, Mexico's transition to democracy has also brought electoral competition into the upper chamber of congress. Figure 3-1 shows the change in the composition of the senate. After more than six decades during which practically all of the seats in the upper

Figure 3-1. *Evolution of Mexico's Institutionalized Democracy, 1985–2011*[a]

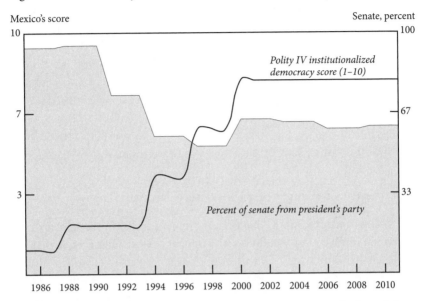

Sources: *Political Regime Characteristics and Transitions, 1800–2011*, Center for Systemic Peace (www.systemicpeace. org/polity/polity4.htm); World Development Indicators 2012 (Washington: World Bank, 2012) (https://openknowledge. worldbank.org/handle/10986/6014).

chamber belonged to the incumbent president's party, the leading party has held less than two-thirds of the seats since the late 1990s.

The evolution of Mexico's democracy can be portrayed by using the framework of the Polity IV project, which measures some of the political characteristics of states for the purpose of comparative and quantitative analysis.[2] In particular, it allows us to follow Mexico's performance in the "institutionalized democracy" indicator, which is shown in figure 3-1. Since 1985 Mexico moved from an institutionalized democracy score of 1, comparable to that of Senegal or Nicaragua at the time, to a solid 8 score, which is shared by countries such as Belgium and South Korea. Freedom House assessments, wherein higher scores indicate less freedom, show a similar trend, with Mexico's score falling from 8 in 1991 to 4 ten years later.[3]

Thus, over a relatively short period and without major episodes of civil unrest or violence, Mexico moved from a hegemonic party system to multiparty electoral competition.[4] Under the Polity IV framework, Mexico's democracy can now be defined as "one in which political participation is unrestricted, open, and fully competitive, where executive recruitment is elective, and where constraints on the executive are substantial."[5] For evidence, the decreasing control of the incumbent president's party over the senate in Mexico can also be found in figure 3-1. While things are far from perfect, Mexican society has clearly transitioned toward an increasingly open, competitive, and inclusive democracy.

Unfortunately, electoral competition is not sufficient to consolidate democracy fully. Democracy in Mexico emerged in the context of political institutions designed for an authoritarian political order, and some inherited formal and informal arrangements have undermined the quality of the political process, making governing Mexico a challenge.[6] Following below is a description of some of the pillars of the country's new status quo.

Governance Challenges of a Democratic Mexico

With Mexico's transition to democracy came a parallel fundamental transformation in the country's political structure: the end of hyperpresidentialism. While the country's 1917 constitution closely emulates that of the United States in providing for a clear separation of powers, until recently the Mexican president exercised nearly absolute control over the nation, choosing his own successor and even designating party officials and candidates all the way down to the local level. Much of that power, however, came from unwritten rules within the corporatist structures of the hegemonic PRI. As the new parties began to increase their presence in congress and win municipal and state elections, excessive presidential privileges disappeared.

Moreover, as Levy and Walton suggest, the transition to democracy in Mexico caused another significant shift in the country's political equilibrium by creating incentives for both the president and congress to support the decentralization of federal spending and the expansion of government-financed programs.[7] That has allowed state governors to become powerful political forces, and many have reproduced in local areas some of the same anti-democratic behaviors that presidents displayed previously at the national level. Finally, perhaps the most evident transfer of political power over the last two decades has taken place between the executive branch of the federal government and the congress, mainly because the legislative authority of the Mexican president, as established by the constitution, is actually relatively limited.

Mexico's lawmakers found themselves in a completely new setting after the democratic transition. The PAN and PRD had, for the first time in history, the option of saying no to a president, and the PRI had to learn to act as an

Figure 3-2. *Legislation and Political Power in Mexico*[a]

Percent

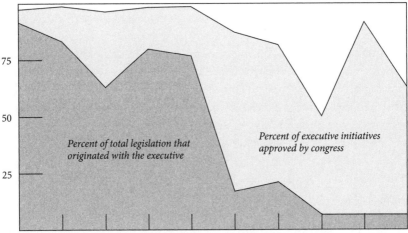

Percent of total legislation that originated with the executive

Percent of executive initiatives approved by congress

1985–88   1988–91   1991–94   1994–97 1997–2000 2000–03   2003–06   2006–09

Sources: Manuel Alcantara Saez, Mercedes Garcia Montero, and Francisco Sanchez Lopez, *Funciones, procedimientos y escenarios: un analisis del poder legislativo en America Latina* [Functions, Proceedings, and Scenarios: An Analysis of Legislative Power in Latin America] (University of Salamanca Press, 2005); Servicio de Información para la Estadística Parlamentaria (INFOPAL) [Parliamentary Statistical Information Service], Camara de Diputados [Chamber of Deputies] (Mexico: May 2012) (www.diputados.gob.mx/sistema_legislativo.html).

a. Does not include reforms to transitory laws, which address implementation and secondary regulation of a common law.

opposition party. Figure 3-2 shows that after 1985, both the approval rate and the proportion of executive-initiated laws have dropped substantially. During the last decade, the percentage of laws coming from the presidential office in Los Pinos has remained way below 20 percent. Mexico's congress has displaced the executive branch as the principal arena for policymaking.

The 57th legislature (1997–2000), which served during the PRI's last term in office, still passed about 80 percent of the executive's initiatives. In this sense President Zedillo did not fare too badly, but his party had 48 percent of the seats in the lower chamber of congress, almost an absolute majority. In 2000 President Fox came to power with a smaller parliamentary group; only 41 percent of the deputies were from the PAN-led coalition. However, in the 58th legislature eleven of thirteen of President's Fox initiatives were approved, a number almost identical to that of President Zedillo; therefore the cause of the pronounced drop in the upper graph in figure 3-2 was not a lower approval rate but the much lower number of reform initiatives presented. Finally, during Fox's last three years in office, the 59th legislature approved only half of his legislative initiatives, almost a 30 percent drop. That may be explained by the fact that during this period, the PAN held only 30 percent of the seats in the lower chamber.

In contrast, the graph shows a rebound in the rate of approval of executive initiatives after the election of Felipe Calderón in 2006, enabled in part by the fact that between 2006 and 2008 the PRI and PAN presented a common legislative agenda with significant reforms to the state pension and public finance systems. However, in July 2009 a stronger executive-legislative confrontation surfaced, and Calderón's ability to get important bills approved by the 61st legislature was even lower than President Fox's during his second term. During this period, the PRI determinedly blocked all major initiatives—including major political reform, comprehensive labor reform, and regulation of private monopolies—presented during President Calderón's administration. Given the current composition of congress, in which three parties together hold 90 percent of the seats but none of them holds more than 48 percent of the seats, every law requires a political coalition.[8]

Reform Paralysis

After 2000, as Mexico's presidents began to lose their unquestionable authority and political control over the legislative agenda, approval of initiatives from the executive became, as is the case in many modern democracies, the object of negotiations between political parties. However, as figure 3-3 shows, during the end of Zedillo's term and more profoundly during Vicente Fox's administration, the number of constitutional reforms—changes that require approval by two-thirds of the legislature—plummeted. Reform paralysis, defined as the inability of government to pass constitutional or structural reforms because of partisan differences in the legislature, emerged as the biggest challenge of the new political equilibrium.

However, the data show only part of the story. A more insightful way of looking at Mexico's reform paralysis is to focus on specific reform agendas. Here, the biggest challenge for those who seek reform in Mexico is that there is no single political party to blame for the country's prolonged stalemate. For example, a series of comprehensive fiscal reforms proposed by presidents Zedillo and Fox—which included a proposed increase in the federal IVA (*impuesto al valor agregado* [value-added tax])—were publicly attacked and

Figure 3-3. *Constitutional Reforms in Mexico, 1997–2006*[a]

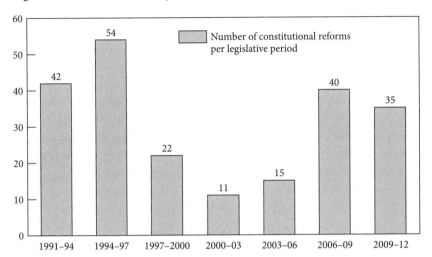

Sources: Manuel Alcantara Saez, Mercedes Garcia Montero, and Francisco Sanchez Lopez, *Funciones, procedimientos y escenarios: un analisis del poder legislativo en America Latina* [Functions, Proceedings, and Scenarios: An Analysis of Legislative Power in Latin America] (University of Salamanca Press, 2005); Servicio de Información para la Estadística Parlamentaria (INFOPAL) [Parliamentary Statistical Information Service], Camara de Diputados [Chamber of Deputies] (Mexico: May 2012) (www.diputados.gob.mx/sistema_legislativo.html).

a. Does not include reforms to transitory laws, which address implementation and secondary regulation of a common law.

defeated by the opposition. More recently, political games in congress destroyed any chance of increasing the government's fiscal revenue in 2010 when the PRI rejected the PAN's proposed 2 percent increase in the IVA. What followed was a long series of partial and sometimes technically flawed fiscal reforms, some of which were approved at the last possible minute and two of which had to be reversed in subsequent years as they created more societal costs than benefits.

Energy reform presents another interesting example of the dynamics underlying Mexico's reform paralysis. The constitution creates a public monopoly for the state-run petroleum company, PEMEX (Petróleos Mexicanos), which controls all aspects of the oil industry, from offshore exploration to gasoline stations. As a result of underinvestment in the sector and PEMEX's continuing loss of efficiency, Mexico has to import more than 40 percent of its gasoline because it lacks refining capacity. During the presidential term of Zedillo, the PAN, with a simple majority in the lower chamber, rejected a proposed reform by Los Pinos that would have allowed private businesses to participate in the energy sector. The president of the PAN's national executive committee at the time was a young and ambitious Felipe Calderón. Four years later, congress once again rejected an almost identical energy reform proposed by President Vicente Fox. This time, it was the PRI that used its majority vote to stop the reform.

Almost a decade later, Calderón, now the president, proposed a package of energy sector reforms after months of behind-the-scenes negotiation with the PRI. The leftist PRD took to the floor of the chamber of deputies to prevent its passage; it then delayed the reform by subjecting it to several months of expert testimony in the senate. The end result was a disappointing series of minor changes. In early 2012, President Calderón announced that he would seek another round of reforms for the oil sector. Yet, as frequently happens during national election years, congress could not reach consensus on the previous government's final attempts for reform. Without a doubt, energy sector reform will be a hot item for the Peña Nieto administration, but how can one expect significant reform after almost fifteen years of opportunistic efforts to impede reform?

Political capture of potential reforms by various interest groups is another fundamental issue in Mexico. For example, one has only to look at the long-standing project for labor reform. The current federal labor law in Mexico has never seen a comprehensive reform since its introduction in 1970. Over the past thirteen years, almost 500 labor-related reform initiatives have been presented in congress; most of them were never even voted on. As Carlos Mayer-Serra explains, "The relatively easier decisions, such as opening up the economy, were taken, but more difficult ones, such as reforming the Labor Law, were not taken. In other words, liberalization happened externally but not internally."[9] With yet another flop in the latest bid to introduce democratic practices for electing labor union leaders, an initiative that was supported by both the incumbent and elected presidents during the 2012 transition, the political influence of these interest groups appears to be stronger than ever.

It is common knowledge in Mexico that the structural reforms of the 1980s and 1990s and privatization of government corporations allowed private business groups to increase their market power and influence. Before the 2000 election, relationships between the national government and big business were handled almost exclusively within the executive branch of government. In the democratic era, business has acquired greater access to political parties and through them to congress. Consequently, business leaders have blocked many attempts to create a pro-competitive regulatory framework, and the result is quasi-monopolies in a large number of sectors, particularly in services and non-tradable activities. On the other hand, the continued opposition to reform of the state-owned oil and electricity companies has allowed powerful and outmoded unions to survive in the new political equilibrium. Perhaps an even more troubling example is that of a teachers' union, the CNTE (Coordinadora Nacional de Trabajadores de al Educación [National Coordinator of Educational Workers]), which has very explicitly, publicly, and creatively used its vast voting and organizational power for political gain during the last two decades.

Finally, outside of the economic agenda, other necessary institutional, judicial, and political reforms also continue to fall short. One example is the long-standing proposal to create a national identity card, which has been presented to congress more than twice since 1997. In 2011, a proposed political reform aimed at producing well-functioning political parties and increasing democratic accountability of elected officials through reelection was held back in spite of popular support.

Are Mexico's Legislators Asleep? Measuring Legislative Efficiency

Mexicans have celebrated the growing independence of the federal legislature in relation to the other two branches of the government. A natural consequence of the legislature's increased autonomy is the claim that legislators are now more effective. However, a 2012 article from *The Economist* painted Mexico's legislature as inefficient and unproductive, calling it the Siesta Congress. The article, which was heavily criticized by members of all parties in Mexico, went on to say:

> Mexico's lawmakers sit for only 195 days a year, the second-fewest among Latin America's bigger countries. (Their $11,200-a-month pay, however, is the highest after Brazil's.) When they do stir themselves to vote, it is more often to block rivals' bills than to pass reforms. Gridlock in the palace of San Lázaro partly explains why Felipe Calderón's presidency, which ends in December, now looks like a six-year damp squib.[10]

Some quantitative and qualitative evidence presented earlier in the chapter questions the hypothesis of reform paralysis in Mexico. Clearly, many opportunities to push important reforms forward have been lost during the last years, and congress has fallen short on its primary responsibility. However, is that a consequence of a lousy work ethic in Mexico's federal legislature, or is the

Figure 3-4. *Mexico's "No Time for Siesta" Congress*

Number

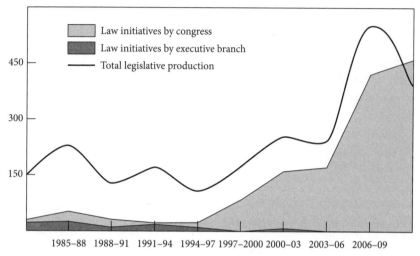

Source: Servicio de Información para la Estadística Parlamentaria (INFOPAL) [Parliamentary Statistical Information Service], Camara de Diputados [Chamber of Deputies] (Mexico: May 2012) (www.diputados.gob.mx/sistema_legislativo. html).

capacity to deliver on critical laws constrained by other factors? To answer that question, we must begin by understanding that the work of congress includes a much wider array of legislation than big reforms to the constitution. Second, in order to assess the efficiency of congress, we need to look not only at the output, namely the number of approved laws, but also at the input.

How has legislative productivity evolved over the last decade? As shown in figure 3-4, in terms of the total number of approved laws, there has never been more production in San Lázaro. The chamber of deputies has managed to pass almost 1,000 laws in the last two legislatures. During the last decade there has been an explosion in the total number of initiatives introduced, as shown in the shaded area in figure 3-4. The previous legislature introduced 20 times as many initiatives as its counterpart in 1997. This exponential growth in law initiatives led to the introduction of new procedures requiring congress to rule on introduced bills within a maximum of sixty days, with a possible extension for another sixty days. The new legislative timeframe left almost 2,000 initiatives in the freezer during the 61st legislature. Consequently, Mexico's chamber of deputies has been able to process and vote on less than one-third of the initiatives that have been presented in the last six years.

Another way to look at productivity is to consider the significance of the bills passed. In the last decade Mexico has passed fundamental reforms with respect to health care, social security, and judicial power. Congress has also approved a freedom of information law, important changes to electoral laws, and enhanced regulation on human rights issues. Some analysts have argued that in a comparison with the legislatures of other democratic governments, the Mexican legislature would have a relatively good track record, given these and other approved reforms. In other words, the end of hyperpresidentialism has not reduced the ability of the Mexican political system to generate policy changes. The empirical evidence presented here on the legislative process suggests that with a divided government, the executive branch has simply lost its grip on the policymaking process, while lawmaking in Mexico is at an all-time high. As O'Neil put it, the exercise of higher levels of freedom by federal legislators has led to greater activism, which is expressed by the presentation of more initiatives and more political claims in the legislature.[11]

However, the greater production of laws during the last six years could simply reflect an increase in non-significant changes in legislation, as the data do not distinguish between major and minor legislative changes. It is clear that when we evaluate the relevance and impact of the recent legislative agenda—not just the number of approved initiatives—lawmakers have failed to tackle many of the most pressing challenges confronting Mexican society. A question arises: Will they ever?

Reforms That Allow for More Reform?

Late in 2009, President Calderón put forward a comprehensive political reform initiative. Among other bold proposals, Calderón advocated allowing mayors, city council members, and federal lawmakers to be elected for multiple terms, up to twelve years. Allowing reelection of these officials would mark a significant change in the country's political habits. In addition, the reform package proposed a run-off election for presidential candidates, seeking to avoid "an election by the largest minority" and to increase political legitimacy. Calderon's daring reform initiative was followed by a PRI proposal in February 2010. Published as an op-ed by their senate leader, Manlio Fabio Beltrones, it sought to establish referendums on issues of national importance.[12] Later, the PRD also pitched its own proposal, which introduced some additional elements such as the referendum, revocation of mandate, and independent candidacy.

While national polls at the time showed broad support for the concept of political reform, with an almost 90 percent approval rating, it was yet another reform attempt by the then-current administration that fell victim to the rancorous relations between parties. However, it remains unclear if such reform could succeed in forming a governing majority in the national legislature. In other words, could the proposed changes really put an end to Mexico's reform paralysis?

First, many in Mexico believe that the current political stalemate is the outcome of the particular constitutional structure of the Mexican state and that therefore it is susceptible to correction by some of the proposed institutional adjustments. Those that adhere to this view are implicitly questioning the depth of change within Mexico's political system. To them, the introduction of competitive elections and reforms that strengthened the system of political checks and balances, discussed previously, has not been enough to create a functional democracy in Mexico. Improving the quality and effectiveness of the Mexican political system requires erasing the legacy of its authoritarian past.[13]

Second, many believe that the obstacles to forming a governing majority in congress can be addressed at the individual or behavioral level. For instance, the historical prohibition of reelection in both chambers of congress creates little incentives for lawmakers to fulfill their campaign promises. Instead, as they seek to remain in office, they express their loyalty by voting as their party coordinators suggest. A recent report by Integralia presents a measure of party unity in the Mexican congress that is defined as the level of cohesion within parliamentary groups. Theoretically, the scores for this index would range from 33 percent, when an equal number of lawmakers from the same party vote differently, to 100 percent, when they all vote in the same way. In the case of Mexico, the scores have remained closer to 100 percent in both chambers. In terms of this measurement, the most cohesive party in 2011 was the PRI, followed closely by the PAN, with the highest scores in the range of 99.7 and 99.6 percent respectively for the senate.[14] Creating incentives for lawmakers to showcase their individuality and independence of thought could be a parallel line of action for breaking Mexico's reform gridlock.

Third, some of the major difficulties encountered by different reform agendas in Mexico seem to arise from social factors, including pressure from certain interest groups to undermine reform initiatives that threaten their own existence. As Rubio noted, "While Mexico's political institutions have experienced a profound transformation, the non-institutional side of the nation's politics has not; organizations representing vested interests continue to operate as they always have."[15] The informal rules of engagement with business and unions ultimately hinder the effectiveness and accountability of the legislature. To change that, Mexico needs better regulation of activities inherent in the decisionmaking process in congress. Formalizing lobbying activities and enhancing transparency throughout the legislative process would be a good start.

In short, regardless of which of these factors is emphasized—the role of institutions, incentives, or interests—the solution for Mexico's current political predicament can be reached only through a combination of constitutional reengineering, improved regulation, and leadership. However, while Mexico seems to require a comprehensive reform of its political system— such as by allowing for the reelection of legislators, run-off elections for presidential candidates, reduced campaign costs and public financing of parties, participation of independent candidates in elections, and referendums that increase the say of the Mexican electorate—those changes will be insufficient if they are not accompanied by a more vibrant civil society and stronger engagement from Mexico's citizenship. Fortunately, many civil society organizations, advocacy groups, and social movements have recently adopted a series of common stances on the improvement of democratic governance in Mexico. From the students of the YoSoy132 movement, to the many social groups participating in the México ¿Como Vamos? (Mexico, how are we doing?) initiative, to the proliferation of independent media websites, blogs, and analyses, Mexican society seems to be raising the bar for government accountability and change.[16]

A Look into the Future: Breaking the Gridlock

In the last two decades, Mexico's democracy has come a long way. Yet Mexican citizens are far from satisfied with their current political representation. It is not surprising to learn from a 2010 survey on opinions about congress that more than 65 percent of respondents gave lawmakers less than a 50 percent score for overall performance and that almost 70 percent believed that legislators did not represent the national interest.[17] "It is unrealistic to expect a country to turn instantly from a closed corporatist economic system to an open competitive market, or from an authoritarian one-party state to a truly open, competitive, and inclusive democracy," reads a Council on Foreign Relations report.[18] True, but after more than a decade of working with democracy, what should Mexico expect? There are some reasons to believe that the country will experience less political quarreling and hopefully more reform in the coming years. The Pacto para Mexico (Pact for Mexico), signed on December 2, 2012, by President Enrique Peña Nieto and the presidents of the PRI, the PAN, and the PRD, is a truly positive sign. In somewhat of a 1987 déjà vu and with the approval of 86 percent of the chamber of deputies and 88 percent of the senate, this "new deal" places ninety-five commitments on the table touching on many of the previously mentioned reform priorities. Yet as some critics have already pointed out, the agreement could be more politics than policy because only around 60 percent of the commitments require changes in law and more than half refer to a single initiative, namely the fiscal reform.[19] The biggest risk for Peña Nieto's consensus strategy is the potential for rapid disappointment. The combination of raised expectations, built on a hurried and weak political equilibrium and channeled through a highly ambiguous "laundry list" agenda, could easily become a recipe for disaster.

Ultimately, any attempt at breaking the current political gridlock should address the deep causes of the impasse. The stakes for Mexico are very high. A 2011 survey conducted by Latinobarómetro indicates that indifference to democracy in Mexico has doubled since 2006 and that less than half of the population believes that democracy is the best political system.[20] Nostalgia for the days when "things seemed to work" is in the air. Authoritarian DNA still runs in the veins of many politicians, from all political parties, and worrying undemocratic gestures are painfully common. The temptation to revert to the ways of the past is as present as ever.

Breaking the gridlock in Mexico's political system is about something more fundamental than any particular reform or development objective. Today, Mexican society needs to prove to itself that it can transform its own future without violence or external imposition. Citizens need to point the political class toward a path of prosperity and freedom and punish politicians when they go astray. To every woman and man in the country, in every state, city, and community, defending these hard-earned liberties and rights should be an imperative and a life-long battle. Ultimately, doing so is about making democracy work not only in Mexico, but for Mexico.

Notes

1. "The Siesta Congress: Reforms Languish While Overpaid, Underworked Lawmakers Bicker," *The Economist*, January 21, 2012.

2. See Polity IV dataset, *Political Regime Characteristics and Transitions, 1800–2011,* Center for Systemic Peace (www.systemicpeace.org/polity/polity4.htm). The Polity IV project offers this operational definition of democracy: "Institutionalized Democracy is conceived as three essential, interdependent elements. One is the presence of institutions and procedures through which citizens can express effective preferences about alternative policies and leaders. Second is the existence of institutionalized constraints on the exercise of power by the executive. Third is the guarantee of civil liberties to all citizens in their daily lives and in acts of political participation. Other aspects of plural democracy, such as the rule of law, systems of checks and balances, freedom of the press, and so on are means to, or specific manifestations of, these general principles."

2. Adrian Karatnycky, *Freedom in the World: 2000–2001: The Annual Survey of Political Rights and Civil Liberties, 2000–2001* (Google eBook, 2001) (http://books.google.com/books/about/Freedom_in_the_World_2000_2001.html?id=Mz57SSzuYecC); and Freedom House, *Freedom in the World 2000* and *2001* (www.freedomhouse.org/reports).

4. Sartori defines a hegemonic party system as follows: "The hegemonic party neither allows for a formal nor a de facto competition for power. Other parties are permitted to exist, but as second class, licensed parties . . . the possibility of a rotation in power is not even envisaged." See Giovanni Sartori, *Parties and Party Systems: A Framework for Analysis* (Cambridge University Press, 1975), p. 230.

5. Definition is that of Ted Robert Gurr, informed by foundational, collaborative work with Harry Eckstein. See Ted Robert Gurr and Harry Eckstein, *Patterns of Authority: A Structural Basis for Political Inquiry* (New York: John Wiley and Sons, 1975). The democracy indicator is an additive eleven-point scale (0–10). The operational indicator of democracy is derived from coding of the competitiveness of political participation, the openness and competitiveness of executive recruitment, and constraints on the chief executive.

6. See Pamela Starr, "Neither Populism nor the Rule of Law: The Future of Market Reform in Mexico," *Law and Business Review of the Americas* 15, no. 1 (Winter 2009).

7. Santiago Levy and Michael Walton, "Equity, Competition, and Growth in Mexico: An Overview," in *No Growth without Equity? Inequality, Interests, and Competition in Mexico,* edited by Santiago Levy and Michael Walton (Washington: World Bank, 2009), pp. 1–44.

8. See Shannon K. O'Neil, *A (Partial) Defense of the So-Called "Siesta Congress" in Mexico* (2012) (http://blogs.cfr.org/oneil/2012/01/20/a-partial-defense-of-the-so-called-siesta-congress-in-mexico/).

9. Carlos Elizondo Mayer-Serra, *Por Eso Estamos Como Estamos: La Economía Política de un Crecimiento Mediocre* [That's Why We Are as We Are: The Political Economy of Mediocre Growth] (México, DF: Debate Editorial, 2011).

10. "The Siesta Congress: Reforms Languish While Overpaid, Underworked Lawmakers Bicker."

11. Shannon K. O'Neil, "Mexico: Development and Democracy at a Crossroads," Markets and Democracy Brief (Washington: Council on Foreign Relations, 2011).

12. Manlio Fabio Beltrones, "Citizen Political Reform," op-ed, *El Universal*, 2010 (www.eluniversal.com.mx/editoriales/47494.html).

13. See Starr, "Neither Populism nor the Rule of Law: The Future of Market Reform in Mexico."

14. Reporte Legislativo: Numero Tres: LXI Legislatura (2009-2012), Integralia, pp. 25–26, (www.integralia.com.mx/files/ reporte_legislativo_lxi.pdf).

15. Luis Rubio, "Democratic Politics in Mexico: New Complexities," in *Mexico under Fox*, edited by Luis Rubio and Susan Kaufman Purcell (Boulder, Colo.: Lynne Rienner, 2004).

16. *YoSoy132* was created after candidate Peña Nieto visited the Universidad Ibero-Americana. Only a limited number of students were admitted into the candidates' meeting. The 132nd student was excluded, thus creating a name for an anti-establishment social movement.

17. Milenio Diario, *Legislators, Flunked in a Survey*, 2011 (www.milenio.com/cdb/doc/impreso/8948177).

18. O'Neil, "Mexico: Development and Democracy at a Crossroads."

19. José Merino, *La viabilidad del Pacto por México* [The Viability of the Pact for Mexico], 2012 (www.adnpolitico.com/opinion).

20. Marta Lagos, *Reporte Latinobarometro 2011* (www.latinobarometro.org/latinos/LATAnalize.jsp).

DUNCAN WOOD

4

Energy Challenges for the Peña Nieto Administration

A s Mexico enters a new political era following the presidential election of July 2012, its energy sector faces the prospect of radical reform. Mexico's problems with oil production and reserves are, of course, well known in the global energy community, and after years of discussion in the relatively elevated circles of national and international energy experts, Mexico's political elites finally appear to have accepted the fact that a crisis is looming. They have now shown that they are ready to engage in debate and dialogue aimed at reforming the sector.

This chapter examines the remaining challenges facing the energy sector in Mexico, going beyond the problems facing PEMEX (Petróleos Mexicanos [Mexican Petroleum]) in terms of reserves and production. While PEMEX's problems are the most obvious and immediate energy problems facing Mexico, a wide range of underlying problems can be identified that reflect the country's broader developmental challenges. Corruption, failure to produce long-term public policies, and failure to invest in industrial development have had a negative impact throughout the Mexican economy, but they are especially acute in the energy sector.

This chapter does not go into any great depth regarding the historical development of PEMEX or the debates surrounding the energy reform of 2008; I have done that elsewhere.[1] But it is important to note that the evolution of a national consciousness with respect to Mexico's energy challenges can be traced back to the reform process that took place that year. The debates and the government's public awareness campaign to try (unsuccessfully) to achieve a far-reaching reform in 2008 have borne fruit by easing the way for meaningful reform after the federal elections in 2012.

Production

PEMEX's problems with declining production have been well advertised in international energy circles and beyond in recent years. From a high point in 2004, oil production went into a near free fall in the years that followed, as extraction from the Cantarell field, for years the mainstay of Mexican oil production, collapsed. While there had been a dramatic increase in production from the Cantarell reserve in the early 2000s, brought about by intensive nitrogen injection, it had rapidly declined. Cantarell was producing 2.136 million barrels per day (bpd) at its peak in 2004, but by 2008 production had dropped to 1.047 million bpd and by early 2012 to around 400,000 bpd. That precipitous drop meant that PEMEX's production from all fields fell from a high point of 3.4 million bpd to 2.55 million bpd in 2012. Despite impressive levels of new production from fields such as Ku-Maloob-Zaap (KMZ) to compensate for Cantarell's decline, PEMEX has been unable to resurrect its production numbers. While it is true that production has stabilized and that PEMEX has added more new barrels of production over the past two years than any other company in the world, questions remain about the firm's capacity to prevent further declines and to raise its numbers.

Mexico's Estrategia Nacional de Energía (ENE) (National Energy Strategy) for the 2012–26 period, issued in February 2012, sets a goal for PEMEX of producing 3.354 million bpd by the end of the period.[2] To achieve that goal, PEMEX will have not only to add significant new production from as yet undiscovered wells but also and more immediately to replace production that will be lost from fields that will begin to decline in the near future. KMZ, for example, is expected to remain the mainstay of Mexican oil production until 2015, but then its production also will begin to drop. PEMEX needs to find another significant source of oil if the decline of KMZ is not to result in an overall drop in production similar to what has been seen since 2004.

The energy reform of 2008 provided one way to stem the fall in extraction. Under the reform, PEMEX is authorized to issue contracts to private firms to exploit oil reserves; the contracts provide a guaranteed price per barrel and an economic incentive to the oil company to produce more oil than was stipulated in the original contract. This policy innovation, first used in August 2011, has thus far not added huge numbers to PEMEX's production, but it has

Figure 4-1. *PEMEX Oil Production, 2009–26*[a]

Cubic feet, millions

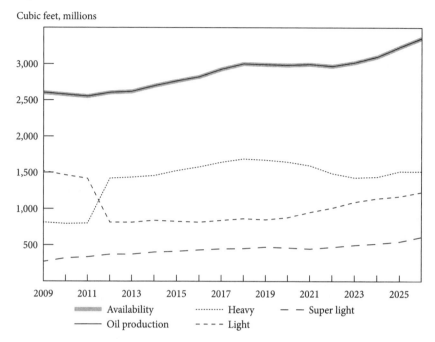

Source: Secretaría de Energía [Secretary of Energy], "Outlook for Crude Oil: 2012–2026."

a. Totals may not add due to rounding. The variation in production and availability of the three types of crude oil are due to mixing to adjust weights. For example, an extra-heavy crude can be mixed with a light crude to obtain a product with the characteristics of heavy crude. The 2009–11 data are historical; the 2012–26 data are estimated.

served as an example of how the contracts can be used to reactivate old fields that no longer were profitable for the national oil company but that can be exploited efficiently by smaller, specialized firms.[3] Three blocks—Magallanes, Santuario, and Carranza—are currently operating under this scheme, and production there has begun to increase (figure 4-1). The second round of contracts went into effect in spring 2012, and it will be intriguing to evaluate the long-term impact of the new arrangements.

The failure of PEMEX to maintain its production at the levels seen in the early 2000s, when it consistently pumped more than 3 million bpd, should be seen in the light of a failure to invest in finding new reserves (see below) and to develop technologies that would allow the firm to enter new fields in the deep waters of the Gulf of Mexico. Instead, in the late 2000s, PEMEX decided to focus on the on-shore Chicontepec field, also known as Aceite Terciario del

Golfo (ATG) (Tertiary Gulf Oil Project). This reserve, which lies under the states of Veracruz and Puebla, consists of many billions of barrels of oil. However, due to the area's complex geological formation, in which oil is trapped in small pockets with minimal porosity or flow, the business of getting the oil out of the ground is difficult as well as energy, time, and capital intensive. It also results in significant disruption of the local population's daily lives as the above-ground footprint of the project is enormous.[4] Most important, production from the field has been disappointing; back in 2009 PEMEX predicted that it would reach 176,000 bpd by 2010, but it had reached only 61,000 bpd by late 2011.[5] While it is true that PEMEX has managed to almost double production from the field over the past four years and has developed some intriguing new technologies and techniques for extracting oil from the field, Chicontepec is unlikely to ever become the backbone of Mexican production.

To increase production in the years to come as indicated in the ENE for 2012–26, Mexico's energy planners face a difficult choice. The first option is for the government to cut taxes on the company and allow PEMEX to keep its profits (thereby forcing the government to collect tax income from other sources to maintain a healthy fiscal balance). Doing so would give PEMEX the financial freedom to invest in the creation of new technologies and to invest more heavily in exploration and production. The second option is to effect a constitutional change that would allow PEMEX to enter into production-sharing arrangements with private and foreign firms, which in turn would provide the needed investment and technologies to increase oil production, particularly in the deep waters of the Gulf of Mexico. At the biannual meeting of the PRI (Partido Revolucionario Institucional [Institutional Revolutionary Party]) in early March 2013, members agreed unanimously to allow private investment in the oil sector. Details of how that investment might be structured are unknown at this time, but the vote opens the way for congressional debate on article 27 of the Mexican constitution and the interpretive regulations. This decision within the PRI demonstrates the broad recognition that without private investment, Mexican oil production will remain stagnant for years to come.[6]

Reserves

Mexico's oil reserve problem mirrors the oil production problem. Inadequate investment in exploration and in developing new technologies, combined with the prohibition against PEMEX's entering into production-sharing deals

Figure 4-2. *PEMEX Hydrocarbon Reserves, 1999–2012*

Barrels of oil, millions

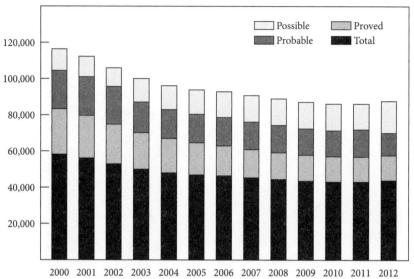

Source: Secretaría de Energía, Sistema de Información Energética [Secretary of Energy, Energy Information System], with information from PEMEX.

with private oil firms, resulted in a dramatic deterioration in the country's reserves during the 1990s and 2000s. As can be seen in figure 4-2, not only did PEMEX's overall "3P" (proven, probable and possible) reserves fall from 57.7 billion barrels in 1999 to only 43.8 in 2012, the individual shares of proven, probable, and possible reserves have changed dramatically, with the amount of proven (1P) reserves diminishing year after year. That reflects the massive exploitation of Cantarell with no view to replacing its barrels through new exploration.

A major cause of the failure to discover new reserves stems from PEMEX's underinvestment in exploration activities over the past twenty years. As seen in figure 4-3, PEMEX began to significantly increase its investment in production activities only in the early 2000s, when it invested heavily in boosting production from Cantarell and then in trying to replace Cantarell's barrels with oil from KMZ and Chicontepec. However, in terms of exploration, PEMEX still invests less than 15 percent of its total portfolio in exploration activities, far below the levels of its international peers such as Brazil's Petrobras. Despite an increase in PEMEX's investment in exploration from around

Figure 4-3. *PEMEX Investment in Exploration and Production, 1997–2011*

Pesos, billions

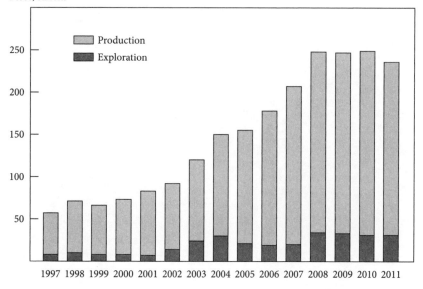

Source: Secretaría de Energía [Secretary of Energy], *Estrategia Nacional de Energía: 2012–2026* [National Energy Strategy: 2012–2026].

20 billion pesos a year in the early years of the last decade to around 31 billion pesos a year in 2011, that represents only a minor increase when calculating the total in dollars because of the depreciation of the peso against the dollar since 2008. In fact, after the depreciation of the peso is factored in, the dollar amount spent on exploration today remains more or less equal to the amount spent in the early 2000s.

The good news for PEMEX is that increased investment over the past decade has resulted in the achievement in 2012 of a 100 percent restitution (or replacement) rate for reserves—a target that PEMEX failed to achieve in the previous twenty years or more. In fact, the ENE claims that PEMEX will achieve a 110 percent restitution rate for its reserves by 2025 if it is permitted to increase its investment still further. However, the cost of producing each barrel of oil from both new and mature fields has increased, as can be clearly seen in figure 4-3. In the 2008–11 period, PEMEX spent more than 200 billion pesos to produce 2.5 million bpd, while in 2004 it spent only 120 billion pesos to produce 3.4 million bdp.

Nevertheless, PEMEX has a chance to boost its reserves in the coming years in a hitherto unexplored area, namely the border regions of the Gulf of Mexico. Thanks to the recent signing and ratification of the Transboundary Oil Agreement, a bilateral agreement with the United States on transboundary reserves, Mexico now has the opportunity to extract oil from the deep waters of the gulf at the border.[7] For years the two countries were unable to come to an agreement over the issue of cross-border reserves, but with the signing of the agreement, exploration and production (E&P) activities can now begin.[8] It is estimated that there are upward of 9 billion barrels of reserves in the cross-border regions of the gulf; perhaps more important, cooperation between PEMEX and private oil firms may help to change attitudes about opening up the oil sector in Mexico.

The best hopes for oil discoveries in the border region, particularly in the area known as the Western Polygon, or "Donut Hole," lie in very deep waters. In this area of the gulf, extraction will have to be carried out at depths of 2.5 kilometers (1.5 miles) or more below the surface of the ocean and then several kilometers below the sea bed. That would normally present PEMEX with an insurmountable problem because PEMEX lacks the technology to produce oil at such depths. Now, under the terms of the Transboundary Oil Agreement, the way is open for private firms to carry out the extraction and then share the oil with PEMEX according to a predetermined formula. Given the flow of oil within an oil field, it is possible for an oil company operating on the U.S. side of the border to extract oil from the Mexican side, but the oil would be given back to PEMEX in return for a fee. The Transboundary Oil Agreement met with minimal opposition in Mexico, a sign of the changing mood in the country, which allowed smooth and rapid passage of the legislation through the senate. The agreement marks an important new departure for bilateral energy relations, and it should be seen as a first step toward a future opening of the oil sector in Mexico.

The Multiple Corporate Challenges of PEMEX

In recent years a number of diagnostic studies of PEMEX, undertaken by government and nongovernment actors, have all pointed to the multiple problems facing PEMEX's corporate governance. The first problem is that the company does not, in fact, operate like a for-profit company; it operates like an organ of government. PEMEX has little control over its budget, it loses almost all (and some years more) of its profits in the form of taxes and royalties to the government, and it needs approval from the Secretaría de Hacienda y Crédito Público (Ministry of Finance and Public Credit) for all major new investment projects. The high level of government interference means that the company has been unable to make the kind of strategic long-term planning decisions that might have prevented the current depressed production and reserves outlook.

A second challenge faced by the company is that it is riddled with corruption. Every month the Mexican press reports another incident of bribery, fraud, or misappropriation of funds. This situation is caused in part by the political interference mentioned above and, more important, by the failure on the part of the company or the government to put in place measures that guarantee transparency and accountability. PEMEXgate, a scandal involving PEMEX payments to a presidential candidate in the 2000 election, was widely viewed as merely a high-profile example of what is common practice at the corporation. Corruption takes many forms within PEMEX: from paying too much for shipments of refined products and receiving a cut of the profits from the company that sells the products to PEMEX, to diverting funds for political purposes, to skimming profits directly from the various departments within PEMEX.[9]

Relations between the company's management and the oil workers' union, the STPRM (Sindicato de Trabajadores Petroleros de la República Mexicana [Mexican Oil Workers' Union]), are a further drag on PEMEX. The union not only plays a direct role in decisionmaking at the corporation through its presence on the administrative board but also is an essential party in making strategic decisions if worker compliance is to be ensured. Most important, the generous salary, benefits, and retirement packages that have been negotiated by the STPRM over the years mean that PEMEX is, for all intents and purposes, bankrupt. PEMEX faces total worker liabilities of almost 787 billion pesos, most of which is tied up in the pension scheme.[10] When that amount is combined with its overall debt (around US$56 billion at the end of 2011), there appears to be little prospect that the corporation will be able to meet its obligations without assistance from the federal government.[11] Two options are available. One is to nationalize the debt, with the government assuming PEMEX's liabilities. That would free the company to divert more resources to E&P, but the current problems would likely recur in a few years' time. The other option is to restructure the pension liabilities through negotiations with the union, which would provide a longer-term, more sustainable solution.

The second option would require a government with the political will to confront the union and the solid backing of the Mexican public. President Peña Nieto now appears to be in a position to take on this challenge.

Mexico's Natural Gas Deposits

Although Mexico is well endowed with natural gas deposits, they have been underexploited for many years because PEMEX has simply flared the gas associated with oil production (to the dismay of environmental and energy-efficiency groups) and has failed to invest adequately in the development of non-associated gas fields. That has led to the current situation, in which the country imports natural gas from the United States through cross-border gas pipelines and from global markets through liquefied natural gas (LNG) terminals.

The situation changed in 2011 when the U.S. Energy Information Agency (EIA) announced that Mexico holds the world's fourth-largest reserves of shale gas. The EIA estimates that Mexico has 681 trillion cubic feet (tcf) of technically recoverable resources, an amount that places the country behind only China, the United States, and Argentina in terms of shale gas reserves.[12] The announcement caused great excitement in Mexico's energy circles, and the Calderón administration immediately began to talk of developing the resource and constructing a nationwide gas pipeline network to finally bring natural gas to the majority of Mexico's population.[13]

Almost immediately, however, questions were raised about PEMEX's capacity to extract the natural gas and, more important, the economic logic of doing so. While it is true that lower gas prices offer the prospect of lower energy costs for the entire economy and therefore of improved economic competitiveness, it is not clear that developing Mexican shale gas in the short term is the best way to achieve that goal. Given the high level of technical sophistication and operational flexibility needed to engage in large-scale shale gas extraction, it may make more sense to import shale gas from the United States, benefiting from the low prices and large volumes there.

By early 2012 PEMEX had drilled only one exploratory well, and it is clear that the nature of the gas fields will require the drilling of thousands of wells every year. PEMEX, as a corporation, lacks the resources to engage in such an ambitious drilling program and would require private companies to drill on its behalf. As yet, no contractual mechanism is available to PEMEX that would make such an arrangement attractive to the private sector.

The second point concerns the economics of shale gas production. Although the shale gas boom has been heralded around the world and has had a major impact on gas production in the United States, a side effect has been rapidly falling prices for gas. From a high in 2006 of almost US$15 per million BTUs (MMbtu), prices collapsed to less than US$2 per MMbtu in April 2012. Given the unusually low price of gas in North America, it makes little immediate economic sense to develop and exploit Mexico's shale gas reserves; Mexico should instead import gas from the United States.

North of the border, shale gas production is profitable thanks to two factors: the high level of technical expertise employed by the large number of specialized firms in the business and the extraction of high-value liquids (shale oil) that can be sold to boost revenue. In fact, without the profits from the sale of shale oil, shale gas would not have been developed to the extent that it has. In Mexico's case, PEMEX lacks the technology and know-how to extract shale gas efficiently (not to mention the severe problem of lack of access to water for the fracking process). Nor is PEMEX equipped on an operational level to drill thousands of new wells in rapid succession. Furthermore, under current legal restraints, which prevent any private firm from owning oil reserves in Mexico, private firms would not be permitted to keep the associated liquid and gaseous hydrocarbon products were they allowed to exploit the gas reserves.

Intriguingly, all three of the major presidential candidates in the 2012 election emphasized shale gas in the energy components of their campaign proposals. That emphasis appears to have been based mainly on the Calderón administration's overly optimistic forecasts, contained in the ENE for 2012–2026, for natural gas production (see figure 4-4) and failure to understand the economics of the issue. The current administration faces a tough choice over whether to invest heavily in shale gas and thus bring jobs and other economic opportunities to Mexico or to import cheap gas from the United States and invest the funds in other productive projects. What is certain is that dramatically lower gas prices in North America present Mexico with a golden opportunity to improve its national competitiveness by significantly reducing the cost of energy for manufacturing and electricity generation.

Mexico's Carbon Challenge

During his administration, Calderón became one of the most vociferous proponents of fighting climate change. Through the Mexican government's foreign policy, Calderón sought to broker agreements in the United Nations

Figure 4-4. *PEMEX Natural Gas Production, 2011–26*[a]

Cubic feet per day, millions

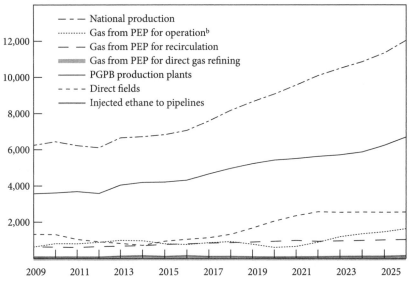

Source: Prepared by Instituto Mexicano del Petróleo [Mexican Petroleum Institute] with data from BANXICO, CFE, CNA, CONAPO, CONUEE, CRE, EIA, IEA, INEGI, PEMEX, SENER, and private companies.

a. The 2009–11 data are historical; the 2012–26 data are estimated. PEP = Pemex Exploración y Producción (PEMEX Exploration and Production). PGPB = PEMEX Gas y Petroquímica Básica [PEMEX Gas and Basic Petrochemicals].

b. The gas mixture referred to here is considered equivalent to dry gas (gas seco).

Framework Convention on Climate Change (UNFCC) to bring about a post-Kyoto consensus. At the same time, his government pushed a domestic legislative agenda that was committed to cutting Mexico's greenhouse gas emissions (GGEs). In April 2012, the Mexican senate approved a climate change bill that is among the most ambitious in the world. Under this legislation, Mexico is committed to

—reducing emissions growth by 30 percent by 2020 and by 50 percent by 2050

—obtaining 35 percent of energy from renewable sources by 2024

—mandating that government agencies use renewable energy

—establishing a national mechanism for reporting on emissions.

In order to reach these goals, Mexico must invest heavily in alternative energy, including both renewable and nuclear options. Indeed, Mexico's long-term energy outlook is extraordinarily positive, given the country's impressive natural endowments with regard to renewable energy. Although to date the development of non-hydro renewable options in Mexico has focused on wind and geothermal energy, it should be noted that Mexico has one of the world's best solar resources and that biofuels hold enormous promise, particularly with regard to second- and third-generation technologies.

Mexico has a long and impressive history with respect to geothermal energy, and it has the potential for significant future development. Since the 1970s the Comisión Federal de Electricidad (CFE) (Federal Electricity Commission) has been exploiting the geothermal resource at Cerro Prieto in Baja California to produce clean electricity, both for the local market and for export to the United States. In addition to the plant at Cerro Prieto, Mexico has three other major geothermal facilities, at Los Azufres, Los Humeros, and Las Tres Virgenes. Total installed capacity is 953megawatts (MW), or around 3.23 percent of national electricity-generating capacity. The CFE estimates that the country has a further 2,400 MW of economically viable capacity that can be developed; however, at the present there seems to be little momentum for proceeding with development. That seems strange because geothermal energy is a relatively "low-hanging fruit" for energy planners, given the advanced level of the industry in Mexico.

Wind energy was the real success story among renewable options under the Felipe Calderón administration. Since 2006, total installed wind capacity in Mexico has increased by 600 percent, and hundreds more megawatts of generating power are due to come online in the next two years. To date, Oaxaca has been the main focus of development, but two northern regions, Baja California and Tamaulipas, show enormous potential, and investment and planning are beginning to bear fruit in those two states.[14] Overall, Mexico has around 71,000 megawatts of wind potential, more than enough to satisfy national demand for electricity. To proceed with further development of the resource, however, the CFE must commit to building the required transmission capacity.

Transmission capacity is also the key issue when it comes to exporting wind energy from Mexico to the United States. California's 33 percent renewable portfolio standard has created a huge market for clean energy in the state, and authorities recognize that California needs to import electrons from neighboring regions, including Mexico and Canada, to satisfy requirements. Regretfully, until now, the development of wind energy resources at neighboring La Rumorosa in Baja California had been held back by the failure of the Mexican and U.S. governments to advance bilateral talks on cross-border electricity transmission. A speedy resolution to this issue is vital if large-scale development of Baja's wind resource is to move ahead.

With regard to solar energy, Mexico's average insolation rate of more than 5 kilowatts per square meter (kwh/m^2) gives it one of the best solar resources in the world. In the northwest of the country, the rate increases to more than 6 kwh/m^2. A commonly quoted statistic is that a 650-meter-by-650-meter area of the Sonoran or Chihuahua desert, covered in solar photovoltaic (PV) panels, would generate enough electricity to satisfy national demand. To date, meaningful solar development has been held back by a lack of subsidies, the high cost of solar PV technology, and the abundance of cheaper alternatives.[15]

Biofuel development in Mexico has thus far been limited, both by the overwhelming dominance of the use of hydrocarbons as liquid fuels and by the absence of a meaningful government strategy for developing biofuels. Ethanol production has been further held back by long-standing problems in Mexico's sugar industry, in which investment has been depressed due to a restrictive pricing policy and labor problems. However, alternative biofuel sources, such as jatropha, algae, and even succulents (like agave) offer enormous hope for the future as technologies advance.

Of more immediate interest may be the prospects offered by municipal solid waste. Municipal authorities working with private companies are beginning to harness the energy potential of garbage landfills in Mexico. Two products are readily available: methane gas from the landfills, which can be easily and cheaply converted into electricity in simple generators, and liquid ethanol produced through distillation of the fluid runoff from organic matter.[16]

Renewable energy development in Mexico offers an opportunity to make a positive impact in the environment, energy, and employment arenas. If that impact is to become a reality, however, the federal government must enact policies and legal and regulatory frameworks that encourage investment by the private sector. It must also ensure a level playing field for renewable energy options with respect to conventional hydrocarbon fuels.

However, it is improbable that the development of renewable energy alone will be enough for Mexico to meet its reduced emissions targets. One of the strategies identified by the Calderón administration in the ENE of 2012–26 calls for the construction of two new nuclear power plants in addition to the existing nuclear power station at Laguna Verde. However, there is little enthusiasm for nuclear power in Mexico, especially after the Fukushima accident in Japan. Siting would be a major obstacle, and the rise of civil society in Mexico makes major development of the nuclear sector even less likely.

Mexico's Energy Future

President Peña Nieto has announced that he will present an energy reform initiative to congress in the second half of 2013. The exact nature of the reform remained unknown at the time of writing, but a number of different proposals are being discussed within the PRI and among key factions in the legislature. The Mexican and international press have speculated that the reform will not involve a constitutional change, but it is the opinion of most leading experts that a meaningful reform—that is, one that both significantly improves the prospects for reserves and production and also brings in the appropriate technology and expertise—cannot be achieved without such a change.

Given the public and private statements of the administration's team, the reform initiative is expected to be ambitious, proposing increased participation for the private sector in the E&P process. That suggests the possibility of a new tax regime for PEMEX and of changes that would permit the company to participate in joint ventures and production-sharing agreements with private firms.

Of particular importance are two unconventional hydrocarbon resources: shale gas and oil resources and deepwater oil resources. Given PEMEX's technological, technical, operational, and financial limitations, the huge resources that remain untapped on land and under the Gulf of Mexico cannot be efficiently and effectively exploited and national energy security concerns cannot be adequately addressed. It is therefore possible that the energy reform will propose separate regimes for conventional and unconventional resources.

Experts predict that by 2015, the nation's most productive oil field, Ku-Maloob-Zaap, will enter into decline. If the reform initiative does not meet with success, the Peña Nieto administration will face a potentially catastrophic drop in production. In fact, without urgent action during the Peña Nieto *sexenio* (six-year presidential term), Mexico could lose as much as half a million barrels of daily production. Given the time required to implement the new legislation and for new public and private investment in E&P to take effect, the nation still faces the prospect of significant further declines before production begins to increase, even if the reform process is successful.

What is certain is that the current situation must change. Mexico's oil and gas sector desperately needs to be modernized, and the existing legal and constitutional framework is not flexible enough to make that possible. Opening of the sector, either partial or complete, is needed to bring the technology, expertise, and financing needed to boost hydrocarbon production and to transform hydrocarbon resources into products that the Mexican economy needs. Furthermore, continuing investment in renewable energy generation is absolutely fundamental to ensuring that Mexico meets the mandated limits on carbon gas emissions that will come into force in coming years. Perhaps most important in the short term, Mexico must find a way to take full advantage of plummeting prices for natural gas in North America and employ those low energy costs to improve Mexico's national competitiveness.

Conclusions

There can be little doubt that the energy sector will continue to be a central component of Mexico's economy in the years to come. Despite the multiple challenges facing oil and gas production, Mexico is fortunate to have massive reserves in this area, many of which have yet to be discovered. Furthermore, Mexico has the potential to become a superpower in nonconventional areas such as geothermal, wind, solar, and biofuel energy. It is to be hoped that technological and policy progress will make exploitation of those resources a reality. Meantime, in order to maximize the benefits for the nation from the exploitation of these resources, the energy sector must be fundamentally reformed and the energy mind-set among Mexico's policy elites must be modernized. New thinking on efficiency and working with the private sector, domestic and foreign, must take priority over the traditional attachment to exclusive state ownership of Mexico's oil. The Peña Nieto administration has now begun to plan strategically to prepare the country for the energy challenges that will affect Mexico and the world during the course of this century, including climate change.

Notes

1. Duncan Wood, "The Administration of Decline: Mexico's Looming Oil Crisis," *Law and Business Review of the Americas* 17, no. 1 (Winter 2011).

2. Secretaría de Energía [Ministry of Energy], *Estrategia Nacional de Energía: 2012–2026* [National Energy Strategy: 2012–2026] (www.sener.gob.mx/res/PE_y_DT/pub/2012/ENE_2012_2026.pdf).

3. Duncan Wood, "PEMEX Issues Contracts: A Small Step into the Future," CSIS Americas Program's Blog, 2011 (http://csis.org/blog/pemex-issues-contracts-small-step-future).

4. Carlos Manuel Rodriguez, "Pemex Increases Chicontepec Output Estimate for 2011," *Bloomberg Businessweek*, October 29, 2010.

5. Karim Meggaro, "Chicontepec Announcement Is the Silver Lining in Pemex's Q3 Earnings Call," October 29, 2011 (www.oilandgasmexico.com/tag/cnh/).

6. Edgar Sigler, "Petróleo seguro para hoy . . . ¿ Y mañana? [Oil Secure for Today . . . and Tomorrow?]," CNNExpansión, 2012 (www.cnnexpansion.com/economia/2012/02/29/petroleo-seguro-para-hoy-y-manana).

7. Duncan Wood, "U.S.-Mexico Cross Border Energy Cooperation: A New Era in the Gulf of Mexico," Woodrow Wilson International Center for Scholars, 2012 (www.wilsoncenter.org/sites/default/files/March_2012_Transboundary_Oil_Agreement_0.pdf).

8. Should the Transboundary Agreement be considered an international treaty, the U.S. Senate will have to approve it. However, should it be considered an executive agreement, only the House of Representatives will have to approve funds for its implementation.

9. "Por corrupción Pemex pago sobreprecios por $14 mil mdp [Because of Corruption Pemex Paid Overcharges of 14,000 Million Pesos]," Animal Politico, February 8, 2012 (www.animalpolitico.com/2012/02/por-corrupcion-pemex-pago-sobreprecios-por-14-mil-mdp/).

10. Luis Carriles, "Pemex da solución a costo de pensionados [Pemex Has a Solution for the Cost of Retired Workers]," El Universal, April 23, 2012 (www.eluniversal.com.mx/finanzas/94593.html).

11. Carlos Manuel Rodriguez, "Pemex Sees Debt Soaring to Record 56 Billion in 2011," Bloomberg Businessweek, December 15, 2010.

12. "Mexico's Shale Gas Potential Untapped," Natural Gas Americas, August 31, 2011 (www.naturalgasamericas.com/mexico-shale-gas-potential).

13. "Anuncia Calderón avance en infraestructura de gas natural [Calderón Announces an Advance in Natural Gas Infrastructure]," Milenio, March 19, 2012 (www.milenio.com/cdb/doc/noticias2011/ba3affde584f0c18a954d6a7777b358f).

14. Duncan Wood and others, Wind Energy Potential in Mexico's Northern Border States (Washington: Woodrow Wilson International Center for Scholars, 2012).

15. Sergio Romero-Hernandez and others, Solar Energy Potential in Mexico's Northern Border (Washington: Woodrow Wilson International Center for Scholars, 2012).

16. Omar Romero-Hernandez and others, Bioenergy Potential in Northern Mexico: An Exploration of the Potential Presented by Municipal Solid Waste (Washington: Woodrow Wilson International Center for Scholars, 2012).

CHRISTOPHER E. WILSON

5

Toward a Regional Competitiveness Agenda: U.S.-Mexico Trade and Investment

Though hidden from the public eye behind headlines on organized crime, violence, and illegal immigration, the economic relationship between the United States and Mexico is strong and growing. Economic cooperation has the potential to act as a strategic driver for the entire bilateral relationship. While migration and security are understood primarily as problems to be solved, trade and investment are areas of immense opportunity. In this respect, a significant and high-level focus on regional economic issues could deliver real economic benefits to both countries while improving the tone of their relationship, thereby facilitating progress across the bilateral agenda.

As shown in figure 5-1, since the 1990s the scale of the economic relationship between the United States and Mexico has grown enormously as the United States, Mexico, and Canada have joined together to become a tightly integrated market and production platform. In fact, with little fanfare or recognition, annual U.S.-Mexico trade in goods and services reached an estimated half-trillion dollars for the first time in 2011.[1] Mexico is the United States' second-largest export market, and the United States is by far Mexico's largest export market. Merchandise trade has more than quintupled since 1993, while bilateral foreign direct investment (FDI) has grown sixfold.[2] The North American Free Trade Agreement (NAFTA), which was implemented in 1994, has certainly facilitated this growth, but the complementary nature of the U.S. and Mexican economies and geographic proximity have also worked to link the region's economies in fundamental ways.

As impressive as the magnitude of the economic relationship is, its depth is equally important. Spurred by the opening of trade, Mexican and U.S.

73

Figure 5-1. *U.S.-Mexico Bilateral Trade and Investment, 1993–2011*[a]

Billions of U.S. dollars

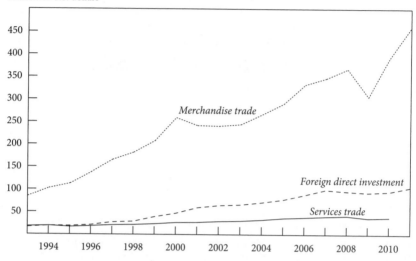

Source: U.S. Department of Commerce, Census Bureau, "Trade in Goods with Mexico," 2012 (www. census.gov/foreign-trade/balance/c2010.html); U.S. Department of Commerce, Bureau of Economic Analysis, "Private Services Trade by Area and Country," 2012 (www.bea.gov/international/interna-tional_services.htm); U.S. Department of Commerce, Bureau of Economic Analysis, "International Data: Direct Investment and MNC," 2012 (www.bea.gov/iTable/iTable.cfm?ReqID=2&step=1#reqid =2&step=1&isuri=1).

a. Imports plus exports for trade; inward plus outward investment positions.

manufacturers now work together to produce goods. Trade in intra-industry and intermediate goods has skyrocketed as companies ship parts back and forth across the border in the process of manufacturing a final product, but perhaps the most striking indicator of this phenomenon is the composition of regional trade. Mexican exports to the United States include, on average, 40 percent U.S. content.[3] As a point of comparison, imports from China contain just 4 percent U.S. parts (see table 5-1 for further comparative data).[4] That means that imports from Mexico, unlike imports from any extraconti-nental partner, strongly promote U.S. exports, industry, and jobs.[5] Through this process of production sharing, the competitiveness of U.S. and Mexican manufacturers has been tightly linked. Improvement in the productivity of industry on either side of the border therefore lowers the total cost of pro-duction for manufacturers on the other. With integrated supply chains, the United States and Mexico must work together to make goods produced in the region competitive for export to the global market.

Table 5-1. *Value of U.S. Content in Imports from Select Economies*

Country	Percent
Mexico	40
Canada	25
Malaysia	8
Korea	5
China	4
Brazil	3
European Union	2
Japan	2
India	2
Russia	1

Source: Robert Koopman and others, "Give Credit Where Credit Is Due: Tracing Value Added in Global Production Chains," Working Paper 16426 (Cambridge, Mass.: National Bureau of Economic Research, September 2010, revised March 2011), p. 38.

Through trade, investment, geography, and shared production, the business cycles as well as long-term growth prospects of the United States and Mexico are tightly intertwined. This interdependence suggests that collaborative and coordinated efforts to strengthen regional competitiveness would offer significant mutual benefits. Nonetheless, the domestic political challenges to their implementation are substantial, especially in the United States. Much of the general public and a large number of policymakers are neither aware of the enormous size of bilateral trade nor conscious of just how important Mexico is to the U.S. economy. There is also significant ambivalence about the value of trade and skepticism regarding free trade agreements. Public opinion does support expanding trade with Mexico, but nonetheless free trade agreements like NAFTA are viewed negatively.[6]

Finally, with NAFTA already in place as the central mechanism for undertaking regional trade and investment, the next set of measures to promote trade, including harmonization of regulations and simplification of customs policies, are both uninspiring and difficult to communicate to the general public. Policy options are discussed at the end of this chapter, but simply put, there is a need for the leaders of the United States and Mexico to articulate and promote a comprehensive competitiveness agenda that comprises both reforms to enhance domestic productivity and bilateral (when possible trilateral) actions to support manufacturers. With such a regional plan, North America can meet the challenge posed by increasing economic competition from emerging markets in Asia and create export-dependent jobs.

The U.S.-Mexico relationship involves, on a daily basis, a web of cross-border interactions among a mix of federal, state, and local government and nongovernment actors. With such a large and dispersed group of players, the only way to enact a coherent strategy is through strong top-level leadership. The U.S. and Mexican presidents must create a strategic framework for the relationship and facilitate the interagency cooperation needed to achieve results. By placing economic relations at the center of that framework, U.S. and Mexican leaders could take advantage of an opportunity to balance the bilateral agenda so that the American public sees Mexico primarily as an opportunity and a partner rather than as a security risk and economic competitor.

Boom, Bust, and an Opportunity for Renewal: Trade and Production Sharing since 1993

Over the past two decades, there have been three major turning points in the U.S.-Mexico economic relationship. First was the implementation of NAFTA, which eliminated most tariff barriers to trade and created a strong legal framework for investors. As a result, trade skyrocketed. Between 1993 and 2000, trade grew at an average annual rate of 17.3 percent, more than tripling in value.[7] Still, many had hoped for even more: a shortcut to the first world for Mexico that would result in an end to illegal immigration into the United States. NAFTA must be recognized both for what is was, a boon to trade and investment, and for what it was not, a broad framework for enhancing development and competitiveness.

The second turning point occurred in 2001 when the roaring growth in bilateral trade that had spurred the integration of the U.S. and Mexican economies in the 1990s slowed down considerably. During the period between 2000 and 2008, U.S.-Mexico trade grew at a modest annual rate of 4.5 percent.[8] The terrorist attacks of 9/11 caused the United States to focus on the defense of the homeland, and the government redoubled border security. Real security advances were made, but the border became more difficult to cross for positive legal traffic as well as potentially dangerous illicit traffic.[9] NAFTA had lowered the barriers to trade, but long and unpredictable wait times at the border ate away at its benefits, adding cost and uncertainty to cross-border supply chains. Several studies have shown how inefficiencies in border management (see table 5-2 for a summary of their findings) and lack of investment in infrastructure and technology at the ports of entry have cut away at the competitiveness of regional industry. Especially affected have been those manufacturers who, because of production sharing, ship materials and parts across the border several times during the production process.[10] As the border became more difficult to cross, the number of people legally entering the United States at the U.S.-Mexico border began to fall. After rising by 22 percent between 1990 and 2000, entries declined by 41 percent in the following decade (see figure 5-2).[11]

Also in 2001, China joined the World Trade Organization, gaining access to most-favored-nation tariffs for its exports to much of the world, including the three North American nations. This shift, along with the more long-term growth of the Chinese economy, resulted in an important new source of competition for U.S. and Mexican producers alike. In Mexico, industries associated with the use of lower-skill labor, like the textile industry, were especially hard hit as factories closed and production shifted to Asia in search of cheaper labor. Largely due to exchange rate fluctuations and the economic rise of China, between October 2000 and March 2002 *maquiladora* production in Mexico declined by 30 percent.[12] Figure 5-3 shows the corresponding drop in total Mexican manufacturing production during this period, as well as its recent recovery.

The third major turning point was the Great Recession. Because of regional economic integration and Mexico's dependence on the U.S. market, when the United States experienced its financial and economic crisis, Mexico's economy crashed even harder, despite its sound macroeconomic footing. While U.S. GDP fell 3.5 percent in 2009, Mexico's economy shrank by a full 6.3 percent (see figure 5-4).[13] Despite the real and significant negative impact of the recession on Mexico, from the depths of the recession and the resulting restructuring of the global economy came a resurgence in Mexico's competitiveness, revival of its manufacturing sector, and a remarkable expansion of trade. After trade fell by 16.8 percent between 2008 and 2009 during the Great Recession, bilateral trade grew at an average annual rate of 23.7 percent from 2009 to 2011, faster than in any two-year period during the NAFTA boom of the 1990s and faster than the growth in U.S. trade with China during the same period (17.3 percent).[14]

Some of the structural factors behind Mexico's resurgence include rising wages in China, an increasingly skilled labor force in Mexico, rising fuel costs, and an important shift in exchange rates. Between 2007 and April 2012, the value of the Mexican peso fell by 17 percent against the value of the U.S. dollar and by a full 33 percent against that of the Chinese yuan, dramatically improving the competitiveness of Mexican exports to the United States and

Table 5-2. *Studies of the Costs of Border Congestion to U.S. and Mexican Economies*[a]

Region of crossings	Region of economic impact	Wait time (minutes)	Year of potential impact	Cost to regional economy (billions of U.S. dollars)	Cost in jobs	Source
San Diego–Tijuana	U.S. and Mexico	No data	2007	7.2	62,000	SANDAG
Imperial Valley–Mexicali	U.S. and Mexico	No data	2007	1.4	11,600	HDR|HLB
Tijuana	Mexico	180	2007–08	1.9	57,000	Del Castillo Vera
Ciudad Juárez	Mexico	132	2007–08	1.5	87,600	Del Castillo Vera
Nuevo Laredo	Mexico	174	2007–08	3.7	133,800	Del Castillo Vera
Nogales	Mexico	66	2007–08	0.2	18,000	Del Castillo Vera
U.S.-Mexico border	U.S.	63	2008	5.8	26,000	Accenture
U.S.-Mexico border	U.S.	99	2017	12.0	54,000	Accenture
El Paso–Ciudad Juárez	El Paso–Ciudad Juárez	2008 peak times: ~45–220	2035	54.0	850,000	Cambridge Systematics

Sources: Cambridge Systematics, El Paso Regional Ports of Entry Operations Plan (Texas Department of Transportation and Cambridge Systematics, June 2011); Gustavo Del Castillo Vera, "Tiempos de espera en los cruces fronterizos del norte de México: una barrera no arancelaria [Wait Times at the Border Crossings in Northern Mexico: Not a Tariff Barrier]," *Comercio Exterior* 59, no. 7 (July 2009), p. 555; SANDAG, *Economic Impacts of Wait Times in the San Diego–Baja California Border Region: Fact Sheet, 2007 Update* (www.sandag.org/index.asp?projectid=258&fuseaction=projects.detail); Accenture, *Draft: Improving Economic Outcomes by Reducing Border Delays*, Accenture and U.S. Department of Commerce, March 2008; HDR|HLB, "Imperial Valley – Mexicali Economic Delay Study" (HDR|HLB Decision Economics, Imperial Valley Association of Governments, and California Department of Transportation, District 11, November 19, 2007).

a. "Year of potential impact" refers to the year in which the listed monetary and employment effects take place. For dates before 2009, it refers to the estimated costs for the year of the study. For future years, it refers to the estimated cost if the border is not made more efficient.

Figure 5-2. *Legal Entries to the United States at the Southern Border, 2000–10*[a]

Millions of legal entries

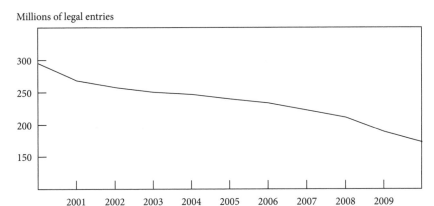

Source: U.S. Department of Transportation, Bureau of Transportation Statistics, "Border Crossing/Entry Data," 2012 (http://transborder.bts.gov/programs/international/transborder/TBDR_BC/TBDR_BCQ.html), based on data from the Department of Homeland Security, U.S. Customs and Border Protection, Office of Field Operations.

a. Figures were calculated by summing the registered number of pedestrians, personal vehicle passengers, bus passengers, train passengers, and trucks entering the United States at the southern border.

Figure 5-3. *Manufacturing Production in Mexico, 1993–2011*

Index 2005 = 100

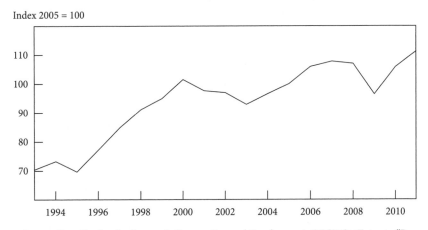

Source: Organization for Economic Cooperation and Development, OECD StatExtracts, "Production and Sales (MEI): Production in Total Manufacturing SA, 2005 = 100," 2012 (http://stats.oecd.org/index.aspx?queryid=90#).

Figure 5-4. *Mexican GDP and GDP Growth, 1993–2017*[a]

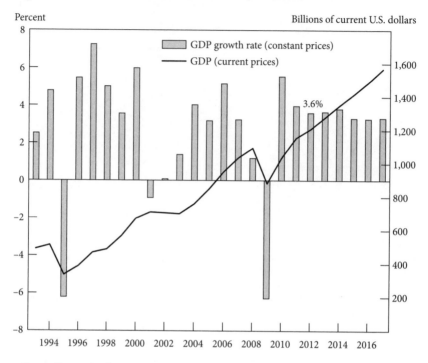

Percent   Billions of current U.S. dollars

Source: International Monetary Fund, World Economic Outlook Database, April 2012 (www.imf.org/external/pubs/ft/weo/2012/01/weodata/index.aspx).

a. Values after 2010 are IMF estimates.

the world, especially relative to that of Chinese exports.[15] At the same time, oil prices continued their more than decade-long period of secular growth, with a 35 percent increase in real crude oil prices between 2007 and 2012, thus raising shipping costs and providing an incentive to use regional rather than global supply chains.[16]

Many of the same factors that led to the resurgence of Mexican manufacturing resulted in similarly positive pressures on U.S. industry. While globalization is still alive and well, the latest trends in manufacturing demonstrate a resurgence of regional production. Offshoring to China is being replaced with nearshoring in Mexico and even reshoring, bringing factories back to the United States.[17] With the technological and logistics improvements that make up advanced manufacturing, labor costs constitute an ever shrinking portion of total production costs.[18] A recent study, for example, found that only 5.3 percent of the price of an iPhone goes to offshore manufacturing wages.[19]

As a result of the advances in manufacturing, firms are less likely to move their factories abroad in search of low wages and more likely to seek out locations with plentiful and skilled human capital and robust supply chains.

A perfect example of the resurgence of regional industry is the auto sector, the industry at the heart of NAFTA. Amazingly, Detroit, rather than Dallas, Houston, or Los Angeles, is the U.S. city with the largest volume of exports to Mexico.[20] Just as the European Union began as the European Coal and Steel Community, NAFTA began as the 1965 Canada-U.S. Automotive Products Trade Agreement. The industry is truly regional. Between 80 and 90 percent of the trade in vehicles and auto parts is intra-industry.[21] Vehicles built in the region are said to cross U.S. borders eight times as they are being produced.[22] The integration of the regional auto sector has allowed the creation of economies of scale and specialization in a way that uses each country's comparative advantages to improve the overall competitiveness of the industry.

After several of North America's largest automakers were on the brink of collapse during the 2008–09 crisis, a robust recovery is under way. There is little doubt that the regional nature of the auto industry is one of the drivers of the recovery. In fact, Mexico and the United States each experienced a sharper rise in vehicle production than any other of the world's top-ten auto producing nations over the 2009–11 period, growing 51 and 72 percent respectively.[23] Mexico's rapid growth in auto production seems likely to continue. In 2011, Nissan, Mazda, Volkswagen, Honda, Chrysler, and General Motors announced investments totaling several billion dollars to increase capacity in Mexico with the intention of serving both their North and South American markets. Then in 2012, Audi announced its intention to build its first North American plant in Mexico, in part because Mexico has free trade agreements with both the European Union and the United States.[24] Despite such gains, the industry faces tough global competition. Predominantly because of the meteoric rise of China's automotive production (from 2 million vehicles in 2000 to more than 18 million in 2011), North America's share of global production declined from 30 percent in 2000 to 14 percent in 2009 before climbing to 17 percent in 2011.[25]

A timid response would be to protect the regional market from imports, but the ambitious and proper response is to aggressively seek to increase productivity in an effort to tap into the markets created by the growing global middle class. A regional competitiveness agenda that lowers barriers to regional trade while promoting U.S. and Mexican investment in human capital and transportation infrastructure could aim for such a lofty target.

Investment: Fueling Industry and Innovation

Bilateral investment boosts trade and employment, supports entrepreneurs and business development, and forms a fundamental component of the production-sharing arrangements that are so vital to regional competitiveness. Foreign direct investment has grown significantly since NAFTA was implemented nearly two decades ago, and each county's FDI position in the other is now at more than six times its 1993 level (see figure 5-5).[26] Foreign direct investment has continued at a fairly steady pace, and it is certainly a driver of economic growth and job creation. In 2009, U.S.-owned companies in Mexico created $25 billion in value added and employed 965,000 workers.[27] Mexican investment in the United States is smaller but has been growing quickly, especially since 2005. In 2008, Mexican companies operating in the United States employed more than 46,000 people and operated 124 production plants.[28] Mexico's top companies have increasingly important U.S. and global operations. Grupo Bimbo, for example, which is the largest baked-goods company in the Americas, has recently grown even more, purchasing Sara Lee's North American business for $709 million.[29] In addition, CEMEX, Grupo Lala, América Móvil, Grupo Alfa, Televisa, Gruma, Grupo Salinas, Grupo Modelo, and several other Mexican companies have established important U.S. operations.

Significant steps have been taken in recent years to strengthen the climate for business and investment in Mexico. The World Bank's Doing Business project, for example, found that the average number of days needed to start a business in Mexico declined from fifty-eight in 2006 to nine in 2012.[30] During the same period, Mexico's score for protecting investors rose from 3.7 to 6.0 of a possible score of ten.[31] The World Economic Forum's Global Competitiveness Index, which ranks the countries of the world from most to least competitive, shows similar advances: Mexico's competitiveness rank rose from 66 among approximately 140 countries in 2010–11 to 58 in 2011–12.[32] Mexico has achieved a remarkable level of macroeconomic stability since its 1994–95 financial crisis, supporting economic growth, keeping inflation in check, and making government borrowing affordable. Mexico's sovereign debt was estimated by the International Monetary Fund to be a manageable 43 percent of GDP in 2012.[33]

Access to credit and the ability to attract investment have increased significantly and helped drive economic growth and the rise of the middle class. As shown in figure 5-6, Mexico's stock exchange exemplifies the trend. It has

Figure 5-5. *U.S.-Mexican Foreign Direct Investment Positions,*
Historical Cost Basis, 1993–2011

Billions of U.S. dollars

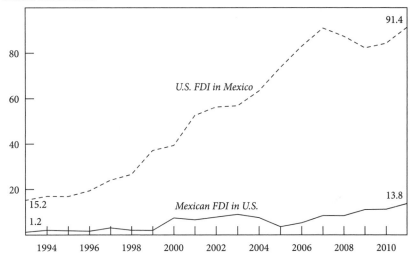

Source: U.S. Department of Commerce, Bureau of Economic Analysis, "International Data:
Direct Investment and MNC," 2012 (www.bea.gov/iTable/iTable.cfm?ReqID=2&step=1#reqid=
2&step=1&isuri=1).

more than doubled in size over the past two decades, with $525 billion in
market capitalization at the end of 2012. Moreover, it proved remarkably
resilient by recovering all of its financial crisis losses in terms of market capitalization in a year and a half, something that the New York Stock Exchange
had not yet done by the end of 2012.[34] Nonetheless, there is still much room
to grow. Businesses often fail to reach their potential due to lack of adequate
access to credit and investment. There remain both untapped opportunities
for investors and significant impediments to greater investment in the Mexican economy.

Two major rule-of-law challenges exist. First, according to an April 2012
article in the *New York Times*, Wal-Mart paid more than $24 million in bribes
to speed up the permit process as the company quickly grew to become the
third-largest company operating in Mexico.[35] Subsequent reporting was quick
to point out that paying such bribes is a relatively common practice, and Mexico does have the poor distinction of being considered more corrupt than
ninety-five other countries by Transparency International's Corruption Perceptions Index. [36] The alleged corruption does not bode well for the way that

Figure 5-6. *Mexican Stock Exchange, Market Capitalization, 1993–2012*

Billions of U.S. dollars

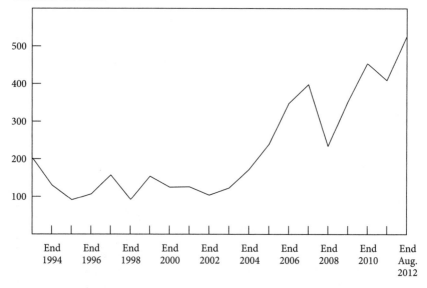

Source: World Federation of Exchanges, "Market Capitalization," 2012 (www.world-exchanges. org/statistics/time-series/market-capitalization).

potential investors see the business climate in Mexico. Second, according to a survey of foreign companies operating in Mexico, investors have been concerned though largely undeterred by the rise of organized crime–related violence in some parts of Mexico.[37] Nonetheless, crime and violence are a drag on economic growth, disproportionately hurting small businesses, and probably have prevented some potential investments. Mexico's largest bank, BBVA Bancomer, estimated the cost of increased violence at approximately 1 percent of GDP growth a year.[38]

Aside from rule-of-law challenges, important limitations on investment in Mexico derive from the lack of competition in the energy and telecommunications sectors and the need for several of the structural reforms mentioned by Franco in chapter 2.[39] Foreign investment in Mexico's energy sector is severely restricted by Article 27 of Mexico's constitution, but Mexico's significant deepwater oil and shale gas reserves mean that energy reform could open the way to significant investment and economic growth. In contrast to Mexico's energy sector, which is run predominantly by state-owned enterprises, Mexico's telecommunications industry was privatized in the late 1980s and early 1990s. Nonetheless, competition in Mexico's television broadcasting and telephone communications industries is quite limited, with one or two companies dominating the markets. Stronger competition policy, including cutting restrictions on foreign investment in these industries, would bring new investment and lower prices.[40] Expanding the size and reach of the banking system by strengthening property rights and fostering greater domestic and international competition in the financial sector would also create incentives for greater investment from both domestic and international sources.[41]

Policies and Strategies for Competitiveness

Four distinct but related factors affect Mexico's ability to compete within the global market and achieve the productivity required to be a newly industrialized nation: global trade and the Trans-Pacific Partnership; the Mexican-U.S. border; regulatory standards; and customs simplification and convergence.

GLOBAL TRADE AND THE TRANS-PACIFIC PARTNERSHIP. As three tightly integrated, open economies, the United States, Mexico, and Canada have much to gain by working together on a global trade agenda designed to increase exports by countering protectionism and opening markets. The fact that each of the North American nations has joined the Trans-Pacific Partnership (TPP) negotiations to create a free trade agreement that would link them to eight other Pacific Rim countries could be interpreted as a sign that the NAFTA partners are ready to work as economic allies on the global stage. Their inclusion in the TPP negotiations protects the regional integration achieved by NAFTA while creating an opportunity to update NAFTA without reopening the still divisive agreement. Nonetheless, a look at the complicated path that brought the three countries together suggests that they may not yet fully embrace the advantages of acting in concert as an economic bloc. Both Mexico and Canada were latecomers to the TPP because of complicated domestic politics and the protectionist leanings of protected industries, and the United States was slow to welcome its neighbors after they had at last signaled their interest in joining. The TPP has the potential to become the new model for trade agreements (with an updated approach to services, intellectual property, and technology), and if it is successfully negotiated and implemented, China may decide that it has more to gain by joining in than by sitting out. If so, that would in turn create a strong incentive for progress on the global trade agenda at the World Trade Organization (WTO). Although the United States, Mexico, and Canada seem to have not yet decided to work together as a bloc, the pieces are in place and there is great potential for them to use the TPP as a first move in a strategic process to encourage the opening of markets and expansion of exports.

THE BORDER. Trade has skyrocketed since NAFTA, but increasingly the ports of entry that should serve as the gateway for regional trade have become bottlenecks. As described above, increased security and lack of investment in infrastructure at the U.S.-Mexico border have led to long and unpredictable border crossing times. To resolve these problems, presidents Obama and Calderón launched the 21st Century Border Initiative, which outlines strategies to simultaneously strengthen security and improve efficiency. One area especially ripe for further action is the promotion and expansion of trusted traveler and trusted shipper programs. With these programs, individuals and companies voluntarily submit to extensive background checks to prove that they present little risk of illicit trafficking. In exchange, they are granted expedited passage across the border. That saves both the individual and the U.S. Department of Homeland Security time and money, allowing border inspectors to focus on those individuals presenting greater or unknown levels of risk.

Also helpful would be expanded use of partnerships with cities and private industry to fund infrastructure projects, which would free up the budget of the U.S. Customs and Border Protection Office of Field Operations and allow the agency to more fully staff each port of entry during peak hours. Public-private and federal-local partnerships have been successful in some locations. However, an ongoing and cooperative dialogue between federal agencies and border stakeholders—for example, local governments, companies with interests in the border region and border management, and private sector groups such as local chambers of commerce—is needed to fully leverage the funding that local governments and the private sector can bring to the table.

REGULATORY STANDARDS. From soup cans to cereal to vehicles, Canada, the United States, and Mexico have their own rules and regulations for product safety. Unfortunately, the artifices of each country's policies to protect domestic consumers often unnecessarily force companies to run separate production lines for goods destined for each country. Overcoming this "tyranny of small differences" is the subject of the U.S.-Mexico High-Level Regulatory Cooperation Council and the U.S.-Canada Regulatory Cooperation Council. The two bodies could be unified and their mandate renewed in an effort to create a truly continental market.

CUSTOMS SIMPLIFICATION AND CONVERGENCE. Despite the free trade framework created by NAFTA, companies must meet significant customs requirements each time they take goods across the border. They must meet complex rules of origin, which in today's world of globalized supply chains can be a complicated and time-consuming task. This regulatory burden acts as a tax on the very cross-border transactions that NAFTA sought to promote. Small and medium-sized businesses—the motor of job creation—are especially affected. Customs requirements on both the U.S. and Mexican sides could be simplified, streamlined, and further computerized. Both countries should redouble efforts to put in place an electronic "single window" system, through which all the needed customs information for imports and exports would be collected in one place and automatically distributed to the many pertinent federal agencies, thus avoiding the significant cost of filing multiple forms.

A more ambitious goal would be to begin product-by-product efforts to harmonize external tariffs, incrementally working toward a common external tariff.[42] As tariffs are harmonized, regional trade in the affected products would be freed of most customs documentation requirements. The need for rules-of-origin recordkeeping, for example, would be entirely eliminated. A natural place to begin would be identification of products for which each North American country charges a similar most-favored-nation tariff rate. For those products, harmonization would require the smallest tariff adjustments, making them less politically contentious and less disruptive to domestic industry.

Conclusion

Currently North America is a region without a regional economic agenda. Ambivalent public attitudes toward trade, a pressing need for domestic economic reforms, and a focus on security issues in Mexico have kept U.S. and Mexican leaders from pursuing an economic agenda robust and coherent enough to inspire public support. Despite the absence of a strategic plan, regional manufacturing has been integrated through production sharing and has recovered its competitiveness, so one can imagine what might occur if the United States and Mexico were to articulate and enact a competitiveness agenda to support regional industry and promote its exports. Tied together by geography, trade, investment, and an integrated manufacturing sector, the United States, Mexico, and Canada are deeply dependent on one another. To effectively meet the challenge presented by China and the rest of emerging Asia, to create good jobs in advanced manufacturing and design, and to compete in a rapidly evolving global market, the United States and Mexico must work together to strengthen North American productivity and competitiveness.

Notes

1. Adding actual 2011 merchandise trade (exports plus imports) to projected bilateral trades in services (exports plus imports) results in a figure of $499.8 billion in total 2011 U.S.-Mexico bilateral trade. The projected services trade figure was calculated by applying the 2009–10 growth rate to the 2010 level. Merchandise trade source: U.S. Department of Commerce, Census Bureau, Foreign Trade Statistics, "Trade in Goods with Mexico," 2012 (www.census.gov/foreign-trade/balance/c2010.html). Services trade source: U.S. Department of Commerce, Bureau of Economic Analysis, "Private Services Trade by Area and Country," 2012 (www.bea.gov/international/international_services.htm).

2. Trade refers to imports plus exports: U.S. Department of Commerce, Census Bureau, Foreign Trade Statistics, 2012. Investment refers to the sum of U.S. FDI in Mexico and Mexican FDI positions in the United States: U.S. Department of Commerce, Bureau of Economic Analysis, 2012.

3. Robert Koopman and others, "Give Credit Where Credit Is Due: Tracing Value Added in Global Production Chains," Working Paper 16426 (Cambridge, Mass.: National Bureau of Economic Research, September 2010, revised March 2011), p. 38.

4. Ibid.

5. For more on this issue, see Christopher E. Wilson, *Working Together: Economic Ties between the United States and Mexico* (Washington: Woodrow Wilson Center, November 2011).

6. Public opinion supports greater trade with Mexico (52 percent for, 37 percent against) but opposes free trade agreements "like NAFTA" (44 percent against, 35 percent for). Pew Research Center for the People and the Press, "Americans Are of Two Minds on Trade," November 9, 2010 (http://pewresearch.org/pubs/1795/poll-free-trade-agreements-jobs-wages-economic-growth-china-japan-canada).

7. Author's calculations based on data from U.S. Department of Commerce, "Trade in Goods with Mexico," 2012.

8. Ibid.

9. For evidence and analysis of this issue, see Edward Alden, *The Closing of the American Border: Terrorism, Immigration, and Security since 9/11* (New York: Harper Collins, 2008); and Robert Pastor, The *North American Idea: A Vision of a Continental Future* (Oxford University Press, 2011).

10. Kei-Mu Yi, "Can Vertical Specialization Explain the Growth of World Trade?" *Journal of Political Economy* 111, no. 1 (February 2003): 52–102.

11. Author's calculations. Comparable data were not available throughout the entire 1990–2010 period, so separate sources were used for the 1990–2000 calculation and the 2000–10 calculation. Data from FY 1990–2000 come from U.S. Department of Homeland Security, Immigration Statistics Office, PAS G-22, as cited in Pastor, *The North American Idea: A Vision of a Continental Future*, p. 117. Data from 2000–10 come from U.S. Department of Transportation, Research and Innovative Technology Administration, Bureau of Transportation Statistics, Border Crossing/Entry Data (http://

transborder.bts.gov/programs/international/transborder/TBDR_BC/TBDR_BCQ. html), based on data from the Department of Homeland Security, U.S. Customs and Border Protection, Office of Field Operations.

12. Total manufacturing in Mexico over the 1993–2011 period, shown in figure 5-3, declined much less than *maquiladora* production. The decline in *maquiladora* production was caused by exchange rate fluctuations, uncertainty, and fluctuations in the way that *maquiladoras* were taxed as well as the fact that much lower-skill assembly work moved to Asia. Source for *maquiladora* production data: U.S. General Accounting Office, "Mexico's Maquiladora Decline Affects U.S.-Mexico Border Communities and Trade; Recovery Depends in Part on Mexico's Actions," GAO-03-891 (July 2003).

13. International Monetary Fund, World Economic Outlook Database, April 2012 (www.imf.org/external/pubs/ft/weo/2012/01/weodata/index.aspx).

14. Author's calculations based on data from U.S. Department of Commerce, "Trade in Goods with Mexico," 2012.

15. Author's calculations based on data from International Monetary Fund, "Exchange Rate Archives by Month," 2012 (www.imf.org/external/np/fin/data/param_rms_mth.aspx).

16. Author's calculations based on data and price projections for 2012 from U.S. Energy Information Administration, 2012 (www.eia.gov/forecasts/steo/realprices/).

17. "The Boomerang Effect," *The Economist*, April 21, 2012 (www.economist.com/node/21552898).

18. "A Third Industrial Revolution," *The Economist*, April 21, 2012 (www.economist.com/node/21552901).

19. Kenneth L. Kraemer, Greg Linden, and Jason Dedrick, "Capturing Value in Global Networks: Apple's iPad and iPhone," July 2011 (http://pcic.merage.uci.edu/papers/2011/Value_iPad_iPhone.pdf).

20. Detroit exported $11 billion in goods to Mexico in 2009. U.S. Department of Commerce, International Trade Administration, Office of Trade and Industry Information, Manufacturing, and Services (http://tse.export.gov/METRO/).

21. Isabel Studer, "The North American Auto Industry," *Mapping the New North American Reality*, working paper series 2004-09 (Montreal: Institute for Research on Public Policy, 2004), p. 1.

22. Robert Pastor, "The Future of North America," *Foreign Affairs* (July–August 2008), p. 89.

23. Author's calculations based on data from the International Organization of Motor Vehicle Manufacturers, 2012 (http://oica.net/category/production-statistics/).

24. Adam Thomson and John Reed, "Audi to Open Mexico Production Plant," *Financial Times*, April 18, 2012 (www.ft.com/intl/cms/s/0/ab3abae8-8987-11e1-85b6-00144feab49a.html#axzz1uaxlppJh).

25. Despite China's growing auto production, its car companies have made little headway in non-Asian markets. Production data from International Organization of Motor Vehicle Manufacturers, 2012 (http://oica.net/category/production-statistics/).

26. U.S. Department of Commerce, Bureau of Economic Analysis, "International Data: Direct Investment and MNC," 2012 (www.bea.gov/iTable/iTable.cfm?ReqID= 2&step=1#reqid=2&step=1&isuri=1).

27. Kevin Barefoot and Raymond Mataloni, "Operations of U.S. Multinational Companies in the United States and Abroad: Preliminary Results from the 2009 Benchmark Survey" (Washington: Bureau of Economic Analysis, Department of Commerce, November 2011) (www.bea.gov/scb/pdf/2011/11%20November/1111_mnc.pdf).

28. Thomas Anderson, "U.S. Affiliates of Foreign Companies: Operations in 2008" (Washington: Bureau of Economic Analysis, U.S. Department of Commerce, November 2010); Gabriel Nieto, "Las mexicanas más globales de 'Las 500' [The Most Global of the 500 Most Important Mexican Companies]," *Expansión*, June 23, 2011.

29. Sara Lee, "Sara Lee and Grupo Bimbo Receive U.S. Department of Justice Approval on North American Fresh Bakery Sale," press release, October 21, 2011.

30. World Bank, "Doing Business: Measuring Business Regulations," 2012 (www.doingbusiness.org/Custom-Query/mexico).

31. Ibid.

32. World Economic Forum, *Global Competitiveness Report 2011–2012* (2012), pp. 258–59.

33. International Monetary Fund, World Economic Outlook Database, April 2012 (www.imf.org/external/pubs/ft/weo/2012/01/weodata/index.aspx).

34. Both the Mexican and New York stock exchanges reached their 2008 high points in terms of domestic market capitalization in May of that year, before the economic crisis. Mexico's exchange surpassed that level in December 2010. World Federation of Exchanges, 2012 (www.world-exchanges.org/statistics/time-series/market-capitalization).

35. David Barstow, "Vast Mexico Bribery Case Hushed Up by Wal-Mart after Top-Level Struggle," *New York Times*, April 22, 2012 (www.nytimes.com/2012/04/22/business/at-wal-mart-in-mexico-a-bribe-inquiry-silenced.html?_r=1&ref=walmartstoresinc).

36. Transparency International, "Corruptions Perceptions Index 2011," 2012 (http://cpi.transparency.org/cpi2011/results/); Crayton Harrison and Nacha Cattan, "Mexico Facing Cost of Bribe Ethos That Snared Wal-Mart," *Bloomberg Businessweek*, April 25, 2012 (www.businessweek.com/printer/articles/53388?type=bloomberg).

37. American Chamber/Mexico and Kroll Mexico, *The Impact of Security in Mexico on the Private Sector*, 2011 (http://krolltendencias.com/site/images/stories/tendencias/093/kroll-amcham-2010-2011-survey-english.pdf).

38. Alejandro Werner, "Mexico: Recent Developments," in Eduardo Levy-Yeyati, *Latin America Economic Perspectives, All Together Now: The Challenge of Regional Integration* (Brookings: April 2012), pp. 70–71.

39. For a comprehensive set of recommendations to strengthen Mexico's financial system and broader economy, see Claudio Loser and Harinder Kohli, *Mexico: A New Vision for Mexico 2042: Achieving Prosperity for All* (Mexico City: Centennial Group, CEESP, IMCO, and México Evalúa, 2012).

40. Instituto Mexicano para la Competividad (IMCO) [Mexican Institute for Competitiveness], "Indice de Competitividad Internacional 2011: Más Allá de los BRICS [International Competitiveness Index: Beyond the BRICs]" (http://imco.org.mx/images/pdf/Indice-de-Competitividad-Internacional-2011.pdf).

41. Ibid., p. 30.

42. See Gary Hufbauer and Jeffrey Schott, *NAFTA Revisited: Achievements and Challenges* (Washington: Institute for International Economics, October 2005). Also see Carla Hills, "Working Together: Economic Ties between the United States and Mexico," conference keynote address, Woodrow Wilson Center, Washington, D.C., February 14, 2012 (www.wilsoncenter.org/event/north-american-integration-essential-to-renewed-us-manufacturing-prowess).

ARMANDO CHACÓN

6

The Priority of Education in Mexico

Countries with the highest productivity per employed person are, with no exception, countries where education levels have grown consistently and the average education level has reached thirteen years of schooling or more. While in Mexico access to education is nearly universal at the primary and secondary levels, the average length of schooling of the labor force is about eight and a half years.

Education has a positive return in all countries where it has been measured consistently. Mexico is no exception. Despite the evident deficiencies in the quality of education in Mexico, an additional year of schooling increases the lifetime earnings of individuals by 10 percent on average. People who manage to invest more in their education not only have higher incomes but also acquire a better quality of life and other forms of social capital. In addition, people with more education are in a better position to better educate their children and provide them with more capabilities so that they, in turn, are able to live better.

Political debate and conventional wisdom have claimed that the opposition of the teachers' union to universal evaluation is the major obstacle to overcoming the educational gaps in Mexico. Facing the presidential election in 2012, the four candidates in the race seemed to have similar assessments and general proposals to improve the quality of education through performance incentives. The candidates also offered to improve educational curriculums and expand school hours. Those proposals were respected when the winning candidate, Enrique Peña Nieto of the PRI (Partido Revolucionario Institucional [Institutional Revolutionary Party]), submitted his education reforms to congress in December 2012. However, despite the appropriateness of such measures, there are no standard solutions to the problem of increasing the quality of educational outputs, which requires both a long time and a lot of resources. Furthermore, implementing the proposed reforms will be extremely challenging, and the reformed programs will require rigorous impact evaluations to distinguish what works from what does not.

The task of improving the quality and quantity of education falls not only on the government but also on citizens in the private sector. Having better teachers, better facilities, and a better curriculum (the supply side of education) does not eliminate the obstacles that most young people must overcome in order to continue their studies. Like any other market, the market for education also has a demand side. Regardless of the quality of supply, we must examine the demand side, where socioeconomic obstacles limit the ability and willingness of young people to stay in school. In particular, lack of role models, lack of early talent-detection mechanisms, and lack of financing present significant obstacles to a majority of students in Mexico. In overcoming those obstacles, civil society can play an important role. Around the world, evidence on mentoring, tutoring, early detection of talent, and access to financing demonstrates the transformative impact on students from adverse environments that occurs when money from donors is combined with good ideas and the voluntary work of concerned citizens.

Education: The Key to Prosperity

More investment and fewer restrictions on economic activity are needed to generate economic growth and well-being. It is indisputable that with better roads, better hospitals, better laws and judges, more security, and more honest and efficient public servants it would be easier to attract more investors to establish operations in Mexico. It is clear that those advantages translate into lower costs for companies and a better business environment in general.

Mexico is still far from being a developed country. However, there are many examples of professionals, companies, and industries in Mexico that are competitive worldwide, exporting high-value-added products as well as knowledge and best practices. What these world-class companies and professionals have in common is their accumulation of human capital at levels comparable to those seen in developed countries. With their human capital, they transcend the material and institutional gaps that otherwise prevail in the country.

Historically, there have been many episodes in which infrastructure, institutions, and other national resources have been devastated by wars or natural disasters. When such disasters occur in countries that have accumulated high levels of human capital, they return quickly to high levels of material and human development. Germany, for example, recovered its place among the most developed countries in the world after much of its infrastructure and resources were devastated during World War II. In more recent examples— such as South Korea, Australia, Ireland, and Spain—the value added per employee has grown steadily as the stock of human capital has increased. To a large extent China and India also have increased the average productivity of their workers through increases in average years of schooling.

From this perspective, human capital is not just one of the factors that help countries grow; it is the essential source of the wealth of any country and, above all, of the prosperity and well-being of its people. The way in which human capital contributes to economic development is easier to understand than the contribution of the so-called structural factors. That does not mean that the structural conditions are unimportant, but it does mean that in order for people and businesses to develop it is not necessary to wait until institutions and infrastructure comparable to those of the most advanced nations are in place. A greater accumulation of human capital should facilitate structural changes and pending reforms, allowing priorities to be reassigned.

Regrettably, the same argument does not work so well in reverse. If we were magically to wake up tomorrow in a Mexico with low-cost energy and telecommunications as well as a super-efficient bureaucracy, surely we might expect positive changes. Yet such instant improvements would hardly close the huge gaps in productivity per worker between Mexico and countries with significantly larger stocks of human capital.

Human Capital and Productivity

The average productivity of workers can serve as a good proxy of the capacity of each person and each country to generate wealth and prosperity. This indicator lets us track the evolution of Mexico's productivity over time and compare it with that of other countries. In comparing the relationship between average years of schooling and value added per employee in constant dollars between 1980 and 2006, we notice that the increase in average years of schooling in the BRIC group has been significant. With the exception of Russia, which in 1989 already had an average of ten years of schooling, the other BRICs started with an average of only three to four years. At the end of 2006, Russia's average reached twelve years of schooling (completion of high school), while some of the other BRICs reached the eight-year average. Consistent with that educational level, the average value added per worker in this group of countries is less than US$20,000.

In those countries with an average of more than ten years of schooling in 1980, education and productivity have continued to grow consistently. That average ten years of schooling could very well be the barrier that divides developing and developed countries. Today, no countries that have a per-worker productivity level of more than US$40,000 a year have an average of less than ten years of schooling. The countries that in 1980 already had an average of more than ten years have experienced significant increases in productivity per worker, in line with the increases in average years of schooling.

A Swiss, Norwegian, or Danish worker generates on average six times more value added than a Mexican worker. A French, Dutch, Italian, or American generates five times more value added. The average English, Japanese, German, or Canadian worker is four times more productive than the average Mexican worker. To get a more complete picture, we can also compare Mexico with countries where workers generate less value. A Mexican worker generates on average 14 percent more value added than a Russian, 18 percent more than a Brazilian, 25 percent more than a South African, three times more than a Chinese, and six times more than an Indian worker.

In general, the countries where people are more productive are countries where the average number of years of schooling has been increasing steadily. In Mexico, the population of men of more than 25 years of age have an average of eight and a half years of schooling. Countries like the Czech Republic, the United States, Norway, Switzerland, and Canada exceed Mexico's average years of schooling by at least five years. Canada has the highest average in the world. Korea, Japan, Germany, Poland, Sweden, Cyprus, and Lithuania surpass Mexico by four years on average. On the other hand, Mexico records more average years of schooling than India and Brazil by two years and slightly more than China by 0.6 years. Among the BRICs, only Russia outdoes Mexico, with an average of almost thirteen years of schooling.

Establishing a precise causal relationship between average years of schooling and economic growth is a complicated task. In the case of Mexico, while schooling increased significantly during the past thirty years (from 4.5 to 8.5 years on average), GDP per worker has stalled. Although GDP per capita has grown moderately in the same period, the participation of the population in the labor force grew more than proportionally. In other words, the country produces more because more people are in the labor force, not because average value added per worker has increased. The fraction of the working-age population is greater than ever before in Mexico's history, and it will continue to grow during the next two decades. Nevertheless, the so-called demographic bonus would be much larger with more value added per worker. There are several possible reasons why it has not increased. One is that although the average years of schooling of the Mexican labor force has doubled during the past two decades, the country's population, on average, has not reached the secondary level of education. Apart from considerations of quality in the Mexican educational system, the country has failed to achieve the average level of schooling needed for workers to participate in higher value-added activities.

The Stage of Educational Development in Mexico

Educational development in a country occurs in at least three stages. In the first stage, the priority is to expand the coverage of basic education services. In the second stage, coverage is extended to include the middle and higher levels of education. Finally, in the third stage, once there is access at all levels for those with sufficient capacity and willingness to continue studying, the quality of educational services becomes the priority.

The challenges of the first stage can still be seen in the least developed countries of the world. In many African countries, the main battle is to ensure that children attend primary school and that teachers show up at school to teach. In this context, programs for deworming children and programs to verify teachers' attendance have been shown to increase schooling.

The third stage is found in more developed countries, where the priority is placed on achieving a specific standard of quality at all educational levels. In countries such as Finland, which always appears at the top of international comparisons, there are programs that seek to close the gaps between regions and within classrooms. Even in countries like Canada, which has the highest average number of years of schooling in the world, it is necessary to actively support school districts and students whose results are below the national standard. In the United States also there are marked differences in quality that can be traced to the family and neighborhood environment as well as the socioeconomic status of students. Performance and achievement in school districts with high income and high average schooling are consistently better than in districts with low income and low average schooling.

Figure 6-1. *Percentage of Men with Higher Education, per Age Cohort,*
1950–95

Percent

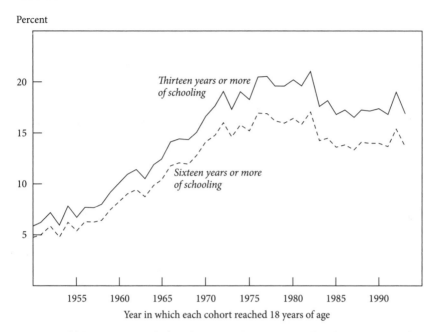

Year in which each cohort reached 18 years of age

Source: Pablo Peña, *Aggregate Shocks and Investment in Human Capital: Evidence on Postsecondary Schooling during the Lost Decade in Mexico* (Universidad Iberoamericana, 2011).

Mexico is probably in a transition between the end of the second stage and the beginning of the third stage. Although the coverage of basic and mid-level education has expanded during the last thirty years, participation in higher education is stagnant. The proportion of each generation that made it to college (students having thirteen or more years of schooling) has been frozen since the late 1970s (figure 6-1). The three decades that followed that period were characterized by a series of economic and financial crises that undoubtedly altered the decisions of individuals and families in Mexico to invest in education.

During economic downturns the relative cost of going back to school goes down since there are fewer opportunities to find well-paid jobs. In developed countries, however, financing is relatively abundant in spite of downturns—financing from the government, financial institutions, and households allows many people to go back to school and complete their undergraduate or postgraduate degrees in order to return to the labor market when the economy improves. In countries like Mexico, where significantly less financing is available, we see the opposite. During economic downturns financially constrained households face additional pressures that force thousands of young students to abandon school in spite of the relative scarcity of well-paid jobs. Without financing, an economic downturn is the worst time imaginable to complete high school or a college or graduate degree.

Economic Return to Education in Mexico

There is much to fix in Mexico's education system, and improving the quality of education in the country is an objective to be pursued urgently. Nongovernment organizations (NGOs) such as Mexicanos Primeros and others concerned with Mexico's performance gaps in education along with international organizations such as the Organization for Economic Cooperation and Development (OECD) and the World Bank have contributed significantly to making education a priority on the policy agenda. There is no doubt that a higher quality of education for all would bring Mexico's population closer to attaining the levels of knowledge and skills observed in developed countries. Despite all the problems and the gaps in quality, more schooling has a positive return. People who study more not only have higher average productivity and earnings, they also enjoy better living standards and can create better opportunities for their children. More education also facilitates investment in other forms of human capital, such as health. It also allows for development of higher civic values and better tools to improve the skills of the upcoming generations.

Higher Income

Returns on education are positive in all countries and periods in which they have been consistently measured. According to George Psacharopoulos, in Sub-Saharan Africa the average return to education is 13.4 percent.[1] In Latin America and the Caribbean, it is 12.4 percent. In Asia, excluding OECD countries, the return is 9.6 percent, while in Europe, the Middle East, and North Africa the average return in each region is 8.2 percent. In the OECD countries, excluding Mexico, the average return to schooling is at 6.8 percent. Worldwide, the return to education is 10.1 percent. Even when different countries have different educational systems and have attained different levels of development, in every country more education is associated with higher income.

According to Juan Ordaz, the average return to education in Mexico is between 10 and 13 percent.[2] In other words, every additional year in school is associated with 10 percent higher lifetime earnings. Figure 6-2 presents

Figure 6-2. *Returns to Education in Mexico*[a]

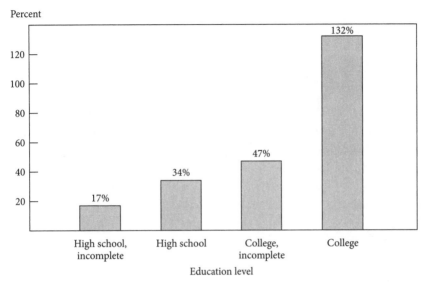

Percent

Education level

Source: Instituto Nacional de Estadística, Geografía, e Informática [National Institute of Statistics, Geography, and Informatics] "Encuesta Nacional de Educación, Capacitación, y Empleo [National Survey of Education, Training, and Employment]" (2001).
a. Percent above the average income for completed middle school.

the percentage of additional lifetime income for different education levels above lifetime income at the secundaria level (middle school or junior high). On average, a person who finishes high school has a lifetime income that is 34 percent higher than someone who finished only secundaria (nine years of schooling). For those who complete a college degree, the difference in income is 132 percent. In other words, the income of a person with a licenciatura is, on average, more than twice the income of a person with only a secundaria diploma.

Moreover, even workers who do not complete a degree are rewarded with higher incomes. Workers with incomplete high school studies have 17 percent more income than those with only a middle school education. Workers who did not complete their studies for a bachelor's degree earn 47 percent more on average than those with only a middle school diploma.

Improved Quality of Life

Education has tangible benefits besides making people more productive at work and allowing them to earn more. Jason M. Fletcher and David E. Frisvold showed that going to college was associated with a greater likelihood of using preventive health care.[3] Furthermore, Nattavudh Powdthavee found that higher education translated into a lower risk of hypertension.[4] Education provides both information and the capacity to acquire and use more information in the future—information that can be used to attain a better quality of life. Health is the best example. Part of the education acquired in school, especially at the most basic level, has to do with health. Basic hygiene to prevent diseases and epidemics, reproductive health, and good nutrition are examples of topics typically addressed in schools. The classroom is a good place to explain health issues and the clear benefits of taking good care of one's personal health and that of one's family. Adriana Lleras-Muney estimates that an additional year of schooling translates into 1.7 additional years of life expectancy. Education enables people to live longer and healthier lives.[5] A person who is exposed to these issues while in school is in a better position to put the lessons learned into practice.

Better Opportunities for Children

Evidence shows that their parents' level of education translates into more and better education for children. The home is a child's first school. Parents are the first teachers of their children, and just as it is a good idea to have well-trained teachers in schools, it is desirable to have better prepared parents at home. Educated parents are in a better position to educate their children. According to the Nobel Prize–winning economist James Heckman and his colleague Pedro Carneiro, "educated parents are more able to school their children, and have skills to direct and assist them in their studies."[6]

Philip Oreopoulos, Marianne E. Page, and Ann Huff Stevens found that an extra year of parental education reduced the likelihood that the children would repeat a school year.[7] It also reduced the likelihood that a teenager would drop out of school. That evidence suggests that the increased educational achievement of one generation benefits future generations. A more educated person will have more educated children, and those children will be better prepared and better able to help educate the next generation.

Benefits for Society

In addition to individual and intergenerational benefits, education also benefits society in general. A society based on law requires its citizens to be aware of their rights and duties. A democracy requires citizens to be aware of alternative political options and to understand the consequences of their electoral decisions. A more educated population is in a better position to benefit from and enjoy the advantages of the rule of law and to sustain a functional democratic system. Robert Barro presents international comparisons that show that higher education in a given population is associated with more voting rights and more civil liberties.[8] According to Thomas S. Dee, higher education has a positive effect on participation in elections and on support for freedom of speech. Markets also function better when consumers are better educated.[9] When people have more information and can process it better, they can improve their assessment of their alternatives, thereby making markets work more efficiently.

According to the Nobel Prize–winning economist Theodore W. Schultz, schooling also improves people's ability to decipher new information, whether it comes from external sources or from their own experience.[10] When there is a technological breakthrough, people with higher levels of education are able to understand its benefits and put it into practice more quickly. Andrew Foster and Mark Rosenzweig showed how farmers in India who had more education were better able to take advantage of the opportunities to use new and more productive seed varieties during the Green Revolution.[11]

Education Reform: Improving the Quality of Education

In December 2012, the Mexican congress approved the Reforma Educativa (Education Reform) by an overwhelming majority of 350 to 51, with 20 abstentions. The most celebrated component of the reform was the amendment to Article 3 of the constitution, which now states,

> The State will guarantee the quality of mandatory education (now including the high school level), ensuring that materials, educational methods, school organization, education infrastructure, and suitability of teachers and school districts guarantee the maximum learning achievement of students.[12]

The constitutional amendment was coupled with the creation of Sistema Nacional de Evaluación Educativa (National Education Assessment System), coordinated by the newly created Instituto Nacional para la Evaluación de la Educación (National Institute for the Evaluation of Education), which is accountable to the senate with a mandate to ensure the quality of education through evaluation. The reform also included the creation of full-time schools and the creation of the Servicio Profesional Docente (Teachers Professional

Service), which is supposed to establish evaluation criteria for granting teachers promotions and offering them incentives.

Elevating such objectives to the constitutional level should carry significant weight, politically speaking. However, Mexico has neither the funds nor the human resources necessary to implement all of these reforms simultaneously throughout the nation. Implementing any one of them will require an enormous amount of money and at least a couple of decades. Curiously, the ambitious plans laid out in constitutional reform measures were not matched with a corresponding increase in the budget approved for 2013.

Role of the Teachers' Union

The reform emphasizes the importance of evaluating teacher performance and the quality of education inputs. The assertion that the SNTE (Sindicato Nacional de Trabajadores de la Educación [National Educational Workers Union]) blocks any effort to improve the quality of education and only wishes to preserve teacher privileges is widely accepted by both analysts and the general public. A recent episode of the visible struggle with the SNTE, the national teachers' union with the largest subscriber base, occurred a couple of months before the July 2012 election.[13] In May 2012, the union broke its agreement with the federal government to implement a universal assessment program, which called for a comprehensive assessment of teachers' training, capabilities, and performance in the classroom. Facing the election, the SNTE put its agreement with the government on hold while awaiting the election's outcome. It was an obvious move to make from the union's perspective, but it met national protest.

The SNTE gave its blessing to the December 2012 educational reforms. The union even mounted a media campaign pledging its support for the evaluation objectives of the reform as long as the evaluations did not jeopardize jobs. The agreement, which is a very valuable political achievement for the incoming PRI administration and an important concession by the teachers' union, may represent a breakthrough in the very tense relationship between SNTE and the government. The evaluation of teachers, their training, and their achievements in the classroom opens the door to greater efficiency through incentives and other mechanisms to improve the quality of teachers and education.

However, the agreement alone cannot solve the problems. It constitutes only the starting point in a process to address the real challenges ahead. If the assessments are well carried out, they can provide valuable information about what the main shortcomings are; that information can then be analyzed to determine how to remedy the deficiencies. Improving the quality of education is a complicated and expensive process that will require many financial and human resources to discover which solutions work to improve performance and which do not.

Improving Quality: A Long and Expensive Process

When factories want to improve the quality of output on a production line, they begin by carefully measuring how many defective parts exist per every thousand items produced. Subsequently, they seek to find the source of the defects, whether in materials, machines, operators, the work environment, or a combination of factors. Yet a high-quality review system does not solve the problem. Punishing or replacing operators or even publishing a national list of bad operators could make them work harder and more carefully. However, neither a positive nor a negative reward system can compensate for operators' deficiencies if they are not caused by lack of effort but instead by lack of skills and knowledge. Nor will a carrot-and-stick strategy resolve failures that are linked to materials or work environment. Therefore, in addition to measurement and evaluation, improving quality requires hard work and training as well as trial and error.

The so-called "universal evaluation" of teachers can help education officials better recognize performance issues and trace them more precisely to particular schools, courses, classrooms, and students. Once that information is obtained, the challenge will be to solve the undisclosed problems. Even if universal evaluation revealed that two-thirds of the teachers in Mexico were poorly prepared, it would be a success. Education officials would then know that they have to train the some 800,000 teachers who demonstrated deficiencies. Positive and negative incentives can contribute to making teachers work harder, but they will not solve the intrinsic deficiencies that result from inadequate training and knowledge. Furthermore, evaluations will not solve problems with the curriculum or the many problems that students bring to school from home.

Overly Ambitious Plans?

If 800,000 teachers are to be trained in English or computer science, at least several thousand computer science and English courses will be required. A two-hour English session every week for groups of twenty teachers adds up to around 2 million sessions a year. If teachers are also to learn computer science or more mathematics or to get an update in science, the training hours add up quickly.

A couple of years ago, Mexico finally implemented a policy to ensure that new teacher vacancies would be filled through a legitimate competitive process instead of through the alleged black market where teaching positions were sold or through inheritance from father to son or another relative. After the first nationwide competence exam for teachers in the country's history, Mexico faced the reality that only 20 percent of the teachers passed the test. In the midst of that scandal, the government was forced to relax the testing criteria in order to get a sufficient number of teachers to cover all of the existing vacancies. This episode is a recent and palpable example of the general claim that assessments must be accompanied by realistic plans for improvements and large enough budgets to sustain them. Anyone who accepted the task of implementing even one of the objectives laid out in the education reform bill would quickly recognize the colossal effort, resources, and time required to advance that objective.

What Can Be Done?

In early 2012, the SEP (Secretaría de Educación Pública [Ministry of Public Education]) announced the release of the first comprehensive database to help guide the efforts to measure performance. RENAME (Registro Nacional de Alumnos, Maestros, y Escuelas [National Registry of Students, Teachers, and Schools]) is a huge repository of information that includes detailed data on school infrastructure and continuous monitoring of the performance of teachers and students.[14] The ability to track the real-time performance of schools, teachers, and students in theory offers the possibility of identifying schools and teachers that add value in terms of student performance and those that do not. With the data currently in RENAME, plenty of projects for educational improvement could be launched, even without results from the aforementioned universal evaluation. The release and publication of RENAME data would be groundbreaking for Mexico's educational system, as it would permit performance evaluation using hard data. In early 2013 there was neither clarity on how the education projects would proceed nor any intention of making the information public.

Even without universal evaluation, RENAME could help in locating major areas of opportunity. The system includes information on academic performance on ENLACE (Evaluación Nacional de Logro Académico en Centros

Escolares [National Assessment of Academic Achievement in Schools]), a standardized test of Spanish, mathematics, and a third subject that varies by year. The test has been given annually since 2006 to students from practically all of the primary and secondary schools, public and private, in the country. In the past five years it has also been used to test high school students. While it does not directly evaluate teachers, the combined data from ENLACE and RENAME should allow for a cross analysis of data on the performance of students and data on teachers.

Closing the gaps in schooling and educational quality in Mexico will require work that goes far beyond reforms to provide incentives and resources. In other words, even if the alleged opposition of the SNTE to modernizing the Mexican educational system were to disappear overnight, implementation of reforms would require massive investments of time and money. Even with the full collaboration of the teachers' union, what kind of concrete results could be expected from educational reforms in the subsequent year? Providing training for the nearly 1.2 million teachers, updating curriculums to meet the needs of the global economy, advancing the use of information technologies, increasing the teaching of the English language, and extending the hours of the school day are all good plans that require considerable resources. For example, before the recent constitutional amendment to make high school attendance universally available and mandatory, some estimates from the SEP indicated that the annual additional cost to reach that goal by 2023 would be around 20,000 million pesos a year (US$1.5 billion). Where the money will come from has yet to be seen.

Maximizing Policy Impact

In order to maximize the impact of the proposed education policies and training plans, implementation should probably begin in the areas of higher dropout risk and lower performance; it is precisely in those areas where the highest added value can be achieved. A bad idea (and one that is heard very often) would be to conceive policies that seek to improve simultaneously the quality of education for all schools at all levels throughout Mexico.

We often hear that Mexico's problems are over-diagnosed, that the reforms and effective education policies needed are clear to all, and that priority should be given to implementing those reforms. In political discourse that proposition may succeed. In practice, however, there are no prepackaged solutions. In addition to requiring additional resources, policies need to be implemented. In practice, this is a process of trial and error. For example, extending school hours can be an effective remedy to improve learning, but it will not happen automatically. The optimal combination of ingredients in any medication depends on the needs of the patient.

Bang for the Buck: The Devil Is in the Details

Implementing plans to improve the quality of education requires accurately defining which specific interventions work and which do not. That distinction is not trivial, and it cannot be made a priori. If the Mexican government is willing to invest a considerable amount of taxpayer money in national programs, its investments must have a positive social return. Proper assessments, including impact evaluation and monitoring of controlled experiments, are required to allocate scarce fiscal resources to achieve social profitability. Before embarking on a national campaign to extend school hours, the purpose of the policy must be accurately defined. Before teachers are given performance incentives, the optimal kind of incentives must be determined. If training is to be provided, which types of training work must be identified first and progress must be measured.

For example, it is common to hear that limiting the number of students in a class (class size) is an effective tool to improve performance on standardized tests. Although reducing class size sounds good in principle, in some contexts it can have huge additional costs. To justify those costs, it must be determined whether reducing class size works and if so, exactly how. The answer to that question is not trivial and has given rise to a vast scholarly literature.

Measuring the impact of programs to improve the quality of education is not a theoretical exercise that contravenes pragmatic and ambitious action plans. If done properly, impact evaluation of programs is a valuable management tool that can help stretch taxpayer money and achieve more of the positive results that Mexico is looking for. For instance, PROBEMS (Programa de Becas de Educación Media Superior [Secondary Education Scholarship Program]) distributes cash transfers equivalent to about US$40 a month directly to students on the basis of financial need. The impact of the program on school dropout rates was determined from the program's administrative data. The impact of PROBEMS is striking. A modest US$40 a month increases the probability that a student will register for the following year by 10 percent. Although the impact evaluation verified a significant positive impact, it also provided information about some aspects of the program that failed to reduce the dropout probability. PROBEMS increases the monetary amount of scholarship according to the student's grade point average. However, it could not be verified that, in general terms, increases beyond $40 made a significant contribution to reducing school attrition. In terms of bang for the buck, the base $40 accounts for most of the effect. Given that information, it appears that reallocating resources to increase the number of beneficiaries instead of increasing the amount of the scholarship would increase the profitability of the program.

Similar assessments can be applied to other innovative proposals to improve education infrastructure or incentives for students and teachers. Providing incentives to influence teachers' efforts sounds like a good idea, and studies that document the positive impact of incentive schemes are frequently found in the literature. However, only specific incentive schemes are successful, in certain places at certain times—the devil is in the details. To get the expected result, choosing the right type of intervention is crucial; there is no cookie-cutter approach to achieving success. For example, an incentive scheme was implemented recently in Mexico to reward teachers from schools with the best results on the ENLACE. Because the best results generally come from the best environments, rewarding the best performers is somewhat misguided. To a large extent, rewarding best performers is equivalent to rewarding more affluent and educated households. Subsequent large-scale efforts to reward teachers with substantial pay increases contingent on improved performance have been proven ineffective when properly evaluated for impact.[15]

Obstacles to Investing in Human Capital: Demand Also Matters

When people talk about improving education, they usually think of building more schools with better infrastructure and equipment, improving the curriculum and teaching materials, providing better training for more teachers, and increasing incentives—the supply side of education. But the education problem cannot be approached from the supply side alone. There are obstacles that prevent people from continuing their studies, even when the return to continued study is attractive. Despite all the benefits of more schooling, many young people in Mexico have dropped out of school prematurely.

Finland has earned a top place in international comparisons of educational achievement. If Finland's educational practices, teachers, incentives, and facilities could magically be brought to Mexico, it would surely improve the nation's school performance. However, in all likelihood Mexican students would still fall below the Finns. Why? Finnish children not only have better schools, they also come from different backgrounds.

To ensure that a child stays in school and learns, it is not enough to have good schools, good materials, and good teachers. What students bring from home is equally important. Children take to school many attributes that they develop at home. In their backpacks they carry not only intellectual ability but also other traits, such as discipline, perseverance, and self-esteem. Children and youth develop at home many types of skills in the intellectual, material, and emotional realms. Their combined abilities make children want to go to school, get more out of it, and go further—or not. Students' willingness and ability to stay in school and make more of it constitutes the demand side of education, about which comparatively little is heard.

Demand-Side Challenges

On the demand side, there are three obstacles to staying in school longer that thousands of students face: lack of role models who have high aspirations; lack of early detection of aptitude and talent; and lack of financing. Children are not born with big plans and high aspirations; their aspirations often are based on those of the people around them. If there are no people with a college degree in a child's family or close circle, why would the child aspire to obtain a college education? Would the child know what it means to have a professional career? How would the child figure out his or her realistic options? In the circle of family and friends of an average low-income household in Mexico, only one of every twenty adults has pursued college-level studies. In a high-income home, children have eight times more access to adults with college education.

In addition, an adverse environment can hide academic aptitude and talent. Many talented children are unaware that they have talent; if they knew that they did, they and their parents would do much more to ensure that they remained in school. But without a way to detect talent in a timely manner, it is wasted. Even in more deficient schools, many children get results similar to the national average. They are compensating for their environment's deficiencies with their aptitude and talent, but in their own view and that of others, they are mediocre; after all, they scored only at the national average. If people do not know that they have talent, their aspirations and their efforts will be low. Parents are also less willing to make sacrifices to allow children to stay in school longer if they do not know that their children have high academic aptitude or talent.

Even when young people have high aspirations and know that they have the ability to reach them, many find that their plans to stay in school are frustrated by lack of funding. A quarter of women and half of men without a professional career in Mexico abandoned school for lack of financing. Most of them had to find a job to help support their family.

The lack of role models, early detection of talent, and financing means that children whose parents have fewer opportunities will inherit fewer opportunities themselves. Thus, parents with little education and low income leave their children at a disadvantage. The children will not benefit as much from schooling, their performance will be lower, and they will leave school earlier. They will most likely end up as adults with low income and little education. If and when they have their own children, the story will repeat itself.

Breaking the Vicious Cycle through Voluntary Action

Although it seems impossible, the vicious circle can be broken. Certain events can change the lives of many children and young people. These events are not coincidences; they are the result of the work of people seeking to help change the stories of others. I am not referring here to a major national program designed by those at the commanding heights. I am not talking about mandatory measures, but the voluntary actions of ordinary people—people who have shown a willingness to help others and have placed achievable goals before them, goals that do not overwhelm but that inspire. Of course, one person cannot solve "the national problem of education." However, individuals, companies, and nonprofit organizations can contribute to supporting the education of children and young people in their surroundings. They can help many children and young people by acting as mentors and tutors or by serving as role models in some other capacity. They can help more children and young people become aware of their aptitudes and talents and help them develop those abilities. And they certainly can help more people not to leave school because of lack of financing. These are actions that individuals, companies, and nonprofit organizations can take now, actions that will allow people to stay in school longer and take more advantage of the opportunities that it offers. The vicious circle can be broken. The stories of children and young people can change, and the stories of their children can too.

Many people, companies, and organizations in Mexico already are taking action. There are also many examples inside and outside of Mexico that can serve as a guide and inspiration. No one has to wait for someone else to do something. When volunteer work is combined with good ideas and the right resources, people's stories can change, as has happened with many mentorship, talent detection, and financing programs. Rigorous evaluation of the results of such programs confirms that they work. It is possible to change individual stories one by one.

With volunteer mentors, school performance improves, and so does the behavior of students, allowing them to get further ahead. Talent detection programs increase the likelihood that students, parents, and society will invest more to develop students' talent. Increased funding for students reduces attrition and dropout rates. Today, volunteers can work to help to change stories. They do not have to spend all of their personal time or money. Sometimes a little is just enough to achieve the needed changes.

Notes

1. George Psacharopoulos, "Returns to Investment in Education: A Global Update," *World Development* 22, no. 9 (1994): 1325–43.

2. Juan L. Ordaz, "México: Capital humano e ingresos. Retornos a la educación, 1994–2005 [Mexico: Human Capital and Income: Return on Education, 1994–2005]," Comisión Económica para América Latina de las Naciones Unidas, Unidad Agrícola [UN Economic Commission for Latin America, Agriculture Unit], 2007.

3. Jason M. Fletcher and David E. Frisvold, "Higher Education and Health Investments: Does More Schooling Affect Preventive Health Care Use?" *Journal of Human Capital* 3, no. 2 (1996): 144–76.

4. Nattavudh Powdthave, "Does Education Reduce the Risk of Hypertension? Estimating the Biomarker Effect of Compulsory Schooling in England," *Journal of Human Capital* 4, no. 2 (2010): 173–202.

5. Adriana Lleras-Muney, "The Relationship between Education and Adult Mortality in the United States," *Review of Economic Studies* 72, no. 1 (2005), pp. 189–221.

6. James Heckman and Pedro Carneiro, "Human Capital Policy," in *Inequality in America*, edited by James J. Heckman and Alan B. Krueger (MIT Press, 2003), p. 100.

7. Philip Oreopoulos, Marianne E. Page, and Ann Huff Stevens, "The Intergenerational Effects of Compulsory Schooling," *Journal of Labor Economics* 24, no. 4 (2006): 729–60.

8. Robert Barro, "Determinants of Democracy," *Journal of Political Economy* 107, no. S6 (1999): S158–S183.

9. Thomas S. Dee, "Are There Civic Returns to Education?" *Journal of Public Economics* 88, no. 9/10 (2004): 1697–720.

10. Theodore W. Schultz, "The Value of the Ability to Deal with Disequilibria," *Journal of Economic Literature* 13, no. 1 (1975): 827–46.

11. Andrew Foster and Mark Rosenzweig, "Technical Change and Human Capital Returns and Investments: Evidence from the Green Revolution," *American Economic Review* 86, no. 4 (1996): 931–53.

12. In the original Spanish: El Estado "garantizará la calidad en la educación obligatoria, de manera que los materiales y métodos educativos, la organización escolar, la infraestructura educativa y la idoneidad de los docentes y los directivos garanticen el máximo logro de aprendizaje de los educandos." The Mexican senate amended Article 3 of the Mexican constitution to add the word *calidad* (quality), thus guaranteeing a higher, but undefined, standard of education. See Israel Navarro and Fernando Damián, "Aprueban la reforma a los artículos 3 y 73 [Reform of Articles 3 and 73 Approved]," *Milenio*, December 21, 2012 (www.milenio.com/cdb/doc/noticias 2011/226d4c649acb22a919d3d8c53def9e18).

13. Although SNTE is the teachers' union with the most members, CNTE (Coordinadora Nacional de Trabajadores de la Educación [National Coordinator of Educational Employees]) has a stronger presence than SNTE in some southern states, like Michoacan and Guerrero. Unlike SNTE, CNTE has opposed the reform and has even laid out a year-round schedule for a resistance movement. In all likelihood, the evaluation agenda will not prosper in those states.

14. The program originally called RENAME is likely to change names under the new PRI administration.

15. Lucrecia Santibáñez and others, "Haciendo Camino: Análisis del sistema de evaluación y del impacto del programa de estímulos docentes Carrera Magisterial en México [Making Progress: Analysis of the Evaluation System and the Impact of Teacher Incentive Programs]," 2006, p. xix–xx (www.rand.org/pubs/monographs/2007/RAND_MG471.1.sum.pdf).

EDUARDO GUERRERO

7

Security Policy and the Crisis of Violence in Mexico

Since 2006 Mexico's federal government has implemented a series of bold interventions to fight organized crime. The last three governments developed vigorous security policies that required each of them to choose among different security priorities, implementing some policy alternatives and rejecting others. In this chapter I discuss those interventions and related issues in an effort to present a balanced overview of the current security situation in Mexico.

Widespread violence has proved to be an increasingly salient feature of criminal activity in Mexico, and much of the current debate among Mexican security pundits and policymakers focuses on violence: its causes, its consequences, and the importance of tackling it. The engagement of criminal organizations in domestic illegal markets, particularly extortion or "illegal protection" and drug dealing, has grown, resulting in the largest increase in organized crime–related violence in recent years.

Security was a key topic in Mexico's 2012 presidential race, and it will remain a top challenge for the Enrique Peña Nieto administration, which seeks to establish an ambitious but feasible security agenda. Two of the main topics on the new security agenda are the ongoing reform of the criminal justice system and the effort to regain control of parts of the penitentiary system from criminal elements. Government officials and other political actors have recently debated what I call "failed security policies" and have sought to promote alternative strategies. Although these policies are appealing, their implementation has proved to be politically and technically unfeasible. At the conclusion of this chapter, I present eight recommendations that have yet to be put into practice at the national level. They stem from success stories both abroad and at the local level in Mexico, and they may be useful in helping to overcome the current Mexican security impasse.

Security Policy during President Calderón's Administration

Several arguments have been made to explain the salience of security policy during President Felipe Calderón's administration. For instance, the former director of Mexico's federal intelligence agency, CISEN (Centro de Investigación y Seguridad Nacional [Center for Research and National Security]), has pointed out that during previous years there was an increase of "criminal density" (more criminals in the streets) and that two large crime syndicates (the Sinaloa and Gulf cartels) gradually accumulated both drug-trafficking enterprises and weapons.[1] However, security was not a central issue during the 2006 presidential race, nor did it loom as a key challenge to Mexico's incoming president. In fact, while running for office, Calderón dubbed himself the "Employment President." During the previous two decades homicide rates had consistently dropped, and security was not the leading preoccupation for most Mexicans. However, by 2012 attitudes had changed. In August 2006, 56 percent had mentioned an economic issue and 35 percent a security issue as a top concern. By August 2012, 49 percent considered an economic issue and 50 percent a security issue their top concern.[2]

It is worth noting that Calderón took the oath of office amid criticism regarding the fairness and legitimacy of the election, which he won by a mere 0.56 percent margin. In December 2006, a few days after taking office, he launched the first "joint operation" involving federal and local law enforcement, sending federal troops to fight criminal organizations in Michoacán, a state that faced a local security crisis and whose governor requested the federal intervention. In the short run the operation rendered results, and during 2007–08 seven additional large-scale joint operations were launched in Baja California, Guerrero, Nuevo León, Tamaulipas, Chihuahua, Durango, and Sinaloa.[3] Security policy swiftly became the central topic in Mexico's public agenda. President Felipe Calderón claimed that his security policy was based on five pillars:[4]

—*Joint operations to support local governments.* A major change implemented by the administration was the massive deployment of the military— and increasingly the Policía Federal (federal police)—to ensure public security in regions that faced mounting organized crime–related violence. Among other tasks, federal forces mounted checkpoints, carried out raids, and seized consignments of drugs; in some cases, they have completely taken over local police operations, even down to traffic control duties. Currently around 45,000 members of the military are participating in joint operations, most of them in the nine states where large-scale joint operations have taken place (which include Veracruz as well as those previously mentioned). However, the operations have not been accompanied by an effective effort to tackle the corruption and low performance of the state and municipal law enforcement institutions, which have allowed security crises to develop. Although resources devoted to enhancing state and municipal security budgets, namely FASP (Fondo de Aportaciones para la Seguridad Publica [Fund for Public Security Provisions]) and SUBSEMUN (Subsidio para la Seguridad Pública en los Municipios [Subsidy for Municipal Public Security]), have increased,[5] neither those funds nor the deployment of federal forces in joint operations has fostered a general revamping of state and municipal law enforcement institutions. On the contrary, at least during the first years of Calderón's administration, the overall response of governors and mayors in organized crime–stricken areas was to rely exclusively on the intervention of federal forces and to refrain from thorough institution-building efforts.

—*Improving the technological and operational capabilities of law enforcement agencies.* The federal government has devoted unprecedented resources to law enforcement, a sector previously neglected. From 2006 to 2012, the federal security budget doubled in real terms.[6] The main effort in institution building has focused on the federal police force, which grew from 22,000 in 2007 to 35,000 members in 2011. The effectiveness of the federal government's other institution-building efforts, such as the creation of a national crime database called Plataforma México, is harder to assess.

—*Reform of the legal and institutional framework.* Security is the only realm where President Calderón's legislative agenda found congressional support; other key proposals have remained frozen for several years. Several federal security-related bills were approved during the Calderón administration:

A general law governing the Sistema Nacional de Seguridad Pública (National Public Security System) was approved in 2009 in order to achieve better coordination among the federal government, states, and municipalities. The general law regulates information-sharing procedures and the distribution of security funds and establishes the basis for professionalizing law enforcement agencies.[7]

A federal anti-kidnapping law was approved in 2010. It establishes harsher sentences for kidnappers and allows the use of undercover agents and telephone tapping in kidnapping investigations.[8]

A new law that streamlines the confiscation of real estate and other assets used in committing crimes has been used in Mexico City to disrupt illegal activities in street markets where a climate of extreme violence reigns. The federal government and other states have yet to develop the institutional framework to systematically apply this law.[9]

A law against money laundering was approved in 2012. It establishes new regulations for a set of activities highly susceptible to money laundering, such as gambling and the issuance of prepaid cards, such as gift and telephone cards.[10]

The establishment of a unified police command in each state that would replace the independent police departments that are responsible for public security in most of Mexico's 2,441 municipalities was rejected.

—*An active crime prevention policy.* Marginal resources have been devoted to Programa Escuela Segura (Safe School Program), a program that seeks to provide a safer environment in schools, and to Programa de Reconstrucción de Espacios Públicos (Public Space Reconstruction Program), a program to improve facilities such as parks in crime-ridden neighborhoods. However, there are no large federally funded programs to prevent illegal organizations from carrying out their recruitment activities. Moreover, data on the detention of criminal organization members and organized crime–related deaths have not been analyzed in a way that would allow the government to design an effective crime-prevention policy. For example, there are no reliable data to assess whether criminal organizations rely on local gangs and criminals as gunmen or whether they recruit gunmen throughout the country and then deploy them in conflict areas. If basic socio-demographic data (age, education, place of birth, and so forth) exist on people killed by criminal organizations (including members of criminal organizations, law enforcement agents, and by-standers), the data have not been shared with the public. Hence it is difficult to assess whether social policy could be targeted more effectively to curb recruitment by criminal organizations.

—*Strengthening international cooperation.* The current crisis of violence has increased international interest in Mexico's security agenda, especially in the United States. The Mérida Initiative, which provides Mexico's law enforcement agencies with funding for technology and training, has been the most important outcome of this renewed interest. The resources allocated through the initiative amount on average to 4 percent of Mexico's federal government expenditure on security. However, the U.S. budget for Mexico's anti-drug operations may decrease 17 percent in 2013, from the $282 million requested for 2012 to the $234 million requested for 2013.[11] Moreover, U.S. Drug Enforcement Administration agents are not allowed to carry weapons openly on Mexican soil. As a general rule, cooperation between the U.S. and Mexican governments takes place on a case-by-case basis and has focused on sharing intelligence stemming from Mexican criminals held in U.S. prisons.

More recently, the United States has become a scapegoat for the Mexican government. For instance, after a fire erupted at a casino in Monterrey in August 2011, causing the deaths of fifty-two people, President Calderón claimed that such tragedies were, in part, a byproduct of the country's proximity to the world's largest drug consumer and weapons retailer. He summoned Americans to consider legalization if they were determined to continue consuming drugs. In February 2012, Calderón again blamed the United States for its alleged responsibility for violence in Mexico and requested that "no more weapons" be allowed across the border into Mexico.

The Evolution of Violence: Emergence, Growth, and Stabilization

Organized crime–related violence has been the most salient feature of the current public security crisis in Mexico. Both the international and the Mexican media report thoroughly on the cartels' seemingly unlimited ability to engage in killings and shootings. Moreover, organized crime–related violence has had deep implications for security policy and for Mexican criminal organizations.

Trends in Violence

The term "organized crime–related violence" is used here to refer to intentional homicides that, given the available information, are thought to be related to conflicts within criminal organizations or between criminal organizations or to law enforcement operations against criminal organizations. This category encompasses bystanders murdered in shootings between criminal organizations and those killed because they were erroneously identified as members of a criminal organization.

In the short run, organized crime–related violence may resemble a "random walk"—which makes it impossible to forecast hikes or slumps—caused by a broad array of events at the local level. However, long-term trends are defined by structural factors. At the beginning of Calderón's administration, the federal government's security policy gave priority to the dismantling of criminal organizations through repeated arrests of kingpins (*capos*). That policy created strains within those organizations. As the permanence of a *capo*'s position became highly uncertain, second-tier leaders within the organization had more incentive to defect before their potential rivals within the organization did so in order to seek control of the drug-trafficking market for themselves. Thus, criminal organizations fragmented and became more unstable, engaging more often in predatory crime and in conflicts with other organizations. That change within criminal organizations was the main factor underlying the dramatic increase in organized crime–related violence from 2008 to 2010.

In addition, crises of violence throughout the country have triggered reactions leading to structural changes in law enforcement agencies, although the effect of these changes has been partial and slow to be felt. Nonetheless, some cities that experienced crises of violence at an early stage have since witnessed a clear and consistent downward trend in violence, even though levels of violence remain much higher than anything observed until 2007. Moreover, data also show that at the national level, organized crime–related violence stopped growing by late 2011 and is progressively declining. The following structural factors underlie this decrease in violence in Mexico:

—*The federal government's shift from a nonselective to a selective law enforcement strategy to dissuade violence.* During the first years of President Calderón's administration, law enforcement did not focus clearly on any specific criminal organization. However, in mid-2011 the federal government launched a large-scale operation that specifically targeted the Zetas, the most violent among Mexican large drug-trafficking organizations. One effect of this shift was that the Zetas displaced the Sinaloa cartel as the federal forces' main target for capturing and killing drug kingpins. Although the Sinaloa cartel is probably larger than the Zetas in terms of drug-trafficking revenue, overall it is less violent. This shift in the federal government's strategy may have provided an important incentive for other criminal organizations to use less violent methods.

—*Increasing social demand to put a stop to violence.* When organized crime–related deaths peaked for the first time in mid-2008, neither the federal government nor civil society leaders identified reducing violence as a priority on the security agenda. However, as violence became increasingly widespread and disruptive of social life, a broad social movement appeared demanding a halt. In 2011, for the first time, an organized movement at the national level made violence reduction its central demand.[12]

—*More effective interventions by the federal government and some state governments.* The deployment of the military to ensure public security started as early as December 2006. However, due to lack of previous experience, the first joint operations did not effectively deter organized crime–related violence. Since then, both the military and the federal police have learned, step by step, from their experiences. For instance, federal forces have become more proactive in taking over municipal police departments that are under the blatant control of criminal organizations. They have also developed special groups that target and disband violent racketeers. A recent event in Acapulco demonstrates the increased effectiveness of joint operations. In October 2011, a 2,000-strong federal force was sent to Acapulco to tackle the increasing levels of violence and predatory crime there. During the operation the most violent and dangerous organizations were targeted and dismantled. Citizens were also encouraged to report crimes.

The professionalization of some police departments and the dissolution of corrupt ones have also played a role in containing or reducing violence. In the city of Veracruz, after a crisis in mid-2011 that prompted federal intervention, the municipal police force was dissolved and the navy temporarily assumed public security duties, contributing to a swift decrease in the level of violence.

—*Reduced availability of new recruits.* Violent conflicts throughout Mexico have been fueled by the ability of criminal organizations to recruit large private armies. In 2011 it was estimated that these organizations' gunmen had a 20 to 40 percent chance of being killed during a year.[13] Even though criminal organizations may recruit among individuals who are accustomed to a high-risk lifestyle and have few options in the legal economy, such high levels of risk constrain the ability of the organizations to keep rebuilding their private armies. There are no systematic figures on enrollment or wages paid by criminal organizations, so it is hard to assess current recruitment constraints on criminal organizations. However, the age of those killed due to organized crime has steadily declined—that is, the proportion of those killed who were 25 years old and younger increased from 24 percent in 2008 to 29 percent in the first semester of 2012.[14] This trend may indicate that criminal organizations are increasingly relying on less experienced gunmen, allegedly due to recruitment constraints.

These four structural factors provide a means for identifying long-term trends in violence at the national level. The data suggest that these factors

Figure 7-1. *Quarterly Organized Crime–Related Deaths, 2007–12*

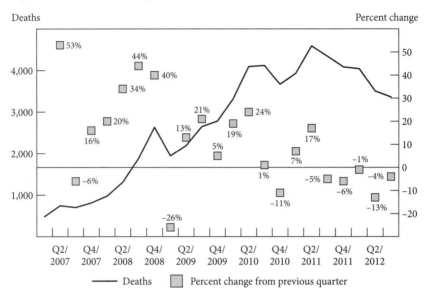

Source: Author's analysis based on data for December 2006 to September 2011 from Secretariado Ejecutivo del Sistema Nacional de Seguridad Pública [Executive Secretariat of the National Public Security System], "Base de Datos de Fallecimientos Ocurridos por Presunta Rivalidad Delincuencial [Database of Deaths Presumably Related to Organized Crime]" (2011) (http://secretariadoejecutivo.gob.mx/en/SecretariadoEjecutivo/Bases_de_Datos_de_Fallecimientos_ocurridos_por_presunta_ rivalidad_delincuencial). Figures for the fourth quarter of 2011 and 2012 are based on data collected by the author from national and local newspapers and adjusted to account for underestimation.

may finally be getting the upper hand over the factors that push the level of violence upward. As shown in figure 7-1, violence levels grew fast until the second quarter of 2010. During the second semester of 2011, violence in Mexico may have begun a downward trend. The third quarter of 2012 was the fifth consecutive quarter in which there was a reduction in organized crime–related deaths. Be that as it may, if the trends in the cities that have experienced the largest and most protracted reductions in violence are any indication, a return to the homicide rate that prevailed until 2007 will take several years. Moreover, there is also some uncertainty about future trends in violence, especially if there is a major shift in the federal government's security strategy or if there is a new outbreak of violence at the national level driven by the fragmentation of either the Sinaloa cartel or the Zetas.

*From Cartels to Mafias: Recent Evolution of Criminal Organizations
and the Consequences for Violence*

In Mexico as in other places in Latin America, criminal organizations that traffic in drugs are colloquially referred to as "cartels." However, I use the term "drug-trafficking organizations" (DTOs) to stress the difference between them and criminal organizations that do not engage primarily in drug trafficking. Following Gambetta, I use the term "mafia" to describe criminal organizations that primarily engage in providing protection—that is, those that obtain rents based on their ability to exert violence.[15]

President Calderón's government claimed that in previous administrations criminal organizations developed "territorial control," which allowed them to engage in systematic extortion of both legal and illegal businesses.[16] That claim implied that extortion was pervasive even before organized crime–related violence was a widespread phenomenon. However, the data suggest that the incidence of extortion peaked after President Calderón came into power in 2006; extortion reports per 100,000 people doubled from 2006 to 2009.[17] In addition, there seems to be a link between violence and extortion. States with a higher rate of organized crime and an elevated number of deaths also have substantially higher extortion victimization rates.

The national victimization survey data refute the claim that criminal organizations developed extensive extortion networks prior to the onset of the current conflicts. For instance, as shown in figure 7-2, Veracruz—a state that experienced a severe outbreak of violence during the second half of 2011— featured moderate extortion victimization in 2010. In Veracruz, 4 percent of survey respondents reported being victims of extortion at least once during 2010, a rate below the 5.4 percent national average. During the 2005–10 period, the Zetas developed strong control over drug trafficking and other illegal activities in Veracruz. However, when the Sinaloa cartel attempted to expand into Veracruz and to contest the strength of the local Zetas network, violence skyrocketed. Organized crime–related deaths in Veracruz leaped from 179 in 2010 to 629 in 2011. In the latter year, 8 percent of survey respondents statewide reported being victims of extortion. The trend in national extortion reports, as well as the experience of Veracruz, shows that conflicts within or between criminal organizations and outbreaks of violence *precede* or *boost* extortion networks, not the other way around.

Current extortion rates across Mexico are related to a change in criminal organizations that took place in recent years. Traditionally, the largest and

Figure 7-2. *Organized Crime–Related Deaths and Extortion Victimization Rate, by State, 2010 and 2011*

Victimization rate, percent

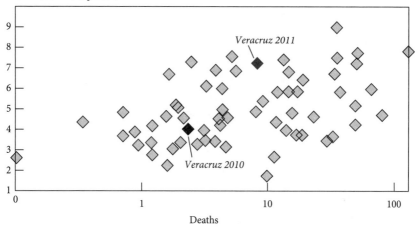

Deaths

Sources: Deaths per 100,000 people (logarithmic scale) in 2010 are based on figures from the Secretariado Ejecutivo del Sistema Nacional de Seguridad Pública [Executive Secretariat of the National Public Security System], "Base de Datos de Fallecimientos Ocurridos por Presunta Rivalidad Delincuencial [Database of Deaths Presumably Related to Organized Crime]" (2011) (http://secretariado ejecutivo.gob.mx/en/SecretariadoEjecutivo/Bases_de_Datos_de_Fallecimientos_ocurridos_por_ presunta_rivalidad_delincuencial). Deaths per 100,000 people in 2011 are based on data collected by the author from national and local newspapers. Extortion victimization rates are based on results from INEGI, "Encuesta nacional de victimización y percepción sobre seguridad pública [National Survey on Victimization and Perceptions of Public Security]" (2011 and 2012). In both cases respondents were asked about events during the previous year.

most powerful Mexican criminal organizations engaged primarily in drug trafficking and had little incentive to use violence intensively or to seek alternative sources of revenue in predatory crime. Drug trafficking was highly profitable and seeking minor rents from predatory crime—which at some point inevitably leads to public anger and police attention—was not a rational business strategy. From 2007 onward Mexico's foremost DTOs quickly began to fragment and engage in increased conflict, processes that I attribute primarily to the government's intensive kingpin arrest policy.[18] Fragmentation and conflict triggered some important changes that eventually led to the conversion of DTO remnants into mafias:

—In order to engage in outright conflicts with other criminal groups—and to resist enhanced government law enforcement—DTOs must invest more resources in developing large private armies. However, those armies are deployed only on a sporadic basis. Hence, predatory crime arises as an alternative activity to help sustain the armies.

—After a large DTO splits, not all the remnants maintain access to transnational drug-trafficking networks. Those remnants must find alternative funding sources, which only predatory crime provides.

—During a conflict, some criminal cells must abandon their areas of operation. Under certain circumstances engaging in kidnapping and extortion affords a natural alternative livelihood for those cells.[19]

As previously mentioned, the development of mafias in Mexico has been an especially violent phenomenon. During the 2010–11 period, the violence was intensive because the mafias were in the consolidation stage and were trying to build their reputations;[20] in some regions several groups were struggling to gain control of extortion over local businesses. Moreover, widespread violence increases citizens' perception of their own vulnerability and enhances the effectiveness of intimidation by criminal groups. Therefore, violence itself boosts the demand for the type of "protection" that mafias may provide.

Extortion of certain businesses and trades, such as nightclubs and taxi drivers, is pervasive in some regions. In 2011 the forms of violence yielding the highest number of innocent victims were those directly related to extortion. In Monterrey, fifty-two people were killed as a consequence of the arson at the Casino Royale, a gambling venue that had already paid illegal protection to one criminal organization but refused to pay a second one. Moreover, extortion may represent an increasing source of income for criminal organizations. Unlike drug trafficking, extortion profits are not capped by consumer demand. There is plenty of room for mafias, including those with limited resources and no international links, to expand into new extortion markets throughout Mexico.

Some media campaigns have effectively warned citizens about telephone extortion, which most of the time relies on unsubstantiated threats designed to intimidate naïve victims. A hotline exclusively devoted to providing assistance to extortion victims has been set up. However, the Mexican government has not implemented specific policies to confront mafias that pose a substantiated threat to citizens and businesses. For instance, in August 2011 an attempt by a local mafia to engage in extortion on a massive scale against teachers in Acapulco was prevented when federal and state authorities arrested the criminals and increased surveillance at schools. Nevertheless, authorities did not act until the teachers' union shut down local schools, announced that classes would not resume until safe conditions were restored, and staged a demonstration on Acapulco's main thoroughfare.[21] The initiative by Acapulco teachers to report the criminal threats and demand government intervention was unusual. Few, if any, professions have the internal cohesion and political clout that teachers have. Authorities will have to engage in proactive and comprehensive interventions if they are to curtail systematic extortion against businesses, trades, and professions.

Illegal Drug Markets and Their Links to Violence

Estimates regarding the size of the illegal drug market in Mexico, as in other countries, have been a subject of debate. The former SSP (Secretaría de Seguridad Pública [Ministry of Public Security]) estimated, without clarifying its methodology, that by 2011 the retail drug market in Mexico was worth US$8.8 billion. However, a respected independent analyst estimated the figure to be around $1.4 billion, using U.S. statistics and adjusting for price, population, and consumption differences.[22] The latter figure is much closer to the amount that I estimated using data from the 2008 National Addictions Survey and domestic retail prices, which yielded an even lower figure.

While uncertainty remains about the actual size of this market, mostly because consumption and price figures are not reliable, it is clear that the value is closer to $1 billion than $10 billion. That means that the current value of the Mexican retail drug market is only about 2 percent of the value of the U.S. market. It also suggests that Mexican criminal organizations obtain only a small, probably negligible, share of their net profits from the domestic drug market and that transnational drug trafficking and other illegal activities account for most of their revenues. Even though the domestic drug market represents only a small fraction of the organizations' income, it does seem to play a key role in the development of criminal networks and thus contributes significantly to the generation of violence.

Drug dealing may be the principal activity that criminal organizations engage in to build up broad social networks. There may be around 60,000 active drug dealers in Mexico, who work in most cases on a part-time basis.[23] Based on location (killings that took place in a drug house or drug-dealing hot spot) and press accounts of organized crime–related deaths, I estimate that at least 8 percent of all such deaths stem from conflicts over the domestic drug market. In most cases the deaths are the outcome of conflicts between local gangs or criminal organizations for control of the distribution of drugs.

Figure 7-3 shows the five states where killings involving drug dealing represent the highest proportion of total organized crime–related deaths. All five

Figure 7-3. *Annual Organized Crime–Related Deaths per 100,000 People and Percent Involving Drug Dealing, 2006–11*[a]

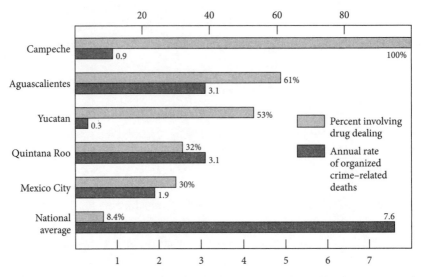

Source: Figure based on data collected by the author from national and local newspapers and adjusted to account for underestimation.

a. States listed have the highest percentages of deaths involving drug dealing.

states are among the areas in Mexico that are *least affected* by organized crime violence. On the other hand, in the most violent states, like Chihuahua and Tamaulipas, most deaths are related to conflicts between DTOs competing for control of transnational drug-trafficking routes. Figure 7-3 shows that even though organized crime–related violence remains a geographically concentrated problem, drug-dealing violence is moderate but pervasive throughout the country. In some places, local drug dealing may be the only source of organized crime–related violence.

It is noteworthy that drug consumption in Mexico seems to have stabilized in recent years. Data show that the percentage of people 12 to 65 years of age who used illicit drugs at least once a year almost doubled from 2002 to 2008 (increasing from 0.8 percent to 1.4 percent). However, data from the same survey series show only a marginal increase in the figure above, from 1.4 to 1.5 from 2008 to 2011.[24] The causes of the stabilization of drug use are still to be determined. However, the federal government claims that the development of a nationwide network of rehabilitation centers played a role in the shift.

Challenges Facing Mexican Security Policy

It has not been possible to address effectively the current crisis of violence and organized crime in Mexico due to the lack of a comprehensive, balanced effort involving all the components of security policy—that is, street-level law enforcement, prosecution of criminals, and the penitentiary system. Mexico has effectively increased the capabilities of its federal police and has intensively implemented its strategy to tackle criminal activities. However, Mexico still lacks the resources necessary to match its efforts in law enforcement with its efforts in the criminal justice and correction systems. Consequently, state coercion cannot be applied strategically and with acceptable standards of legitimacy. Moreover—as is discussed in the section on failed policies—the lack of a reliable criminal justice system fosters systematic human rights violations.

The Criminal Justice System

Most felonies in Mexico are prosecuted at the state level, and fewer data are available on the criminal justice system at the national level. However, as shown in figure 7-4, data from Mexico City suggest that a very large share of sentenced criminals did not commit serious offenses: in 2011, for instance, 80 percent of convicted criminals had committed property crimes.[25] Moreover, research conducted in 2005 showed that 47 percent of prison inmates in Mexico City were convicted for nonviolent theft and 43 percent had stolen money or goods worth less than $30.[26]

The intensive use of "preventive imprisonment" is another salient feature of the Mexican criminal justice system. Even though the law establishes that preventive imprisonment should be an exceptional measure, authorities mandate preventive imprisonment—or at least request bail—for virtually any felony. As a result, a staggering 42 percent of people imprisoned in Mexico have not been sentenced.

Traditionally, the Mexican criminal justice system has been "inquisitorial," with trials of a highly bureaucratic nature. Under this system, the public prosecutor conducts *averiguación previa*, the preliminary investigation of the crime, which consists in the preparation of a series of files regarding the existing evidence. The judge's main task is to examine those files. The procedure could well be described as a "paper trial" because it lacks the vital presentation, in a public space, of contrasting evidence by a prosecutor and defense lawyer in the presence of the accused, elements which are characteristic of the

Figure 7-4. *Criminals Sentenced in Mexico City, by Crime, 2010*

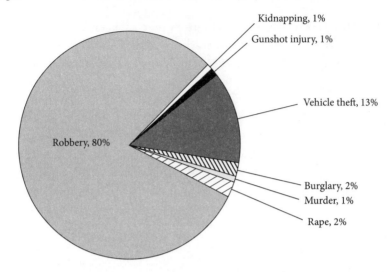

Kidnapping, 1%

Gunshot injury, 1%

Vehicle theft, 13%

Robbery, 80%

Burglary, 2%

Murder, 1%

Rape, 2%

Source: Author's illustration based on data from Procuraduría General de Justicia del Distrito Federal [Mexico City Attorney General's Office], *Quinto Informe de Labores* [Fifth Annual Activities Report] (2011), p. 244 (www.pgjdf.gob.mx/images/Contenidos/Informes/5toInformedeLabores PGJ.pdf).

"adversarial" system of justice. Rulings thus tend to be made on the basis of formalities rather than hard evidence. Such "paper trials" have given rise to a dilatory and unfair system.

The current system has also discouraged the development of investigative skills. The investigative police are currently under the command of prosecutors; hence the responsibility for designing criminal investigation strategies is in the hands of lawyers who lack formal training in detective work. The flaws of the criminal investigation system can be traced to Mexico's recent authoritarian past, when the judiciary was under the overall control of the executive; the attorney general—who could be removed from office by the president—was the key player in the criminal justice system. During this period, courts endorsed procedures that reduced the need to conduct any serious criminal investigation. For example, it is the detainee's initial confession before the prosecutor that is accorded the highest evidentiary value, allegedly because it is the most "spontaneous." Moreover, illegal and protracted detention and even evidence of torture do not nullify confessions to the prosecutor. Likewise, the absence of a lawyer for the defendant does not nullify a confession.[27]

Historically, such provisions meant that there was no need to conduct effective criminal investigations in order to exert effective (although arbitrary) control over criminals. Medical tests, finger print impressions, ballistic analyses, and other "hard" evidence were generally absent in criminal trials. However, this system became dysfunctional as the judiciary gained autonomy during Mexico's democratization process. Recently, the lack of skills necessary to pursue criminal investigations has become evident in some important organized crime–related cases. In May 2009, for instance, thirty-five public officials from Michoacán were arrested by the federal government after authorities found evidence suggesting that the officials received periodic payments from a criminal organization. Ten mayors were among the detainees, and the case swiftly became a major political issue. However, all thirty-five officials were released because federal prosecutors failed to provide sufficient evidence to support their accusations.

There are no systematic analyses of bias and discrimination in the Mexican criminal justice system. However, anecdotal evidence suggests that having sufficient economic resources—especially the money to hire a private attorney and to bribe prosecutors and judges—greatly reduces the probability that an indicted person will be sentenced if he or she is backed by wealthy individuals or a strong criminal organization. Such practices may be hampering current efforts to crack down on large criminal organizations.

In 2008 the Mexican congress approved a major reform to the criminal justice system. The core of the 2008 reform is to replace the "paper trial" with the full trial (*juicio oral*) found in the adversarial system. As a result, prosecutors should now focus on evidence gathering and the preparation of objectively convincing cases. An additional purpose of the 2008 reform is to develop alternative remedies for resolving minor felonies. Regrettably, the pace of implementation of the new system has been sluggish. By December 2012 only three states (Chihuahua, Estado de México, and Morelos) had fully implemented the judicial reforms; eight states had implemented them partially. In addition, twenty states remain in the planning stage and one of them, Nayarit, is still in the initial phase.[28] Furthermore, efforts to enhance the prosecutorial system at the federal level, which has jurisdiction over drug trafficking and organized crime felonies, have not matched the efforts and funds devoted to security and law enforcement. As shown in figure 7-5, from 2004 to 2012, the SSP's budget more than quadrupled in real terms, while the military budget increased by approximately 70 percent. During the same period the budget for

Figure 7-5. *Mexico's Federal Budget, 2004–11*

Constant millions of dollars

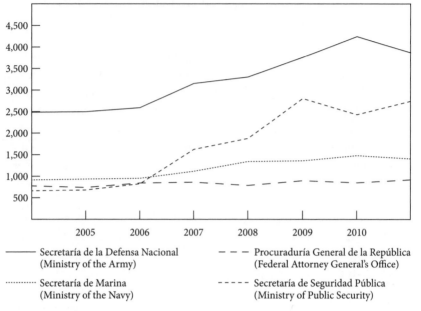

——— Secretaría de la Defensa Nacional   – – – Procuraduría General de la República
       (Ministry of the Army)   (Federal Attorney General's Office)

············ Secretaría de Marina   – – – – Secretaría de Seguridad Pública
       (Ministry of the Navy)   (Ministry of Public Security)

Source: Presupuesto de Egresos de la Federación [Federal Expenditures Budget], 2004–11
(http://www.dof.gob.mx/).

the PGR (Procuraduria General de la República [Federal Attorney General's
Office]) increased by approximately 46 percent.

The Penitentiary System

Along with the growth in homicide rates and public expenditures, a sharp
increase in incarceration has been one of the most salient changes related to
public security during the last decade. In 2000 there were around 135,000
inmates in Mexican prisons for both "ordinary felonies" and "federal felonies."[29]
That figure increased rapidly, and by July 2012 there were 238,000 detainees in
Mexican prisons, for an annual rate of increase of approximately 5 percent.
That number put Mexico on the list of high-incarceration-rate countries. As
shown in figure 7-6, the latest World Prison Population List places Mexico in
the upper range among both the G-20 countries (fifth of nineteen countries)
and Latin American countries (eighth of the twenty countries that were measured). It is noteworthy that Colombia, a crime-reduction success story, has a
lower incarceration level than Mexico.

Figure 7-6. *Inmate Populations in the G-20 Countries and Latin America per 100,000 People*[a]

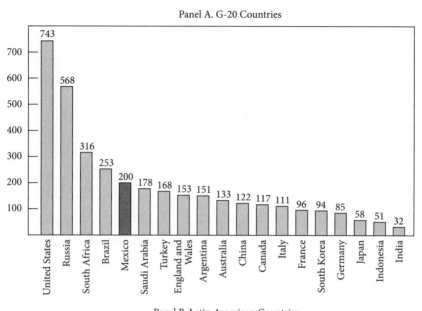

Panel A. G-20 Countries

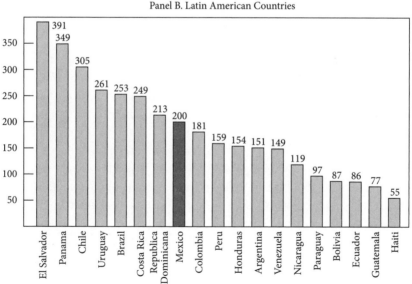

Panel B. Latin American Countries

Source: International Centre for Prison Studies, World Prison Population List, 9th ed. (London, 2011) (www.idcr.org.uk/wp-content/uploads/2010/09/WPPL-9-22.pdf).

a. Figures, the latest available, are as of May 2011.

Stories of crime and overcrowding in prisons are relatively common throughout the world. However, the situation in Mexican prisons is especially catastrophic. Today, the situation in several states may be described as one of outright control of prisons by criminal organizations. Even though overcrowding was a problem before the Calderón administration, the current crisis in Mexican prisons is closely related to the conflict among criminal organizations since 2008.

The authorities have not developed the capacity to place the large influx of criminal organization members in appropriate facilities, and even though these individuals are prosecuted for federal felonies, if convicted they are usually placed in state prisons, along with "common" criminals. This practice, combined with widespread corruption and lack of resources in state prisons, has meant that members of criminal organizations are able to use their networks to gain control of basic prison functions and to continue engaging in criminal activities. For instance, around 70 percent of Mexican prisons are understaffed, with less than one guard for every four inmates, and such understaffing enables hegemonic groups of prisoners to gain effective control of prison functions.[30]

The prison system has been a neglected budgetary item. According to SSP, the agency responsible for running federal prisons, the daily cost per detainee in a Mexican prison hovers around $20, less than one-third of the U.S. figure, which is closer to $70 (it varies by state).[31] Nevertheless, Mexico's federal government transfers to state governments only $4 per day for each federal inmate in state prisons.

The dramatic increase in jailbreaks is the most visible indicator of the level of control that criminal organizations have acquired over the prison system during the last few years (figure 7-7). The number of jailbreaks reported by the media quadrupled between 2007 and 2011, and the number of escaped prisoners increased tenfold during the same period. In 2011 the average jailbreak involved 150 percent more prisoners than four years earlier. An especially large jailbreak—involving eighty-five escaped prisoners—contributes to explaining the 2010 hike. Jailbreaks have become larger because increasingly they have become complex rescue or escape operations planned by criminal organizations, not individual or small-group initiatives.

Increasing incarceration rates while large parts of the prison system remain under criminal control will have the effect of increasing the rents available to criminal organizations. Rent extraction from prisoners is pervasive throughout the prison system. While in some states syndicates of guards control rent extraction, in others criminal organizations that have intra-prison chapters (and sometimes the ability to appoint guards) extract rents from prisoners.

Figure 7-7. *Jailbreaks and Escaped Inmates, 2007–12*

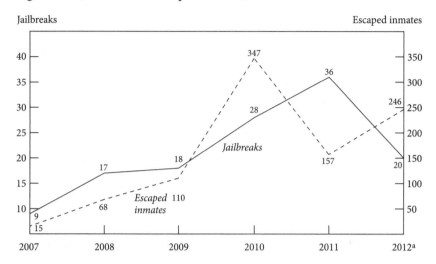

Source: Figure based on data from author's systematic search of national newspapers.
a. Figures for January to October 2012.

Despite the evidence that longer prison sentences have little if any deterrent effect, promising ever longer jail sentences remains popular with Mexican political parties and the electorate.

The Current Security Policy Agenda

The policies discussed below have been fixtures on the public security agenda during recent years, and some were endorsed by candidates during the 2012 presidential race, including the winner, Enrique Peña Nieto. All of the policies, which address pressing security concerns, are appealing, and none should be discarded. However, even though they have been widely promoted and discussed by decision makers, they either have proved unfeasible in practice or have not produced results. Hence, there is no point in keeping them as priorities on the security agenda unless advocates identify novel mechanisms to solve the impediments that have prevented their effective implementation.

Unify State Police Commands

Police forces in Mexico are divided into federal, state, and municipal agencies. Municipal agencies encompass the largest share of agents. However, municipal police forces typically are the least professional and most vulnerable to infiltration by criminal organizations. Moreover, in Mexico City, where municipalities do not exist, a unified police force under a single command seems to favor more effective law enforcement strategies. Hence, policymakers have advocated merging all municipal police agencies into unified state-level police departments. However, municipalities and mayors are the basis of local governance across Mexico, and they have strongly opposed the unified state police project. Even so, some mayors, primarily those overwhelmed by organized crime, have in fact relinquished their right to run their own police departments. That was the case in Navolato, Sinaloa—among the most violent municipalities in the country—where the municipal police was disbanded in January 2012.

Intensify Efforts to Gather Financial Intelligence

Using financial intelligence gathering to fight criminal organizations is a popular idea. Targeting financial networks rather than performing arrests and seizures seems like an ideal violence-free alternative measure to fight crime. However, some practical issues limit the feasibility of the financial intelligence approach in Mexico. First of all, approximately 43 percent of Mexico's economy remains informal, and participants do not have to comply with basic labor, zoning, and fiscal regulations.[32] The broad scope of the informal economy provides criminal organizations with plenty of opportunity for circumventing financial intelligence gathering by authorities, for the simple reason that much of the economy is actually beyond the reach of the authorities.

A law aimed at establishing an ambitious set of regulations to prevent money laundering was published in October 2012, after being stalled in congress for over two years. This bill obliges businesses to report transactions, especially those involving large amounts of cash. The red tape implied by the new law may make compliance unfeasible for informal businesses. At the same time, Mexico's tax collection rate is among the lowest in the Western hemisphere. In a country that systematically fails to collect taxes and to curtail the informal economy, enhancing tax collection rather than creating a new layer of reporting obligations for businesses seems to be a more logical step.

Withdraw Military Forces from Public Security Duties

It is generally accepted that Mexican military forces were not created to engage in public security tasks and that their current deployment as substitutes for ailing police departments in crime-ridden areas is spurring human rights violations and damaging the military's institutional reputation. Increasing reports of human rights violations—along with a military justice system that allegedly protects violators—have boosted demands for the military to return to barracks. On the other hand, the flaws of the criminal justice system, which has proved incapable of successfully prosecuting some dangerous criminals, may foster human rights violations. If criminals cannot be prosecuted, the military has an incentive to make its targets "disappear" instead of arresting them.[33]

In any case, Mexico's security crisis is far from over. Despite successful steps to modernize and improve the capabilities of the federal police and some state and municipal police departments, the Mexican deficit in reliable law enforcement institutions remains large. The army and the navy have a combined force of well over 250,000; the federal police force has slightly over 40,000 officers. Under these circumstances, it is not clear that sending the army back to the barracks is a step that the Mexican state can afford. In addition, it may prove easier to modernize some features of the military forces and to offer incentives for a more open and effective military justice system. Moreover, the Colombian experience shows that the military can play a positive role in an effective public security policy. The Colombian army was successfully deployed to provide public security in areas recovered from insurgent control; the Colombian army also has anti-kidnapping and anti-extortion units.[34] Historically, Mexico's army and the navy have been excluded from Mexican politics. Both have developed their own internal dynamics, a tight institutional identity, and a hermetic stance toward other social spheres. Until 2001, no secretary of defense had ever attended a congressional hearing. In order to attain an army more fit for public security duties, it is necessary to grant military personnel a more active role within democratic institutions. For instance, we might reverse the custom that no member of the military forces, not even the secretary of defense and the secretary of the navy, appear in the media on a regular basis.

Another exceptional feature of the Mexican military is that civilians are tacitly banned from being secretary of defense or the navy. Appointing a civilian defense minister is a step that should be considered in order to signal a stronger commitment to public accountability and human rights while preserving public security responsibilities. Peña Nieto's proposal to establish a national gendarmerie (staffed by military personnel but under the command of a civilian) would require greater accountability from at least those soldiers deployed in public security duties.

Capture all Major Cartel Kingpins

The public perceives the capture of famous *capos* as a major security policy achievement, and authorities may have political incentives to undertake and publicize such captures. However, capture operations are costly in terms of human lives and cause danger and disruption in communities where criminals are hiding. Furthermore, I have shown through empirical analysis that the intensive capture of cartel bosses was one of the main causes of the crises in organized crime–related violence during President Calderón's administration.

In a January 2012 article, a Salvadoran security expert wrote that, following the rationale of those who blame capturing *capos* for the violence, drug barons should be released even if they are captured by chance.[35] Certainly, providing kingpins with legal immunity is not an alternative that I would endorse. However, we should clarify the implications of the more selective use of coercion that critics of the capture-intensive strategy propose. The question is not whether kingpins should be legally prosecuted or not once they are captured. The question is whether capturing them should be a top priority on the security agenda; in other words, what resources should law enforcement institutions devote to capturing them? Following the rationale explained above, such operations—despite their undeniable media impact—should not be a top priority. The fugitive status of kingpins and their associates should mean that they are effectively excluded from the benefits enjoyed by law-abiding citizens, such as the right to lead a public life freely, to acquire property or hold financial assets, and to obtain a passport. Meanwhile, only moderate resources and staff should be devoted to capture operations.

An additional policy shift related to kingpin captures concerns target selection. In 2009 the federal government issued a list of the thirty-seven most wanted criminals. The criteria for the selection of individuals on the list were never disclosed. Selection seems to be based on a mix of wealth, public notoriety, and rank within drug cartels, instead of an individual's record for murder and violent crime, as government publicity claims. The list was not accompanied by any sunset rule to establish under what timeframe or circumstances, other than incarceration or death, it would be updated or criminals would cease to be listed among the most wanted.

This vague and indefinite target selection process nullifies any deterrent effect that the capture operations might have had. On one hand, the criminals on the list have no incentive to change their behavior because doing so does not imply ceasing to be a target in the future. On the other hand, criminals not on the list face no imminent risk of becoming avowed top targets of the federal government. Specifying sunset rules and target selection criteria would maximize the deterrent effect for each captured and incarcerated kingpin. Only those organizations that engage more intensively in violence and predatory crime should be targeted.

The New Security Agenda: Eight Recommendations

I offer eight policy recommendations, based on several criteria that are critical to achieving a balanced and effective security policy during Peña Nieto's administration (2012–18). Table 7-1 provides a classification of these recommendations. Recommendations encompass a combination of short- and long-term interventions. Mexico's security dilemma is complex, and it will require cumbersome changes as well as intensive institution-building efforts. Nevertheless, in order to obtain much-needed public support and cooperation from key actors, the new president will need to send a strong signal that the new administration will implement an effective security agenda. The best way to obtain support is to deliver some significant short-term results. Recommendations therefore are classified in two categories: those that can be implemented within a short timeframe (around six months) and those that will require a lengthier institution-building process (around two years) before they can start to take effect.

The recommendations also encompass the most salient flaws in Mexico's current security policy, described previously. Hence, each of these recommendations addresses at least one of the four central goals:

—reduce predatory crime (extortion, kidnapping, and overall insecurity on the roads)

—reduce violence

—improve the criminal justice system

—regain control of prisons.

Recommendations may also be classified according to the primary mechanisms through which they are implemented. In some cases, recommendations refer to policies implemented through field operations by law enforcement agencies; in other cases it will be necessary to improve intelligence capacities, such as information-gathering capacity within prisons and at the neighborhood level. Legal and administrative changes are also key mechanisms for implementing the recommendations. Finally, some cases call for the assistance of foreign experts or governments in designing effective interventions.

Table 7-1. *Overview of Key Policy Recommendations*

Recommendation	Time frame	Goal	Working mechanism	International cooperation
Restore security on roads	Six months	Reduce predatory crime	Field operations	Colombia
Conduct prison population survey		Regain control of prisons	Increased intelligence capabilities	Not applicable
Issue outbreak-of-violence alerts		Reduce violence	Improved coordination	Not applicable
Launch social media platform on security		Reduce predatory crime	Improved coordination	Not applicable
Crack down on place-specific drug markets	Two years	Reduce violence	Field operations Increased intelligence capabilities	United States
Isolate marijuana market		Reduce violence	Legal/administrative changes	United States
Set incarceration reduction targets		Regain control of prisons	Legal/administrative changes	United States
Implement witness protection program		Reduce predatory crime Enhance criminal investigation Regain control of prisons	Increased intelligence capabilities Increased prosecution capabilities	Italy

Source: Author's compilation.

Restore Security on the Roads

Most of Mexico's current security problems, such as drug trafficking, illegal protection markets, and authorities' collusion with criminals, arise from complex and intertwined phenomena. They are byproducts of both economic dynamics and the shortcomings of law enforcement institutions, neither of which will disappear overnight. In the short run such security problems can only be "contained" and then slowly reversed. While a long-term approach to security policy is vital, the new government should have a strategy in place to produce a visible and relevant improvement in security during its initial months. Such an improvement could shift the current pessimism and negative perception of the outlook for the country; it could also boost broader social and political support for the new government's security agenda. Restoring security on the roads would be a good short-term tangible improvement, and it is a goal that can be achieved. At the same time, such an endeavor would not be purely demagogic. Secure roads would also have a positive economic impact and reduce the mobility of criminal organizations.

As shown in figure 7-8, for ordinary citizens, fear of road trips is among the most pervasive consequences of the current security crisis. In the 2011 victimization survey, 24 percent of the respondents (up from 20 percent in 2011) claimed that they had stopped traveling by road due to security concerns. Nevertheless, in several of the Mexican states worst hit by organized crime, the percentage of people avoiding road travel is closer to 40 percent, and it reaches 61 percent in Tamaulipas.[36]

To date, the government has been reluctant to restrict transit or introduce other measures that might prove unpopular in the short run or that might be construed as acknowledging failure. However, in high-risk areas where it is not possible to provide twenty-four-hour surveillance, temporary road curfews may be an effective way to reduce criminal activity. The curfew is a simple means to increase traffic during working hours and reduce the level of risk on less traveled roads.

Conduct Prison Population Surveys

Prison populations have proved to be key actors in Mexico's criminal sphere. Inmates do not cease committing offenses while in prison; they maintain links with their organizations outside prison and have access to valuable information. They also account for a large and increasing share of organized crime–related violence. Scarce information, however, exists on Mexican prison

Figure 7-8. *States with Highest Number of Travelers Avoiding Roads Because of Security Concerns*

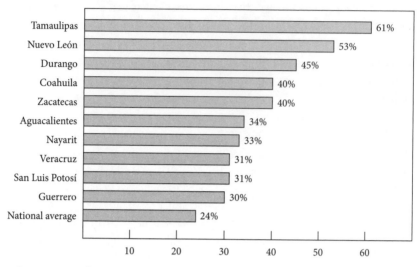

Source: INEGI, "Encuesta nacional de victimización y percepción sobre seguridad pública [National Survey on Victimization and Perceptions of Public Security]" (2012).

populations. The federal government could usefully mandate a series of periodic prison population surveys covering the inmates in the thirty-two state prisons as well as the federal prison system. The surveys should include demographics, criminal record, organization membership, and legal status in the criminal justice system as well as behavior within the penitentiary. Such surveys would help to identify the factors conducive to control of penitentiaries by criminal organizations—for example, by profiling inmates who organize extortion networks from within the prison. They would enable strategic planning on prison capacity, conditions leading to violence within prison, and jailbreaks. They would facilitate identification of inmates as members of competing criminal organizations, which could lead to separation of competing inmates and the diminution of violent conflict between them. The surveys could also identify conditions under which prison staff are bribed and threatened by inmates.

Finally, the survey results would enable evaluation of central features of the criminal justice system, such as the incarceration of violent and dangerous criminals together with those detained for *averiguación previa* (preliminary investigation). That should give state governments an incentive to accelerate

Table 7-2. *Trends in Violence for Selected Locations*

Municipality/ metropolitan area	Violence outbreak	Pre-outbreak average monthly deaths	Post-outbreak average monthly deaths	Percent change
Ciudad Juárez	01/2008	11	169	1,436
Culiacán	05/2008	20	45	125
Chihuahua	06/2008	4	43	975
Mazatlán	07/2008	2	17	750
Tijuana	09/2008	16	36	125
Torreón/Gómez Palacio	02/2009	5	45	800
Zona Metropolitana de Monterrey	03/2010	7	67	857
Zona Metropolitana de Guadalajara	05/2010	7	39	457
Acapulco	10/2010	10	70	600
Veracruz/Boca del Río	06/2011	2	42	2,000

Source: Author's compilation based on data from Secretariado Ejecutivo del Sistema Nacional de Seguridad Pública [Executive Secretariat of the National Public Security System], "Base de Datos de Fallecimientos Ocurridos por Presunta Rivalidad Delincuencial [Database of Deaths Presumably Related to Organized Crime]" (2011) (http://secretariadoejecutivo.gob.mx/en/SecretariadoEjecutivo/ Bases_de_Datos_de_Fallecimientos_ocurridos_por_presunta_rivalidad_delincuencial).

implementation of their respective criminal justice reforms. The survey could also be used to identify and discourage systematic human rights violations.

Issue "Outbreak-of-Violence" Alerts

The analysis of trends from recent years suggests that there is a strong path dependence regarding the amount of organized crime–related violence at the local level. Analyses performed using monthly data on organized crime–related deaths in municipalities and metropolitan areas show that the epidemic of violence becomes self-sustaining whenever there is an increase beyond a statistical threshold for two consecutive months. These two-month episodes, which may be called violence "outbreaks," have proven to be effective predictors of protracted crises of violence. Table 7-2 presents summary statistics on trends in violence in the ten municipalities or metropolitan areas where outbreaks were identified in the 2007–11 period. In all ten cases average monthly organized crime–related deaths were at least twice as high after the outbreak as they were before the outbreak.

Given these findings, the federal government, using currently available information and simple statistical analysis techniques, could identify in a timely fashion municipalities and metropolitan areas that are on the brink of suffering a full-blown security crisis. For example, an "alert" could be issued whenever the level of organized crime–related deaths rose beyond the statistical threshold in any one month. Such an alert would justify a large-scale intervention, which would necessarily divert scarce resources and require a thorough investigation of the municipal police. Such measures, while politically sensitive, are more effective if they are implemented before a full-blown crisis of violence has begun. Moreover, epidemic alerts would foster deeper engagement of state and municipal authorities in efforts to contain violence because mayors and governors would have a clear incentive to avoid alerts being issued for their jurisdictions.

Create a Social Media Platform on Security

During President Calderón's administration, both the federal and state governments adopted a set of commitments to report relevant information on both the incidence of crime and institution-building efforts. Those commitments include the creation of a national database, Plataforma México, aimed at improving information sharing among the federal government, states, and municipalities. However, relatively little information has so far trickled down to citizens. Moreover, conventional media such as newspapers, radio, and television may not be providing reliable reports in crime-ridden areas due to increasing intimidation by criminal organizations. Hence, the federal government should create a social media platform that would allow citizens to obtain real-time information on the incidence of crime and violence, safety on roads, and even the location of authorities who could provide assistance in an emergency. Social media and mobile phone companies could join this initiative to reduce the uncertainty and insecurity that citizens face on a daily basis.

Witness Protection Program

Mafia members are the only individuals who possess information of pivotal importance for dismantling extortion rackets—membership, modus operandi, records of victims, assets bought with illegal proceeds, and so forth. Therefore, the least risky and most successful law enforcement operations against organized crime are those that rely on information provided by defectors or informants within criminal organizations. Due to widespread violence and conflicts among local mafias, which expose members of criminal organizations to a substantial risk of being murdered, members may be willing to defect if a comprehensive program to grant them security and reduce sanctions is established.

The Italian framework for protecting prosecution witnesses and mafia defectors, which has contributed to the weakening of mafias during the last two decades, features witness protection, financial assistance, and the possibility of changing residence and identity as well as reduced sanctions for defectors.[37] The Italian program has been broad but not massive, with no more than 400 witnesses protected each year. The selection of suitable individuals and an adequate government budget are critical to the program's success.

Mexican prosecutors have not developed comprehensive and reliable informant networks, a flaw that is directly linked to the dire situation in Mexican prisons. Authorities can neither stop the influence of criminal organizations over prisoners nor guarantee the safety of imprisoned informants. As a result, extradition to the United States is the only way to obtain reliable intelligence from criminal organization members. However, this intelligence is available to Mexican authorities only to the extent that it serves U.S. law enforcement agencies' interests.

Nevertheless, in addition to major facility-building and staff-training efforts in the prison system, Mexico still needs to set up the legal and institutional framework necessary to run an effective witness and defector protection program. Article 20 of the federal constitution and the federal law against organized crime establish a legal basis for including "cooperative witnesses" in investigations. The law allows for reductions of from one-half to two-thirds of time sentenced for those who collaborate. However, neither adequate staff nor funds have been allocated to run an effective program similar to that in Italy. During the Calderón administration, at least two cooperative witnesses, out of three hundred, were killed.[38]

Along with providing the staff and resources needed to protect and obtain information from participants, rules should be drawn up for classifying the information gleaned from the program. Investigations are frequently discredited due to the opacity that characterizes intelligence collected from cooperative witnesses. Moreover, it is necessary to clarify the conditions under which the evidence provided by a protected witness or defector can be used at trial.[39] The recently approved bill concerning protected witnesses will provide a better framework for running a successful program in President Peña Nieto's administration.[40] This bill calls for construction of a national center to coordinate the program. It also requires the federal attorney general's office to issue an annual report containing budgetary and statistical information about the program.

Crack Down on Place-Specific Drug Markets

There is little evidence that law enforcement or drug use prevention and treatment policies substantially reduce drug consumption.[41] However, some interventions have been effective in altering features of drug markets and limiting the damage from drug trafficking. These interventions generally involve the disruption of "open air," or place-specific, drug markets. In place-specific markets anyone can buy drugs. That makes market participants vulnerable to law enforcement and exposes buyers to conducting transactions with strangers, which often leads to violence.[42] In place-specific markets violence is also a frequent consequence of rivalry between competitors who seek "territorial control" over the market.

Place-specific drug markets are also highly disruptive within the underprivileged communities where they are located; they increase predatory crime, and they are a major source of urban decay. On the other hand, person-specific markets are based on social networks and rely to a large extent on personal reputation. Although person-specific drug markets are not exempt from violence, they are considerably less violent than place-specific markets.

During the last decades Mexico developed a dense network of *narcotienditas* (retail drug venues), which risk becoming a major source of conflict. In recent years place-specific drug markets have produced substantial criminal violence. Although Mexico City has largely remained a safe haven from organized crime–related violence, shootings and killings take place on a regular basis around drug-trafficking hot spots. Tepito—a working-class neighborhood close to the city center—is known as one of the main drug trading areas for consumers as well as for mid-level traffickers. Drug pushing in Tepito is not limited to *narcotienditas;* it is mostly performed at the street level by dealers who are constantly on the move. From 2007 to 2010 at least nineteen people were killed in Tepito as a result of conflicts between criminal organizations. This figure represents 3 percent of all organized crime–related killings in Mexico City. The percentage is high when we take into account that Tepito encompasses only a few blocks (approximately 0.1 percent of Mexico City's developed area). Hence, killings in Tepito illustrate how place-specific drug markets increase violence at the neighborhood level.

Acapulco, a resort town where organized crime–related deaths skyrocketed during 2011, provides another example of the potential harm that place-specific drug markets pose to Mexico's security. Competition for the drug market in Acapulco's nightclubs was at the core of the bloody conflicts between local mafias that emerged in 2009 and 2010 following the disbanding of the Beltrán-Leyva Organization.

Authorities should implement strategies tailored to each place-specific market. These strategies may include a broad array of interventions:

—intensive and unconcealed patrols

—raids

—"buy and bust" exercises

—arrest of drug buyers

—confiscation of properties that function as retail drug venues.

Most successful interventions to disrupt place-specific drug markets are neighborhood or community based. In addition, interventions have a better chance of success when they are supported by an improved relationship or even a partnership between law enforcement agencies and communities.[43] Therefore, state and municipal authorities are in principle better suited than federal authorities to implement interventions aimed at disrupting place-specific drug markets. However, the federal government could lead a national effort to disrupt these markets.

While some information about *narcotienditas* in the Mexico City Metropolitan Area was generated by the federal attorney general's office, authorities lack comprehensive and systematic information regarding place-specific drug markets. The federal intelligence agency, CISEN (Centro de Investigación y Seguridad Nacional [Center for Research and National Security]), could develop and regularly update a national database on drug-dealing hot spots that could guide authorities in designing interventions. It would also help to evaluate the degree of engagement by states and municipalities in the national effort to disrupt place-specific drug markets. The federal government should also provide the training and support necessary for police departments to perform effective interventions.

Isolate the Marijuana Market

Marijuana (cannabis) is by far the most popular illegal drug among Mexican consumers. One strategy that the Mexican government may follow to curb the expansion of illegal drug markets and their most troubling effects is to attempt to split the marijuana market from other illegal substance markets—that is, prevent marijuana users from becoming consumers of other more harmful and more expensive drugs.

While outright legalization of the marijuana trade may prove politically unfeasible—and probably not the best policy option—there are alternatives for dealing with the demand for the drug that are worth exploring. For instance, Mexico has not yet developed a framework to allow the operation of "cannabis social clubs" similar to those existing in several European countries or to license "medical marijuana caregivers," as in some U.S. states and Canadian provinces. Although the scope and details of these alternatives for marijuana distribution vary, they are all based on the principle of limited scale of operation and limited profits for producers and distributors. They provide a legal framework for marijuana production, distribution, and consumption as well as seek to avoid mass media advertising.

Establish Incarceration Reduction Targets

In order to reduce the threat that mafias pose to Mexico's security and stability, it is necessary to address the protracted overcrowding and self-governing problem in prisons. In the long run, the reform of the Mexican judiciary should lead to more timely trials and reduce the number of inmates in preventive detention. However, if the deplorable situation of prisons is to improve during the 2012–18 administration, a more proactive approach will be necessary. The Mexican authorities therefore should consider massive releases of inmates akin to those mandated in California by the U.S. Supreme Court in May 2011.[44] A mass release based on the grounds of prevailing inhumane conditions within prisons should be easy to justify, and the failure to guarantee due process for more than 45 percent of inmates held in preventive detention may also be a powerful justification for a judicial inmate release order. Moreover, the increase in the number of jailbreaks and homicides within prisons provides grounds for a massive inmate release policy. Finally, in 2011 the documentary film *Presunto Culpable* (Presumed Guilty), which portrays the story of a blatant miscarriage of justice regarding an innocent detainee, raised public awareness regarding the vulnerability of citizens vis-à-vis a negligent and corrupt criminal justice system.[45] Hence, public opinion could be more favorable now than before to the swift release of inmates who are likely to be victims of prosecutors' and judges' incompetence.

Conclusion

An increasing number of communities throughout Mexico face a daunting public security challenge. While in previous years certain state and local governments as well as the federal government increased resources devoted to law enforcement, the incidence of crime has not been curbed. On the contrary, there has been a substantial increase in the number of violent crimes. The federal government's public security strategy must focus on the reduction of criminal violence, including the growth of mafias devoted to extortion.

I have proposed a set of recommendations specifically tailored to address the main sources and consequences of organized crime–related violence. To implement these and similar interventions we need more active engagement by state and local governments, which have jurisdiction over the largest share of Mexico's police officers. Unfortunately, in violence-ridden areas criminal organizations have been able to bribe and intimidate state and local officials. Criminals are now also threatening journalists and community leaders in order to prevent civil society and local social movements from advancing their anti-crime strategies.

The federal government, as the actor least exposed to criminal organizations' influence, must play a proactive role in fostering and supporting more effective state and local government policies to reduce violence and crime. Federal funds should be used to leverage broader engagement by state and local governments. The formulas for estimating the federal transfer programs for funding law enforcement institution building—namely those for FASP (Fund for Public Security Provisions) and SUBSEMUN (Subsidy for Municipal Public Security)—could be modified to reward states and municipalities that successfully implement crime- and violence-reduction policies. Due to the fact that performance-based funding is a highly contentious political issue in Mexico, the main resistance to this approach will stem from the reciprocal distrust between political parties. However, the breadth and scale of the current epidemic of violence requires citizens of all political persuasions to unite in combating this scourge.

As described previously, several years will be required to effectively tackle Mexico's foremost security challenges. Regarding the most pressing issue, namely violence reduction, Peña Nieto has already set a goal to reduce the murder rate by half. The recent experience from Ciudad Juárez suggests that it is possible to achieve substantial violence reduction over the medium term. Organized crime–related deaths in that city declined 83 percent from their peak in the third quarter of 2010 to the third quarter of 2012. Hence, as long as the government effectively identifies and contains new violence epidemics, the goal of reducing the murder rate by half during President Peña Nieto's administration seems feasible.

There is more uncertainty regarding potential progress in other realms of security policy. Institution-building efforts such as better law enforcement and effective control of prisons will rely in most cases on the ability of the new government to achieve better coordination with state and municipal governments. The fact that twenty-one of thirty-two governors come from Peña Nieto's party, the PRI (Partido Revolucionario Institucional [Institutional Revolutionary Party]), may foster better coordination. However, the opposite may also be true: governors may have a stronger bargaining position vis-à-vis a president from their own party and thus may be able to avoid adopting policies harmful to their political interests.

Greater engagement by advocacy groups and citizens will be necessary if Peña Nieto's administration is to implement a successful security strategy. Social movements that advocate violence reduction and better security standards have already developed significant notoriety at the national level. However, they must increase the scope of their networks in order to have a greater impact on policymaking, especially at the state and municipal levels. It is noteworthy that in some violence-ridden areas criminal organizations systematically intimidate citizens, especially outside large metropolitan areas like Monterrey, where stakeholders from the business community have been vocal about the need for a better response to the violence crisis. National-level advocacy groups could play an important role in providing visibility to such communities and fostering greater accountability among their authorities.

Transparency and accountability will also contribute to state and local governments' engagement in the implementation of the new security agenda. The federal government has already disclosed information on the level of compliance with agreed-upon standards by state law enforcement institutions. It also publishes data on the states that have failed to perform polygraph tests on senior public security officials.[46] Now, a more systematic and broadly publicized security information and disclosure policy is needed to provide for greater coordination and shared responsibility among all three levels of government throughout the republic.

The eight recommendations that I present in this chapter imply a critical change from the security strategy priorities in the early years of President Calderón's administration. The change means that drug interdiction efforts and other actions against criminal organizations that focus primarily on drug trafficking will rank lower than reduction of violence and crime. This change had already begun with the Calderón administration's targeting of law enforcement operations against Zetas, the most violent of Mexico's large drug-trafficking organizations. The change is likely to continue and deepen during the Peña Nieto administration through the implementation of either these recommendations or similar policies.

There is a lack of thorough analyses of the impact of Mexican drug interdiction efforts on drug availability in the United States. Hence, it would be highly speculative to estimate an impact of the recommendations on cross-border drug trafficking. Nevertheless, bilateral relations are not likely to be damaged even if changes in Mexico's security strategy imply a greater flow of drugs across the common border. On one hand, Mexico is not likely to stop enforcing anti-narcotics law overall. On the other hand, widespread violence in Mexico remains a common security threat (1 million U.S. citizens live or have property in Mexico, many of them in areas already threatened by violence epidemics). Therefore, U.S. authorities are likely to praise violence reduction efforts in Mexico.

The United States may even play a key role in reducing violence and crime in Mexico. For instance, bi-national cooperation to foster better local governance in Mexico may evolve over the following years. Traditionally, U.S. local governments have been strong, and local law enforcement institutions have a remarkable record in the design and implementation of violence- and crime-reduction programs, such as the Boston Gun Project and Chicago CeaseFire. American senior policymakers and practitioners could help their counterparts in Mexican municipal law enforcement agencies to develop the skills necessary to successfully implement similar programs.

Notes

1. Fernando Escalante Gonzalbo and others, "Nuestra Guerra: Una Conversación [Our War: A Conversation]," *Nexos*, November 1, 2011.

2. Consulta Mitofsky, *México: Evaluación de Gobierno* [Mexico: Evaluation of Government], 2012 (http://consulta.mx/web/index.php/estudios/evaluacion-gobierno/96-felipe-calderon-2).

3. See Escalante Gonzalbo and others, "Nuestra Guerra: Una Conversación."

4. Felipe Calderón Hinojosa, *La lucha por la seguridad pública* [The Fight for Public Security], 2010 (http://portal.sre.gob.mx/chicago/pdf/061810SeguridadPublica.pdf).

5. FASP is a federal fund established to allocate resources to each state security budget. These resources are intended to support institution-building efforts (for example, recruitment, training, and evaluation of police officers; purchase of police equipment; and establishment of the national telecommunications network and the national emergency telephone line). SUBSEMUN plays a similar role at the municipal level.

6. The combined budget of the four main federal law enforcement security agencies was $5,258 million in 2006 and $8,979 million in 2011 (adjusted to 2011 prices).

The four agencies are the army (Secretaría de la Defensa Nacional [Ministry of National Defense]); the navy (Secretaría de Marina [Ministry of the Navy]); the Federal Attorney General's Office (Procuraduría General de la República), which is responsible for criminal investigations; and the Ministry of Public Security (Secretaría de Seguridad Pública), which encompasses the federal police and is also responsible for the administration of federal prisons. Figures according to *Presupuesto de Egresos de la Federación para el Ejercicio Fiscal de 2006* [Federal Expenditures Budget for 2006], published December 22, 2005; and *Presupuesto de Egresos de la Federación para el Ejercicio Fiscal 2011*, published December 7, 2010.

7. Ley General del Sistema Nacional de Seguridad Pública [General Law on the National Public Security System], *Diario Oficial de la Federación*, January 2, 2009.

8. Ley General para Prevenir y Sancionar los Delitos en Materia de Secuestro [General Law on Kidnapping Prevention and Enforcement], *Diario Oficial de la Federación*, November 30, 2010.

9. Ley Federal de Extinción de Dominio [Federal Law on Illegal Property Seizure], *Diario Oficial de la Federación*, May 26, 2009.

10. Ley Federal para la Prevención e Identificación de Operaciones con Recursos de Procedencia Ilícita [Federal Law on Money Laundering Identification and Prevention], *Diario Oficial de la Federación*, October 17, 2012.

11. Figure for 2012 is from Clare Ribando Seelke and Kristin Finklea, *U.S.-Mexican Security Cooperation: The Mérida Initiative and Beyond* (Washington: Congressional Research Service, 2011) (http://fpc.state.gov/documents/organization/170503.pdf). Figure for 2013 came from President Obama's request on February 13, 2012. Testimony of Kevin Whitaker, acting principal deputy assistant secretary of state, before the House Appropriations Committee, 2012 (http://appropriations.house.gov/uploaded files/hhrg-112-ap04-wstate-kwhitaker-20120329.pdf).

12. This was the Movement for Peace, led by the poet Javier Sicilia, whose son was murdered by a local criminal organization in Morelos. Large-scale protests demanding more security had taken place in previous years. For instance, in August 30, 2008, Iluminemos México (Let's Light Up Mexico, a social movement that advocates better accountability by authorities) organized a massive protest on Mexico City's main thoroughfare demanding action against kidnapping for ransom. This protest was organized after the teenage son of Alejandro Martí —a sports businessman—was murdered while he was kidnapped. However, prior to 2011 this and similar protests did not stress demands to reduce organized crime–related violence (which in most cases involves members of criminal organizations exclusively and police officers and soldiers to a lesser extent); they focused on reducing other criminal activities, foremost kidnapping for ransom.

13. Alejandro Hope, "¿Qué fumaron mientras medían? [What Were They Smoking While They Were Measuring?]," *Nexos*, September 1, 2011.

14. According to data collected by the author from national and local newspapers.

15. Diego Gambetta, *The Sicilian Mafia: The Business of Private Protection* (Harvard University Press, 1996).

16. Calderón, *La lucha por la seguridad pública*.

17. México Evalúa, *Índice de Víctimas Visibles e Invisibles de Delitos Graves* [Index of Visible and Invisible Victims of Serious Crimes], Mexico City, 2011, p. 8. (www.altoalsecuestro.com.mx/INDICE_VICTIMAS_VISIBLES_INVISIBLES.pdf).

18. A detailed account of this process is provided in Eduardo Guerrero, "Security, Drugs, and Violence in Mexico: A Survey," paper prepared for the Seventh North American Forum, Washington, D.C., October 6–8, 2011 (http://iis-db.stanford.edu/evnts/6716/NAF_2011_EG_(Final).pdf).

19. Federico Varese, "How Mafias Migrate: The Case of the 'Ndrangheta in Northern Italy," *Law and Society Review* 40, no. 2 (2006): 411–44.

20. An analysis of reputation building in the mafia is provided in Gambetta, *The Sicilian Mafia*.

21. Elisabeth Malkin, "As Gangs Move In On Mexico's Schools, Teachers Say 'Enough,'" *New York Times*, September 25, 2011.

22. Alejandro Hope, "La milagrosa multiplicación de los sicarios [The Miraculous Multiplication of Gunmen]," *Animal Político*, October 23, 2011 (www.animalpolitico.com/blogueros-plata-o-plomo/2011/10/23/la-milagrosa-multiplicacion-de-los-sicarios/).

23. This figure is a rough approximation. It is a simple calculation that applies a standard ratio of one drug dealer per 20,000 people (based on information from PGR for the Mexico City metropolitan area) to the national population.

24. Comisión Nacional Contra las Adicciones [National Anti-Addiction Commission], *Encuesta Nacional de Adicciones* [National Addiction Survey], 2011 (http://www.conadic.salud.gob.mx/pdfs/ENA_2011_DROGAS_ILICITAS_.pdf).

25. Procuraduría General de Justicia del Distrito Federal (Mexico City Attorney General's Office), *Quinto Informe de Labores* [Fifth Annual Activities Report] (Mexico City: 2011), p. 244 (www.pgjdf.gob.mx/images/Contenidos/Informes/5toInformedeLaboresPGJ.pdf).

26. Marcelo Bergman and Elena Azaola, "Cárceles de México: cuadros de una crisis [Prisons in Mexico: Scenes of a Crisis]," *Urvio: Revista Latinoamericana de Seguridad Ciudadana* [Urvio: Latin American Security Magazine] 1 (2007): 74–87.

27. Ana Laura Magaloni Kerpel, *Arbitrariedad e Ineficiencia de la Procuración de Justicia: Dos caras de la misma moneda* [Arbitrariness and Inefficiency in Administering Justice: Two Sides of the Same Coin] (Mexico City: CIDE, 2007).

28. Presidencia de la Republica, "Sexto Informe de Gobierno [Sixth Government Report]," 2012 (http://sexto.informe.gob.mx/pdf/INFORME_ESCRITO/Sexto_Informe_de_Gobierno.pdf).

29. Felonies in Mexico are classified under two broad categories: *delitos del fuero común*, including most forms of property crime as well as homicide and violent crime that harms individuals; these are generally prosecuted by courts at the state level. *Delitos del fuero federal* encompass the main activities of criminal organizations, such as drug trafficking and kidnapping; they are prosecuted by courts at the federal level.

30. México Evalúa, *Índice de Desempeño del Sistema Penal* [Prison System Performance Index] (Mexico City: 2010), p. 21 (http://mexicoevalua.org/descargables/180f47_INDICE_DESEMPENO-PENAL.pdf).

31. On average, keeping an inmate in a U.S. federal penitentiary costs $65 to $70 a day. Incarceration in California costs $122 a day. See U.S. Department of Justice, Bureau of Justice Statistics (December 2011) (http://bjs.oip.usdoj.gov/content/pub/pdf/jee8207st.pdf)

32. Santiago Levy, *Good Intentions, Bad Outcomes: Social Policy, Informality and Economic Growth* (Brookings, 2008).

33. "Mexico's Disappeared: The Enduring Costs of a Crisis Ignored," *Human Rights Watch* (February 2013). The report cites extensively from the Comisión Nacional de los Derechos Humanos (National Human Rights Commission) and public information accessed through the Instituto Federal de Acceso a la Información y Protección de Datos (Federal Freedom of Information and Data Protection Institute).

34. Presidencia de la República y Ministerio de Seguridad Nacional de Colombia [Presidency of the Republic and Ministry of National Security of Colombia], *Política de defensa y seguridad democrática* [Democratic Defense and Security Policy] (Bogotá: 2003), p. 52 (www.oas.org/csh/spanish/documentos/Colombia.pdf).

35. Joaquín Villalobos, "Nuevos mitos de la Guerra contra el narco [New Myths of the War on Drugs]," *Nexos*, January 1, 2012. Villalobos is a former leader of Frente Farabundo Martí para la Liberación Nacional [Farabundo Martí National Liberation Front], a Salvadorian guerrilla coalition that later became a political party, and he is currently a consultant in conflict resolution. He has published articles about organized crime in Mexico.

36. Instituto Nacional de Estadística y Geografía [National Statistics and Geography Institute], "Encuesta nacional de victimización y percepción sobre seguridad pública [National Survey on Victimization and Perceptions of Public Security]" (2011) (www.inegi.org.mx/est/contenidos/proyectos/encuestas/hogares/regulares/envipe/default. aspx).

37. Letizia Paoli, "Mafia and Organized Crime in Italy: The Unacknowledged Successes of Law Enforcement," *West European Politics* 30, no. 4 (2007), pp. 854–80.

38. Jesús Zambada Reyes, a nephew of a Sinaloa cartel kingpin, was found dead in November 21, 2009, while he was in a facility under PGR custody. Edgar Enrique Bayardo del Villar, a witness in a police corruption case, was shot while he was in Starbucks in Mexico City, on December 1, 2009; see María de la Luz González, "Matan a testigo protegido de PGR en Starbucks del DF [PGR Protected Witness Killed in Starbucks in the Federal District]," *El Universal*, December 1, 2009.

39. Álvaro Vizcaíno Zamora, *Reflexiones sobre los testigos protegidos* [Thoughts on Cooperative Witnesses], Instituto Nacional de Ciencias Penales, 2011 (www.inacipe.gob.mx/index.php?option=com_content&view=article&id=371:reflexiones-sobre-los-testigos-protegidos&catid=37:alvaro-vizcaino-zamora&Itemid=171).

40. Ley Federal para la Protección de Personas que Intervienen en el Procedimiento Penal [Federal Law for the Protection of Individuals Who Intervene in Judiciary Procedures], *Diario Oficial de la Federación*, published June 8, 2012.

41. Peter Reuter, "How Can U.S. Domestic Drug Policy Help Mexico?" in *Shared Responsibility. U.S.-Mexico Policy Options for Confronting Organized Crime,* edited by Eric Olson and others (Washington: Woodrow Wilson International Center for Scholars, 2011), pp. 121–40.

42. Alex Harocopos and Mike Hough, *Drug Dealing in Open-Air Markets* (U.S. Department of Justice, 2005) (www.popcenter.org/problems/pdfs/DrugMarkets.pdf).

43. Lorraine Mazerolle and others, *Disrupting Street-Level Drug Markets* (U.S. Department of Justice, 2007) (http://cops.usdoj.gov/Publications/e04072678.pdf).

44. In 2011, the U.S. Supreme Court ruled that California must reduce its prison population by more than 30,000 inmates over two years.

45. Roberto Hernández and Geoffrey Smith, *Presunto Culpable*, documentary film, 2009.

46. Secretariado Ejecutivo del Sistema Nacional de Seguridad Pública [Executive Secretariat of the National Public Security System], "Base de Datos de Fallecimientos Ocurridos por Presunta Rivalidad Delincuencias [Database of Deaths Presumably Related to Organized Crime]" (2011) (http://secretariadoejecutivo.gob.mx/en/ SecretariadoEjecutivo/Bases_de_Datos_de_Fallecimientos_ocurridos_por_presunta_ rivalidad_delincuencial).

DIANA VILLIERS NEGROPONTE

8

The Mérida Initiative:
A Mechanism for Bilateral Cooperation

Historically, relations between the Mexican and the U.S. governments have been most productive when both governments share common goals but work independently to achieve them. Close collaboration over time produces friction, with Mexico asserting national sovereignty and rejecting integration of common projects. In the early 1990s the U.S. government collected and passed on to the Procuraduría General de la República (PGR) (Federal Attorney General's Office) information on Colombian aircraft carrying shipments of cocaine that were using landing strips in Mexico. The federal police, sometimes in conjunction with the Secretaría de Defensa Nacional (SEDENA) (Ministry of National Defense), would then take control, apprehending the crew and seizing the drugs and aircraft. That protocol ensured that no offense was given to Mexican sovereignty and furthered the common objective of stemming the flow of Colombian drugs through Mexico to the United States. In contrast, when officers from the U.S. Drug Enforcement Administration (DEA) sought to operate on Mexican soil in conjunction with their Mexican counterparts, popular outrage resulted, particularly if the operation was unsuccessful. Preserving Mexico's territorial sovereignty remained a fundamental principle of national security.

In October 2007, President Felipe Calderón chose a radically different policy. Because Calderón's new "war against drugs" required close collaboration with the United States, he asked President George W. Bush for assistance. In the colonial town of Mérida, far from Mexico City, the two presidents deliberated on how they might work together to bring down the Colombian drug trafficking organizations (DTOs) that had been taken over by Mexican organizations.

From that initial meeting, a bilateral program known as the Mérida Initiative emerged, in which Bush pledged funds for sophisticated equipment, training, and intelligence sharing to destroy the Mexican DTOs. President Barack Obama continued the U.S. commitment but shifted to a more comprehensive approach in which the training of investigative police, prison staff, and judicial officers would play a more important role. In 2009, an offshoot of the initiative, Beyond Mérida, assumed a broader role in reinforcing the border between the two countries and strengthening communities bombarded by drug-related violence.

With a new president in Mexico and a renewed mandate for President Obama, it is time to question the value of the 2007 Mérida Initiative as well as that of Beyond Mérida. President Enrique Peña Nieto has called for a review of current U.S. and Mexican strategies, proclaiming that he will give greater attention to keeping citizens safe from criminal violence, while Washington remains committed to stopping the flow of drugs northward. It is therefore reasonable to ask whether Mexican and U.S. interests still align or whether the Mérida Initiative has run its course as a means of bilateral cooperation. From here forward, should the two governments resume their traditional approach, in which each government pursues its common goals with relative independence? Furthermore, is it time to address broader security issues, such as containing the financial power of drug trafficking cartels and strengthening Mexico's southern border, as well as social issues shared by both nations, such as deportation and youth violence?

The Mérida Initiative: 2007–09

U.S. Assistant Secretary of State Tom Shannon, who accompanied Bush to Mérida in October 2007, understood the radical change in the relationship proposed by Calderón. For the first time, the Mexican government was asking Washington to collaborate on a common project. After decades of distrust on both sides, Calderón was asking for equipment, spare parts, and training for the Mexican armed forces. He requested sophisticated, expensive ion scanners capable of identifying explosives and narcotics, as well as equipment for the electronic tracing of weapons. Shannon argued in favor of closer collaboration with the Mexican government, urging approval of a supplemental appropriation of $1.46 billion to meet the needs of both Mexico and the Central American countries. Calderón and the U.S. State Department intended to
    —break the power and impunity of criminal organizations
    —strengthen border, air, and maritime controls

—improve the capacity of the criminal justice systems in the region
—diminish local demand for drugs by restraining gang activity.[1]

Under the Mérida Initiative, Congress approved a $400 million supplemental appropriation for Mexico in FY 2008; $300 million was included in the FY 2009 budget, plus $420 million more in a 2009 supplemental appropriation; and $210 million was included in the FY 2010 budget, plus $175 million in a 2010 supplemental appropriation. Those funds were to pay, among other equipment, for four CASA 235 maritime surveillance aircraft, nine UH-60 Black Hawk helicopters, and eight Bell 412 helicopters.[2] Nonintrusive inspection equipment was provided for Mexico's border entry points, and polygraph machines were delivered to both the PGR and the Secretaría de Seguridad Pública (SSP) (Ministry of Public Security). The total cost for the equipment was $1.1 billion. Delivery has been very slow, provoking keen annoyance within the Mexican government.[3] In early 2013, the final piece of equipment, an Intelligence, Surveillance, and Reconnaissance Dornier 328-JET aircraft for the federal police, still awaited delivery.

In subsequent years, the administration sought and Congress appropriated lesser sums of money for Mexico. In 2011, Congress reduced Mérida funding to $143 million and provided an estimated $282.8 million for FY 2012.[4] The administration has requested $205 million for FY 2014.[5] This represents a 35 percent reduction from FY 2012 due to the discontinuation of purchases of big-ticket hardware items and a concentration on capacity training programs, which cost less. None of the Mérida funds are transferred directly to the Mexican government. Instead, the State Department's Bureau of International Narcotics and Law Enforcement Affairs (INCLE) uses the funds to purchase equipment and pay for spare parts and maintenance as well as to pay trainers and consultants. Likewise, Justice Department and USAID funds for Mérida are not transferred to the Mexican government but are used to pay Mexican and U.S. contractors to deliver services. Despite increasing levels of trust between individual government officials, the means by which funds are disbursed under Mérida suggests a lack of conviction that the Mexican government will hold itself accountable for the funds.

A significant proportion of the funding goes to pay for training. Under a system of "train the trainer," courses are offered at both the federal and state level for municipal police investigators; judges and prosecutors; customs officials; prison staff; and managers of canine teams. Most training takes place in Mexico, with some taking place in Arizona and New Mexico. The training provided in the United States has proved most beneficial for the Mexican trainees because it is highly practical in nature. Retired U.S. prosecutors, judges, and investigative police with years of experience organize mock trials and crime scene exercises. Furthermore, Mexican prosecutors spend time discussing cases with both the police and judges. That interaction—among officials who rarely talk with each other in their home states—helps to create mutual understanding. It also supports the implementation of the new criminal procedural code, which remains a challenge. A majority of judges prefer Mexico's old inquisitorial justice system, in which they controlled the file and the docket. But with this training, a cadre of progressive professionals is learning how to conduct oral trials, fashion arguments that preserve the presumption of innocence, and collect and preserve evidence while documenting its chain of custody.

Despite the initial delay in delivering equipment, Mexican officials were satisfied with the high degree of cooperation between the two governments and began to develop close ties with individual U.S. officials. Bilateral cooperation developed among law enforcement, military, and intelligence agents in both countries. Advances were made in information sharing and data interoperability through fusion centers and common platforms, such as the Special Investigative Unit (SIU) and the Border Enforcement Security Task Force (BEST). In Mexico City, Mexico's Coordinator of International Cooperation and Security convenes a monthly bilateral implementation meeting (MBIM) of all concerned agencies in the Mexican government as well as the U.S. agencies working in Mexico.[6] This degree of close collaboration has created levels of trust between U.S. officials and their Mexican counterparts rarely seen before. Furthermore, information gathered in the United States is shared with Mexican officers, even though Mexican officials cannot be sure whether they received all the relevant information or only that which served the U.S. national interest.

Mérida's Second Stage: "Beyond Mérida"

With the election of Barack Obama in 2008, Carlos Pascual, the incoming U.S. ambassador to Mexico, brought his keen analytical mind to bear on the bilateral security problems and proposed that President Obama continue the Mérida Initiative but shift focus. He recommended that the initiative take a comprehensive approach, combining effective law enforcement with improved criminal justice, border security, and social programs in key communities. In 2009, Mexico and the United States drew up a new strategic framework for security cooperation under the Mérida Initiative. The two governments agreed to the following four pillars of the revised framework, known in the United States as "Beyond Mérida":

—Pillar I: disruption of organized criminal organizations
—Pillar II: institutionalization of the rule of law
—Pillar III: construction of a 21st century border
—Pillar IV: development of strong, resilient communities that can withstand the pressure from criminal organizations.[7]

The new strategy required the United States to shift from providing support exclusively at the federal level to helping Mexican state and municipal officials confront problems through police assistance and community development programs. With the helicopters, fixed-wing aircraft, and polygraph machines still to be delivered, it was both politic and effective to stress training and technical assistance. The intent was to offer training to judges and prosecutors in the states that had demonstrated their commitment to reforming the criminal justice system, moving from an inquisitorial process with only written pleadings to open trials, the presumption of innocence, and the rejection of evidence gathered by police under torture and ill treatment.[8] By late 2012, funds for the second pillar—institutionalization of the rule of law—were far greater than for other parts of the plan.

Strong cooperation between the two federal governments continued, and on September 18, 2012, at a meeting of the High-Level Consultative Group, both governments endorsed their commitment to the revised strategic framework. The cabinet-level members of the group pledged "to build on and institutionalize the cooperation [that] the Mérida Initiative has established."[9] Together, they would take combating domestic problems that contribute to drug trafficking and crime, including demand for drugs, as part of their accepted "shared responsibility."[10] That meeting represents the high-water mark of bilateral cooperation.

However, the policy of shared responsibility had, and still has, different implications for each national government. Mexico believes that the U.S. government should reduce U.S. consumption of illicit drugs; enforce regulations that limit straw purchases;[11] prohibit the sale of weapons that are known, or should be known, to end up in Mexico; and devote resources to contain money laundering and the shipment of bulk cash southward. The United States believes that Mexico should end the impunity with which the federal police have operated; vigorously implement its criminal justice reforms; and combat corruption among government and political officials.

In 2011, considerable frustration existed on the U.S. side at the lack of coordination between Mexican federal officials and state authorities. With a mandate from Washington to focus on the states most seriously affected by the DTOs, U.S. State Department officers struggled to find a level of federal-state coordination sufficient to allow distribution of Mérida funds. Funds distributed to the PGR and SSP were concentrated at the federal level and rarely distributed to the states to enable local training of law enforcement officers. Beyond Mérida remained a federal-to-federal government program. The constraints faced by Mexican officers in implementing programs became increasingly evident on the U.S. side. On the Mexican side, the lack of progress in curtailing drug-related violence resulted in President Calderón's acute criticism of Washington's lack of political will to reduce drug consumption and control the southward flow of weapons. Though justified, vocal criticism did little to enhance collaboration on the ground. The coordinating agency existed in Mexico City, but out in the field, collaboration was tenuous.

The inadequate effort to track firearms flowing south, dramatized by a misguided undercover operation conducted by the U.S. Bureau of Alcohol, Tobacco, Firearms, and Explosives (ATF) that allowed guns to move into Mexico, reinforced the perception that Washington lacked the political will to contain drug violence in Mexico. The operation, dubbed "Fast and Furious," went awry when ATF lost track of the firearms until one of them was used to kill a U.S. law enforcement official working out of a U.S. consulate.[12] This botched attempt to track the trade in weapons reinforced the conclusion of many Mexican citizens that Washington did not care if their compatriots died in the "war on drugs" as long as the violence did not spill over into the United States. By early 2012, a number of contentious issues had become public, among them the failure to reduce the level of violence and the Mexican abuse of human rights.

Human Rights

An issue of potential conflict and assured irritation lurked just below the surface of bilateral cooperation: human rights. When the Mérida Initiative was initially passed, Congress had debated whether human rights provisions in section 620J of the Foreign Assistance Act should apply. This section states that a unit in, or an individual of, a foreign country's security forces is prohibited from receiving assistance if the U.S. secretary of state receives "credible evidence" that the person or unit has committed "a gross violation of human rights."[13] Because of Mexico's concerns that the provisions would violate its sovereignty, the State Department requested that a modified condition be written into the Mérida Initiative stipulating that 15 percent of funds distributed by the State Department would be withheld until the secretary of state reported in writing that Mexico was taking action to

—improve transparency and accountability of the Mexican federal police forces

—establish a mechanism for regular consultations among relevant Mexican government authorities, Mexican human rights organizations, and other Mexican civil society organizations to ensure that implementation of the Mérida Initiative complied with Mexican and international law

—ensure that civilian prosecutors and judicial authorities investigate and prosecute, in accordance with Mexican and international law, federal police and military forces that have been credibly alleged to have committed violations of human rights and ensure that the federal police and military forces cooperate fully in the investigations

—enforce the prohibition, in accordance with Mexican and international law, on the use of testimony obtained through torture or other mistreatment.

All four conditions were maintained in congressional appropriations for the Mérida Initiative in FY 2010 and FY 2011. However, the U.S. Embassy in Mexico recommended withholding some funding pending improvements in key areas of concern. In September 2010, the State Department withheld $26 million until the Mexican government made further progress in providing transparency and combating impunity.[14] In response, the Calderón administration submitted legislation to strengthen the power of the Comisión Nacional de Derechos Humanos (CNDH) (National Human Rights Commission), and it also sought to strengthen the Code of Military Justice so that military officials accused of human rights crimes against civilians would be tried in civilian courts. The Mexican congress approved moving trials to civilian courts in certain limited cases, but the Mexican senate blocked using civilian courts for all charges of human rights crimes. The new senate, elected in July 2012 and in session after September 1, 2012, has yet to vote on the reach of this provision.

In recognition of Mexican sensitivities over national sovereignty, the U.S. House appropriation for FY2012 omitted the first two human rights conditions on aid to Mexico; however, the Senate Appropriations Committee retained all four conditions. As a result, U.S. funds have been held back on two further occasions.

Acknowledging the need to improve bilateral cooperation in this area and to facilitate release of the withheld 15 percent of aid, the Mexican and U.S. governments have established a human rights dialogue. The dialogue has proposed and now provides human rights training for the Mexican security forces. The parties have also implemented several new human rights programs, including a USAID grant of $5 million to Freedom House to increase protections for Mexican journalists and defenders of human rights. The UN Office of the High Commissioner for Human Rights also received $1.3 million to help Mexican civil society groups monitor abuses by Mexican security forces. Nongovernmental organizations receiving Mérida funding should also report on how security forces respond to reports of human rights abuses.

The leverage exercised through the 15 percent withholding has not improved cooperation with the new PRI (Partido Revolucionario Institucional [Institutional Revolutionary Party]) government, and so far it has had only a minimal impact on the abuse of Mexican journalists. Many of them have left the country, and in early March 2013, a local newspaper in Coahuila announced that it could no longer publish freely and would have to close because of threats of violence. Meantime, Mexican civil society criticizes the U.S. government for its support of the military-led security strategy and for failure to enforce the human rights restrictions. In short, the level of friction between the two neighbors is rising. The State Department must weigh the overall bilateral relationship against pressures from human rights organizations in both countries to prevent the Mérida projects from becoming an abusive security strategy.[15]

Measuring the Success of the Mérida Initiative

Congress has continually requested that the State Department evaluate the various programs under Mérida. In its initial framework for the initiative, the State Department established criteria and benchmarks, but the government has revised its criteria, and outside observers have proposed new benchmarks as the program has evolved. The central question is to determine which criteria best indicate the level of violence, the strength of democratic governance, and the rule of law in Mexico.

QUANTITY OF EQUIPMENT DELIVERED AND NUMBER OF TRAINEES. In the first years of the Mérida Initiative, the quantity of equipment delivered and the number of trainees appeared to satisfy the U.S. Congress. As of September 2012, 4,400 federal police investigators and 5,000 prison staff had completed

U.S.-funded courses. Another 7,500 federal and 19,000 state judicial sector personnel had received training in the new accusatorial criminal justice system.[16] The numbers are satisfactory, but the quality of the training and the implementation of that training in the pursuit of criminal cases remain harder to quantify.

DRUG-RELATED HOMICIDES. On the Mexican side, success was measured by the reduction in the number of homicides. The startling increases that marked the period from 2007 to the third quarter of 2011 raised the question of whether Calderón's "war on drugs" could work. The stabilization of, if not the 17 percent decrease in, intentional homicides from November 2011 to December 2012 indicated that Mexican law enforcement had regained control. However, the first months of 2013 witnessed a rise in intentional homicides in communities away from the U.S.-Mexican border, suggesting that the violence has been displaced from its traditional trafficking routes to new centers. These centers, most notably Guerrero and Michoacán, have become the new focus of criminal violence such as rape, sexual assault, kidnapping, and extortion. Thus, Mexican citizens do not yet feel safer.

VICTIMIZATION RATES AND PERCEPTIONS OF INSECURITY. Measuring the number of kidnappings, assaults, and extortions is problematic because in many cases victims are unwilling to report the crimes to the police. Victimization rates therefore do not reflect the actual level of violence. Instead, perceptions of insecurity may be a more effective tool for measuring progress. However, the data collected by Eduardo Guerrero (see chapter 7) indicate that victimization rates have declined while the perception of insecurity has remained steady, if not increased slightly. A discrepancy exists between reporting that one has been a victim of a crime and the feeling that one is more, or less, secure. That discrepancy also extends to whether citizens feel safer in their own community or in the country as a whole. In general, citizens feel safer in their immediate surroundings. Media accounts of violence in the nation raise fears that violence pervades Mexico, making travel by road and vacations a risky venture. The broad perception is that the nation is subject to widespread threats of violence, not so much from drug traffickers as from transnational criminal organizations (TCOs).

LEVEL OF TRUST. Victims' reluctance to report criminal activities reflects the low level of trust that citizens have in the police, the justice system, and politicians. Measuring that trust is the key metric for determining the relative success of any security strategy, including the Mérida Initiative. If success is to be claimed, trust in public institutions, particularly law enforcement and the judiciary, must increase. In its most recent survey of Mexico, Latinobarómetro found that 85 percent of Mexicans surveyed believed that corruption has increased.[17] Related to that is the finding that only 39 percent of respondents believed that public institutions can resolve security problems. Indeed, 81 percent of those surveyed had "low" or "no" trust in their police.[18] These findings are disturbing because they show that respondents do not believe that key government institutions serve the public. In the absence of trust in public institutions, communities form vigilante groups, such as two groups in Guerrero that recently formed to protect their families from TCOs.[19]

IMPACT ON THE UNITED STATES. The U.S. Congress looks at those elements that directly affect security within the United States, namely the number of drug-related arrests, the size of drug seizures, and the price of drugs in different geographic markets. Congress has asked the Congressional Research Service (CRS) to examine the nature and dimensions of spillover violence on the southwest border. However, in its latest report, CRS was unable to reach a definite conclusion on whether there existed "a significant spillover of drug trafficking–related violence into the United States."[20]

BILATERAL COOPERATION. The State Department has suggested that success should be judged on the basis of bilateral cooperation. U.S. government agencies claim that the increasing ability of U.S. and Mexican law enforcement to share information and "work together to prosecute transnational crime" may be a byproduct of the Mérida Initiative.[21] However, this is a tenuous measurement of success because, as both sides are keenly aware, information sharing is an area of friction as well as close collaboration. Any analysis should examine how those areas of friction are resolved rather than mark bilateral irritations and discord as negatives on the score card. Mérida is a vehicle for collaboration, but not an alliance. Both governments continue to seek collaboration and minimize the impediments to cooperation. How that effort will proceed under President Peña Nieto is a key question that must be examined.

The Peña Nieto Administration and the Future of the Mérida Initiative

Both during his electoral campaign and in the early months after taking office on December 1, 2012, President Enrique Peña Nieto emphasized that his government would give priority to "reducing the violence" in Mexico. The implication of giving priority to citizen security was that pursuit of drug kingpins would be less important. In chapter 7, Eduardo Guerrero notes that one consequence of decapitating the ringleaders has been increased competition among their lieutenants for leadership and the most profitable drug trafficking routes; the losing lieutenants then move into other illicit businesses, such as human trafficking, kidnapping, and extortion. This situation was prevalent in early 2013, with violence spreading to areas previously disconnected from the traditional routes used to ship illicit drugs to the U.S. market, such as Morelos and the Estado de Mexico. New criminal organizations have emerged in these central states, fighting among themselves for the loyalty of the local population.

In his November 2012 meeting with President Obama prior to taking the presidential oath of office, Peña Nieto reiterated his determination to continue security cooperation with the U.S. government as part of a broader reform agenda.[22] U.S. recognition of "shared responsibility" and Washington's willingness to both share information and seek the extradition of criminals who manage drug trafficking rings are critical to Mexico's ongoing effort to contain violence and insecurity. However, although Peña Nieto endorsed this essential bilateral cooperation on security issues, he stated that the nature of the collaboration was under review. In March 2013, no senior officials from the new Mexican administration attended the Trilateral Border Symposium in Phoenix, Arizona, despite the Canadian and U.S. expectation that the Mexicans would participate in significant numbers, as they had done over the previous six years. The excuse from Mexico City was that the government was currently reviewing border security policies.[23]

Overlapping Economic and Security Challenges

With the Mexican president's emphasis on boosting the economic ties between Mexico and the United States, the security dialogue will become less prominent in the bilateral relationship. However, security and economic issues overlap. In Beyond Mérida, Pillar III is devoted to creating a 21st century border—a border that should facilitate the passage of goods between the two countries while ensuring that illicit goods and undocumented migrants are prevented from entering the United States. The construction of access roads to allow pre-inspected trucks carrying valuable merchandise to pass through U.S. border crossings requires considerable private investment in infrastructure, the purchase or taking of land under eminent domain, and the use of secure technology to guarantee the content and security of pre-cleared trucks. By early 2013, U.S. Customs and Border Patrol (CBP) had granted two Mexican companies a permit to participate in pre-clearance, after which a container is sealed and allowed to enter the United States without further inspection;[24] more companies are expected to join the pre-clearance regime in 2013. A GPS device on board participating trucks allows CBP to check whether the container or the driver's cab has been tampered with en route.

The third pillar of Beyond Mérida opened the way to coordinate security measures and commercial trade. We should therefore ask whether the 21st century border program has assumed a dynamic of its own, with considerable potential for expanded commercial trade, particularly in the automotive industry.[25] Will Mérida continue to be the umbrella under which discussions on the 21st century border are held, or has Mérida given birth to a bilateral project of much broader dimensions?

Another area in which security issues overlap with economic challenges is Pillar IV—building strong and resilient communities that can withstand the pressure of criminal organizations. This task originated with the urgent need to address the alarming homicide rate in Ciudad Juárez. Following the shooting of fifteen teenagers in January 2010 as well as the discovery of shallow graves containing the bodies of more than fifty women who had been murdered within the city limits, the horror of the two nations resulted in a coordinated bilateral effort to contain the violence in Ciudad Juárez.

That effort, called Todos Somos Juárez (We are all Juárez), brought together existing and previously funded Mexican government programs, civil society, the business community, and trade unions as well as USAID. If a concerted bilateral effort to address the socioeconomic and law enforcement needs of this border city could result in a reduction in drug-related homicides and a resurgence of business activity, then President Calderón could claim both a success and a model for other Mexican communities to follow. The Mexican and U.S. governments invested close to US$400 million in this comprehensive socioeconomic project.[26]

The principal investor in Todos Somos Juárez was the Mexican federal government, which directly or indirectly supported 168 programs to benefit the Juárez community. USAID, which played a key role in coordinating projects, took twelve community leaders to Medellín, Colombia, to examine how this previously violence-torn city restored relative security and reinvigorated its economic livelihood through a comprehensive law enforcement and socioeconomic approach. The role of both U.S. and Mexican businesses in Juárez was critical. In a project known as Paso del Norte, the private sectors in El Paso and Ciudad Juárez joined together to maintain investments in the southwest border region, donate funds to youth-at-risk programs, and work with the mayor of Juárez to combat corruption.[27]

Given the lack of an honest and effective municipal police force, Calderón ordered federal troops to patrol the city streets. It was intended to be a temporary measure, but the troops remained, although they eventually moved on to patrol the airport and highways leading to and from the city. Later, Calderón transferred retired army colonel Julián Leyzaola Pérez from Tijuana—where he had succeeded in defeating the Arellano-Felix cartel and arresting several corrupt police officers—to Ciudad Juárez. The combination of strong law enforcement and socioeconomic projects produced a significant decline in homicides and violence. In 2011, the number of drug-related homicides in Juárez was 2,086; a year later that number had fallen to 750 homicides.[28] The city remains a critical gateway for illicit drugs entering the United States, and conflict between the Sinaloa cartel and the Zetas continues. However, the homicide level has diminished significantly, and Ciudad Juárez is no longer classified as one of the most violent cities in Mexico.[29]

Partnering with Colombia

Today, Ciudad Juárez has seen the return of business, the opening of sidewalk cafes in the downtown area, and the opening of a new museum for children.[30] The city's recovery began under Beyond Mérida, but the recovery of Mexico's cities no longer requires significant U.S. government help. Instead, the provincial cities of Colombia, with their focus on comprehensive law enforcement and socioeconomic programs to address the underlying causes of violence, have become the model for Mexico. In that connection, candidate Enrique Peña Nieto called on General Óscar Naranjo Trujillo, the former chief of the Colombian national police, to advise him on the appropriate security strategy for Mexico. General Naranjo remains an adviser to the Mexican president and his new team within the Secretaría de Gobernación (SEGOB) (Ministry of Government).

Colombia can also provide trainers in the reformed criminal procedural system. In 1991, Colombia began its own reform of its criminal justice system, transitioning from the inquisitorial system to the adversarial system, in which a defendant is presumed innocent and open trials are held.[31] The U.S. government is committed to supporting Mexico's reforms and has committed substantial funding under Pillar II of Beyond Mérida to training programs for Mexican prosecutors, judges, investigative police, and prison staff. The Mexican federal government recognizes the importance of those programs, and President Peña Nieto has reiterated his government's commitment to strengthen the rule of law. However, the challenge of reforming principles and procedures and reducing the level of police impunity is formidable and will require several years of training. Furthermore, new courthouses must be built. Partnering with the Colombian government, the Mexican government can increase the impact of U.S. investments under Mérida and accelerate the process of introducing a more equitable and independent criminal justice system. By 2016—eight years after introduction of the reforms—the Mexican government should be able to rely more on Mexican and Colombian trainers and less, if at all, on U.S. trainers.

The Future of Mérida?

Where does that leave Mérida? From March 2007 to December 2012, the collaboration between Mexico City and Washington to construct, under the Mérida Initiative, a framework for both integrated intelligence sharing and certain integrated operational activities produced successful strikes against drug trafficking organizations. With the election of the PRI and Peña Nieto's inauguration in December 2012, two factors have become more prominent: first, the PRI has historically held a strong commitment to national sovereignty and suspicion toward the motive and means of U.S. interference; second, the amount of U.S. funding is small compared with the overall Mexican contribution in funds and personnel.[32] Taken together, these factors imply that the Peña Nieto administration will seek a change in, if not a diminution of, the U.S. role. Over the last six years, ideas and plans developed jointly have grown enough to enable the Mexican government to continue with less U.S. involvement. The close bilateral collaboration under Mérida during the 2008–12 period is weakening, and signs of friction between the two governments are more evident. The Fast and Furious fiasco, future U.S. budgetary restraints on Mérida funding, and the maturation of the projects developed under the initiative may result in both governments agreeing that Mérida has accomplished its principal goals. It is now time to reconsider the nature of the bilateral security relationship.

The four pillars of Beyond Mérida have assumed goals and budgetary requirements that far exceed those of the 2007 Mérida Initiative. That initiative gave birth to a previously unseen level of integration between the two governments, which worked well in developing specialized teams of agents to collect and share information, develop security strategies, and, in a few limited cases, combine security forces for special projects. However, integration in security matters has probably reached its limit. The Peña Nieto government review suggests terminating the integrated projects. It is more comfortable returning to traditional bilateral relations, in which the two nations develop common goals but each nation pursues those goals independently. The Mexicans would prefer that the Obama administration focus more on three objectives: reducing illegal drug consumption within the United States; stopping the sale of high-caliber weapons to Mexico; and containing the transfer of bulk cash and electronic funds to Mexico. Achieving those objectives requires concentrated U.S. government actions within the United States.

Mérida was a mechanism with which to organize an ambitious bilateral security program that facilitated the coordination, if not control, of the projects within the U.S. State Department and allowed a single request for funds to be presented to Congress. Under one rubric, funds for distinct but related purposes were gathered together. The winding down of Mérida has complicated ramifications for the U.S. government. It may result in the distribution of tasks to different U.S. government agencies with responsibility for border security, information sharing, rule of law, and socioeconomic programs; it may also result in multiple requests for funding from Congress. Consequently, coordinated security programs for Mexico could well be lost. From the U.S. point of view the winding down of the Mérida Initiative has budgetary and administrative consequences that must be considered seriously. Given the complexity and breadth of the U.S. relationship with Mexico, it would be better to retain Mérida as a State Department program and funding item for Mexico. However, programs should take into account the Mexican government's reduced need to work with U.S. officials in its sovereign territory and the greater need for the United States to concentrate on domestic and border projects that directly affect Mexico.

This is not to suggest that the closeness of purpose and the recognition of "shared responsibility" will evaporate. On the contrary, the presidents of both countries are committed to ensuring that the violence diminishes to levels that civilian law enforcement can manage. To achieve an increased level of security, information must continue to be shared, trust between government institutions retained, and conflicts between the two governments managed.[33] It is highly preferable that Mexico and the United States remain good neighbors!

Notes

1. A separate program, the Central American Regional Security Initiative (CARSI), was created later for the other Central American countries, and a similar program, the Caribbean Basin Security Initiative (CBSI), was created for the Caribbean area.

2. Congressional Research Service, "U.S.-Mexican Security Cooperation: The Mérida Initiative and Beyond," January 14, 2013, p. 9 (www.fas.org/sgp/crs/row/R41349.pdf).

3. Multiple reasons have been given for the delays, the principal one being the complex specifications for the aircraft and helicopters. See General Accounting Office, "Mérida Initiative: The United States Has Provided Counternarcotics and Anticrime Support but Needs Better Performance Measurements," GAO-10-837, July 2010 (www. gao.gov/new.items/d10837.pdf).

4. U.S. Department of State, "Congressional Budget Justification for Foreign Operations FY2008-FY2012" and "FY2013 Executive Budget Summary: Function 150 and Other International Programs." Figures combined in Congressional Research Service, "State, Foreign Operations, and Related Programs: FY2013 Budget and Appropriations," January 2013, table 1 (www.fas.org/sgp/crs/row/R42621.pdf).

5. U.S. Department of State, "Budget and Planning: International Affairs Budget FY2014," press briefing, April 10, 2013 (www.state.gov/r/pa/prs/ps/2013/04/207326.htm).

6. "Understanding and Improving Merida," *Americas Quarterly* (Spring 2010) (www.americasquarterly.org/negroponte-villiers).

7. The new strategy was formally declared at the Mérida High-Level Consultative Group meeting in Mexico City in March 2010.

8. Torture is applied most frequently in the period between when victims are detained and when they are handed to the *ministerio publico* (the prosecutor). See Human Rights Watch, "World Report 2013: Mexico" (February 2013) (www.hrw.org/world-report/2013/country-chapters/mexico).

9. U.S. Department of State, "Joint Statement of the Mérida Initiative High-Level Consultative Group on Bilateral Cooperation against Transnational Organized Crime," March 29, 2010 (www.state.gov/secretary/rm/2010/03/139196.htm).

10. During her visit to Mexico in April 2009, Secretary of State Hillary Clinton declared that the United States and Mexico had a "shared responsibility" for the violence in Mexico.

11. Straw purchases occur when the actual buyer of a firearm is unable to pass the required federal background check or does not want his or her name associated with the purchase and someone else who can pass the required background check purchases the firearm instead.

12. U.S. Congress, Hearings before the House Committee on Oversight and Government Reform, June 2012.

13. Foreign Assistance Act of 1961, as amended by the Consolidated Appropriations Act of 2012, December 23, 2011 (P.L.112-74) (www.gpo.gov/fdsys/pkg/PLAW-112 publ74/pdf/PLAW-112publ74.pdf).

14. See U.S. Department of State, "Mexico-Mérida Initiative Report," known as the "15 percent report," August 30, 2012 (www.state.gov/p/wha/rls/fs/2012/ 187119.htp).

15. Human Rights Watch, "Human Rights Report 2013: Mexico."

16. U .S. Department of State, "Joint Statement of the Mérida Initiative High-Level Consultative Group on Bilateral Cooperation against Transnational Organized Crime," September 18, 2012.

17. Latinobarómetro , *Seguridad Ciudadana: El problema principal de América Latina* [Public Safety: The Principal Problem in Latin America], table 9, "Comparación de percepción de delincuencia e inseguridad [Comparison of Perceptions of Crime and Insecurity]," p. 38 (www.latinobarometro.org/documentos/LATBD_La_seguridad _ciudadana.pdf).

18. Latinobarómetro, *Seguridad Ciudadana,* "Confianza en la policía," p. 56 (www. latinobarometro.org/documentos/LATBD_La_seguridad_ciudadana.pdf).

19. People wearing bandanas and carrying small arms began manning checkpoints on roads into the municipalities of Ayutla de los Libres and Teconoapa in the Costa Chica area of the state of Guerrero. See "Armed Vigilante Groups Policing Two Mexican Towns," *USA Today,* January 12, 2013 (www.usatoday.com/story/news/world/2013/01/12/armed-vigilantes-mexican-towns/1829469/).

20. Congressional Research Service, "Southwest Border Violence: Issues in Identifying and Measuring Spillover Violence," "Introduction" (February 28, 2013).

21. U.S. Department of State, "Assistant Secretary Roberta Jacobson Previews the Pathways for Prosperity Forum," October 18, 2012 (http://govne.ws/item/Assistant-Secretary-Roberta-Jacobson-Previews-the-Pathways-for-Prosperity-Forum).

22. "Remarks of President Obama and President-Elect Peña Nieto of Mexico before Bilateral Meeting," White House press release, November 27, 2012.

23. Rick Van Schoik, president, North American Council for Transborder Studies and co-sponsor of the Trilateral Border Symposium, Phoenix, Arizona, March 18, 2013.

24. CBP operates the pre-clearance system, known as PAPS (Pre-Arrival Processing System).

25. Small and medium-size businesses find that pre-clearance, which requires lawyers to complete government forms, is a very expensive procedure. The high costs affect trucking companies that operate independently and contract with Mexican and U.S. companies to ship their products to the United States.

26. Adam Thompson, "Troubled Juárez Starts to Breathe Again," *Financial Times,* October 11, 2012 (www.ft.com/intl/cms/s/0/bcb0aaf0-12c9-11e2-aa9c-00144feabdc0. html#axzz2O6ojBPP4).

27. The Paso del Norte Regional Economic Development Corporation recently changed its name to BorderPlex Alliance. Its principal purpose is to facilitate commercial relations in the border area, but it has also extended to social projects to meet the security threats in Ciudad Juárez.

28. "Reporte Lantia Violencia y Crimen Organizado [Lantia Report on Violence and Organized Crime]," August 6, 2012. Conclusions can be found at www.sinem bargo.mx/06-08-2012/322753.

29. Consejo Ciudadano para la Seguridad Pública y la Justicia Penal [Citizens' Council on Public Safety and Criminal Justice] (www.seguridadjusticiaypaz.org.mx/).

30. The museum is called Espacio Descubre, Interactúa, Imagina (EDII) (Space Discover, Interact, and Imagine).

31. Michael R. Pahl, "Wanted: Criminal Justice—Colombia's Adoption of a Prosecutorial System of Criminal Procedures," *Fordham International Law Journal* 16, no. 3 (1992).

32. A discrepancy exists in estimates of the relative contribution of each nation. William R. Brownfield, assistant secretary of state for international narcotics and law enforcement, stated that the U.S. government contributes $1 for every $13 that the Mexican federal and state governments contribute. Remarks to the Americas Society and Council of the Americas, March 22, 2013 (http://iipdigital.usembassy.gov/st/ english/article/2013/03/ 20130325144776.html#axzz2Olq4gHG2). Eduardo Medina Mora, the Mexican ambassador to the United States, stated that the U.S. government contributes $1 for every $16 of Mexican government contribution (remarks made to Diana Villiers Negroponte at the Brookings Institution, February 21, 2013).

33. In Mexico, SSP is being incorporated within SEGOB so that security becomes a fundamental aspect of the federal government's relations with the Mexican states. In the creation of a powerful SEGOB, presidential influence is expected to increase and with it the capacity to implement projects at the state and municipal level.

ANDRÉS ROZENTAL

9

Mexico and the United States: Where Are We and Where Should We Be?

Mexico and the United States are not only neighbors—distant or close depending on where you sit—but two equally proud nations with their respective histories of struggles for independence and bloody civil conflicts. Each is fiercely jealous of its sovereignty, although each benefits enormously from our geographical vicinity. The movement of people and goods across the land border, through airports, and by other means of transport is among the most intense anywhere in the world. As befits two countries with such vast disparities in economic strength and political influence, we sometimes find ourselves on different sides of the fence when it comes to foreign policy issues or the bilateral agenda. However, in general there are many more pluses than minuses.

Notwithstanding the asymmetries and occasional political discrepancies, our bilateral relationship has evolved over the past few decades into a much more cooperative and trustworthy interaction than was the case historically. Whereas in the past both governments often viewed each other with suspicion and misgiving, today's situation is very different. Ever since the North American Free Trade Agreement (NAFTA) entered into force in 1994, government officials in Washington and Mexico City have developed a closer, friendlier, and mutually beneficial relationship as they deal with the multiplicity of subjects that characterize the intense, day-to-day dealings between the two nations. Almost every American and Mexican is affected in some way by what happens in the other country, whether in immigration flows, the growth and greater political importance of the Hispanic community in the United States, or the impact of remittances and the influence of bilateral trade and reciprocal investments in the products consumed by Mexicans and Americans on a daily basis.

While the intimacy of bilateral cooperation has grown, problems still remain that bedevil the Mexico-U.S. relationship. These often are much more visible and troublesome than the many positive aspects of our partnership. Media attention in both countries tends to focus on the negatives of illegal immigration, drug trafficking, criminal activity, and trade conflicts, while in reality these are but a part—albeit an important one—of an otherwise vigorous agenda that includes cooperation on cross-border public health issues, legitimate tourism and business travel between both countries, intelligence sharing in the fight against organized crime and terrorism, as well as communications and transport, business facilitation, and infrastructure development.

Citizens in both countries are often unaware of the beneficial parts of the bilateral agenda and tend to focus mostly on the negative aspects that the media prefer to emphasize as the business of selling news becomes increasingly competitive. This leads to a dual-track relationship: in reality, the positives far outweigh the negatives, and the day-to-day interaction is mostly constructive and encouraging. Despite this, public opinion and media perceptions portray two countries that don't get along, often disagree on how to tackle different aspects of the relationship, and are far from being the partners or strategic allies that NAFTA intended. While it is undeniable that in recent years Mexico has been plagued by an upsurge in violent criminal activity, it is no less true that other aspects of the country's economic performance, social progress, and political maturity have far outweighed the relatively recent increase in homicides related to organized crime and drug trafficking.

Mexico's foreign policy historically claimed a consensus within a fairly diverse spread of political and ideological currents of thought. Based on the same principles enshrined in the United Nations Charter, successive PRI (Partido Revoluncionario Institucional [Institutional Revolutionary Party]) governments were able to give Mexico a diplomatic profile that hewed closely to the noncontroversial ideals of sovereignty, self-determination, and noninterference in the internal affairs of others and friendly relations among states.[1] Up to the 1990s these tenets were enough to govern foreign policy and guide Mexico's behavior in the international arena, but during the Salinas administration an activist foreign policy replaced the country's more traditional diplomacy, with a subsequent shift in how Mexico viewed its role in the world.[2] Along with an opening up of the country's economy, and the decision to negotiate a free trade arrangement with Canada and the United States, came a simultaneous shift in the conduct of the country's foreign policy: from a mostly defensive and passive role to the establishment of bold, new priorities in the Asia-Pacific region, in Latin America, and in Europe. Mexico began to assert itself as one of the world's largest economies and trading nations, while it simultaneously became an even more attractive destination for foreign investment targeting the North and Central American markets.

The days of Mexico's hobnobbing with the G-77 and nonaligned movement gave way to a clear political objective: the country wanted to be seen by the rest of the world as one better suited to developed-country status than as part of the developing world. Although Salinas's decision to negotiate NAFTA and give Mexico a new global presence was viewed by some of the more traditional elements of Mexico's establishment as moving the country away from its natural space on the international stage, a powerful, highly autocratic presidential system allowed him to undertake the strategy notwithstanding internal opposition, even within his own political party.

During this period Mexico became a member of OECD (Organization for Economic Cooperation and Development),[3] negotiated a third-generation economic and political cooperation agreement with the European Union, became a party to APEC (Asia Pacific Economic Cooperation), concluded a free trade arrangement with Japan, and substantially expanded its diplomatic presence in regions where it had been historically underrepresented.

In Latin America, Mexico spearheaded the creation of the Rio Group as a successor to the Contadora Group, which helped end decades of civil war in Central America; became actively involved in Colombia's efforts to make peace with its guerrilla movements; and promoted the establishment of the Ibero-American summits and secretariat. Among others—including a hotly disputed decision to normalize relations with the Vatican and change Mexico's antiquated anticlerical laws—these initiatives signaled a new era in Mexican diplomacy and projected the country globally as never before.

There was a very clear objective guiding the country's foreign policy: to take advantage of Mexico's geostrategic position as a natural link between the United States and Canada to the North, to Latin America and the Caribbean to the south and east, to Europe across the Atlantic, and to the Pacific Rim and Asia. Few nations have had such an advantageous position, allowing them to simultaneously expand political and economic relations in all directions in an increasingly globalized world.

In the specific case of Mexico–U.S. relations, the last decade of the twentieth century and first ten years of the twenty-first brought a sea change in the conduct of Mexican policy toward the United States. President Salinas and NAFTA played an important part in this shift, but the victory in 2000 of the first opposition government to take the reins since World War II also played a significant role. Many of the traditional taboos that had characterized Mexico's defensive policies toward its northern neighbor were discarded when it became clear that they were no longer compatible with a North American partnership that, at least theoretically, placed Mexico in a new and very unique relationship with the other two developed economies. The country's business leadership and more forward-looking segments of the political establishment realized that Mexico could no longer foment anti-American sentiment by using the historical baggage associated with the loss of territory resulting from the Mexican-American War and the two military occupations by American troops during the 1914–17 revolutionary period. Nor could the country continue to blame the United States for many of its ills, thus ending a custom that had become habitual.

When Vicente Fox won the presidency in 2000, expectations were extremely high for a radical change in both domestic and foreign policy in a government no longer burdened by the traditional PRI-dominated agenda. With a young, creative foreign minister full of new ideas and initiatives, the first PAN (Partido Acción Nacional [National Action Party]) government wasted no time in putting its stamp on Mexico's foreign policy. Instead of basing the government's diplomacy on time-honored caveats of non-intervention and absolute sovereignty, Fox and Jorge Castañeda designed a new strategy based on increased activism in international forums and a new relationship with the United States based on trying to forcefully and openly address the major irritants that troubled the bilateral agenda. This, together with an unprecedented move to open Mexico's political, legal, and social system to greater outside scrutiny, allowed the new government to establish greater legitimacy with its North American neighbors. Perhaps of greater significance, it reversed Mexico's traditional defensive view of what non-intervention and sovereignty meant.

History has shown that every time a Mexican government takes office, expectations are high for a new era in U.S.-Mexican relations, but these soon give way to disappointment and frustration when facing the complex, hard realities of the relationship. The year 2000 was no exception. Vicente Fox had a background of working for a U.S.-based multinational and spoke colloquial English, thus spurring expectations of enhanced bilateral interaction.[4] However, the hope for a substantively different type of relationship never truly materialized.

Although many of the country's established politicians were wary of this new, more aggressive approach, the Fox administration began its bilateral strategy with a somewhat daring and unprecedented initiative in its dealings with Washington: instead of waiting to hear what the incoming George W. Bush government would propose for the two countries' agenda, Mexico immediately put on the table a significantly different strategy to address the long-standing immigration conundrum—sometimes referred to as "the whole enchilada." Castañeda met with the new Washington foreign policy team to push for a novel, bilateral approach to the problem. In exchange for normalizing the status of several million Mexicans living in the United States without papers, and agreeing on a temporary worker program to rationally and legally address the constant demand by American employers for Mexican labor, the Fox government would, for the first time, recognize its responsibility to ensure that Mexican citizens who went to the United States would, as far as feasible, do so with proper documentation and through established ports of entry.

For years the conventional wisdom and politically expedient excuse in Mexico was that no government could impede or interfere with Mexicans' constitutionally guaranteed freedom of movement within and outside of Mexico, notwithstanding the fact that the country's immigration laws clearly established that any such freedom was conditional on leaving Mexico with the receiving country's permission and through authorized border crossings, airports, or maritime ports. In practice, for many years this had already been an existing procedure for anyone flying out of Mexico by commercial or private aircraft. Passengers traveling to countries that require immigration papers are required to show that they have a valid visa *before* they are allowed to board a flight to the United States or other international destinations. Nevertheless, Mexico's politicians continued to conveniently espouse the myth that their countrymen should never be restricted from leaving the country because that would interfere with their constitutionally guaranteed freedom of transit.

The Post-2011 Era

When the new Mexican government presented its strategy to the Bush administration in early 2001, the response was initially positive. The "whole enchilada" idea seemed like an attractive and workable quid pro quo that could simultaneously bring millions of undocumented Mexicans out of the shadows into a normalized status of legal aliens, although they would be penalized for having broken U.S. laws. The proposal ensured that the need for immigrant labor from Mexico would be met with a bilateral guest worker program matching supply and demand in an orderly and legal fashion. Negotiators from both governments were appointed to discuss the details of how this would work in practice, and it appeared that, for the first time in decades, there was enough political will both in Mexico City and in Washington to search for a mutually acceptable solution to the immigration problem.[5]

Hardly had the negotiators exchanged first drafts when the tragic events of September 2001 changed everything. After the attacks on New York City and the Pentagon, and the downing of the aircraft in Pennsylvania, the Bush administration abruptly terminated the bilateral discussions on the immigration issue, and any hope for a solution that would resolve the supply and demand nature of the flow of Mexican labor north was dashed. Instead, many politicians from both sides of the aisle in Washington found solace in clamoring for a more secure border as a way of addressing a dysfunctional immigration system. This rhetoric quickly became synonymous with homeland security and protecting the United States against new terrorist threats, even though none of the events of 9/11 had anything to do with the country's land borders. The bilateral nature of the threat to national security and its eventual solution were quickly forgotten and replaced with a purely unilateral policy aimed at thickening both the southern and northern land borders in order to protect the homeland. It didn't seem to matter that a very first requirement was for the authorities to know who was already *inside* the country. In 2001 the estimated 11 to 12 million individuals who resided in the United States at the time (only a minority of whom were Mexican) without proper documentation, and whose names and whereabouts were unknown to U.S. authorities, did not seem to figure in the government's calculations of how to guard against potential outside threats.[6]

Shortly after 9/11, the Fox government decided to propose to the Canadians a joint approach to demonstrate to President Bush that both NAFTA partners were seriously concerned about the damage caused to the structure of the three-way trade agreement by the new restrictions imposed unilaterally at U.S. borders, many of which affected manufacturing and just-in-time supplier deliveries to integrated facilities in all three countries. It seemed logical for both neighbors to propose a new trilateral border agreement that would ensure that free trade did not become a victim of the new U.S. policy of dramatically increasing supervision and enforcement along its borders with Canada and Mexico. Unfortunately, a short-sighted Canadian government at the time decided that the two countries' issues with the United States were so substantially different that it would be better off negotiating a bilateral "smart" border treaty with the United States, leaving Mexico to do the same on its own. As a result, a unique opportunity to show trilateral solidarity with the United States was lost. Eventually both Canada and Mexico reached separate agreements with Washington, which were for all practical purposes similar, except for issues relating to refugees and asylum.

U.S. Comprehensive Immigration Reform

In the intervening decade, very little progress has been made on comprehensive immigration reform in the United States, until President Obama, at the outset of his second term, made the issue a priority for his administration. Both Presidents George W. Bush and Barack Obama in their first terms were unable or unwilling to spend the political capital needed to get immigration reform through Congress, in spite of campaign promises to the American Hispanic population that the issue would be addressed as a matter of high priority. With the additional four years that American voters gave President Obama in November 2012, together with a realization by many Republicans that the 2012 election was lost to a large extent because of the anti-immigrant rhetoric alienating Hispanic voters, there is now a good opportunity for comprehensive immigration reform to finally become a reality during 2013 and for progress to be made in fixing the existing broken system.

The global economic and financial crisis that broke out in 2008 significantly impacted the bilateral immigration picture. Together with disgruntled state legislatures that have passed drastic anti-immigrant laws in the absence of federal action, the realities for Mexicans—either those living in the United States or those seeking to migrate without papers—have changed dramatically. Immigrants who lived and worked in localities that had made life difficult for them began to move to more immigrant friendly parts of the United States. Although figures from official reports attempt to show that net undocumented immigration of Mexicans to the United States has almost reached zero—with approximately the same number returning to Mexico as entering—it may be premature to conclude that the immigration "problem" is over. The increased legal difficulties for undocumented Mexicans living in the United States, together with the economic downturn and a somewhat encouraging growth picture in Mexico, may have contributed to reducing the "pull" factor that historically encouraged people to attempt the trip into the United

States. Additionally, Mexico's demographic profile is rapidly moving toward an aging population with a substantial drop in the annual increase in the number of young people entering the job market. Presumably, if the Mexican economy continues to pick up and returns to steady growth, there will be increased opportunities for employment at home and fewer incentives to migrate.

A further dynamic in the immigration equation comes with the growing pressures on Washington to "do something" about reforming federal legislation that is both out of date and does not work. Americans often ask why Mexicans do not just patiently apply, wait in line, and get their visas legally if there are job offers waiting for them north of the border. Few realize that this is simply a nonstarter. The immigration backlog currently averages 730 days, and the categories under which Mexicans can apply for visas are extremely limited. It is much easier for a potential migrant to slip across the border—often at enormous cost in smuggler fees or physical risk—than to attempt a legal method of entry. Until the concept of a North American free market, in labor as well as in goods, becomes a reality, there will always be people who find it simpler to overstay a visa or cross a border without proper documentation. Even in times of economic recovery, it is an uphill battle to convince U.S. politicians that North America would become much more competitive in the global marketplace if we had a system whereby citizens of all three nations could come and go freely to work in any of the three NAFTA partners.

Mexico's Northern Border with the United States

Since 2006 the cost to the U.S. government of building, policing, and enforcing its southern border against undocumented immigrants has amounted to an average $18 billion a year. If only a small proportion of those funds was redirected toward improving border infrastructure, building new transportation hubs instead of fences, and helping bring more prosperity to border communities, the violence that has recently characterized the Mexican side might very well diminish because the criminality associated with smuggling people into the United States would no longer have a raison d'être. In 2009 the Mexican Council on Foreign Relations and the Pacific Council on International Policy jointly sponsored a task force that produced a report with specific short-, medium-, and long-term recommendations to both governments on how to manage and improve the border.[7] An earlier Council on Foreign Relations–Instituto Tecnológico Autónomo de México task force also addressed the issue. Sadly, only a handful of both reports' recommendations were ever implemented.[8]

A second aspect of the bilateral relationship that has become a major worry for both countries is the drug trafficking and organized crime situation in Mexico and across the border. For the past six years, this issue has overshadowed almost all others and has led to the relationship being viewed, on both sides, almost entirely from a security perspective. This was already the case after 9/11 when the United States decided that securing the homeland was its highest priority. In the case of Mexico, this has meant strengthening an already highly controlled border with 698 miles of new fencing and approximately 18,516 border patrol agents—with costly new high-technology resources. None of this made a substantial difference following 9/11 in reducing immigrant flows.

However, fewer Mexicans now cross into the United States because of diminished job opportunities due to the 2007–08 economic recession and anemic recovery north of the border, as well as the improved strength of the Mexican economy. In 2002 U.S. border patrol agents apprehended 929,809 persons on the U.S. Southwest border, 95 percent of whom were Mexican citizens. In 2011 agents apprehended 327,577 persons, only 40 percent of whom were Mexicans.[9] For Mexicans migrating northward, the crossings have become more difficult and more expensive. Meantime, the criminals who prey on these migrants have become stronger, richer, and more omnipresent throughout the border area just as it became harder to reach the United States and remain there safely and avoid apprehension and deportation.

Calderon's War on Drugs and Organized Crime Cartels

By the time President Felipe Calderón took office in December 2006, the situation on the border and in surrounding parts of Mexico had deteriorated considerably. Organized crime and drug cartels had reached into the very heart of several municipal and state governments. They controlled territory where law enforcement was either absent or totally corrupt. Frequently, they ingratiated themselves with a population that saw their social largesse as a welcome substitute for an often absent national or local government unable to satisfy their needs. A *narco* culture began to spread in some rural areas, and increasing numbers of unemployed young people became vulnerable to the siren song of traffickers and criminals offering relatively large sums of money for seemingly small-time smuggling and petty crime.[10]

With the lifting of the assault weapon ban in the United States in 2004, heavy arms began finding their way into Mexico, ending up in the hands of the cartels and criminal organizations. These often have better weaponry, more money, and larger numbers of recruits than the government and as a result pose a formidable threat to law and order. The "Fast and Furious" scandal involved Bureau of Alcohol, Tobacco, Firearms, and Explosives (ATF) agents who knowingly allowed weapons to enter Mexico from the United States in order to allegedly trace both the routes and individuals who smuggle arms. This became a potent symbol of how the U.S. government unsuccessfully deals with an increasingly criminalized Mexican border.[11] What few Americans realize, or accept, is the fact that drug consumption in the United States is a fundamental driver in the growth of these criminal organizations, which thrive on the illegality of the phenomenon. One still continues to hear Americans bemoan the fact that "Mexicans are poisoning our children," while few are ready to admit that a culture that pushes drugs and violence on young people is equally responsible.

At the outset, the Obama administration was slow to grasp the threat that the drug traffickers and organized crime posed to Mexican and U.S. law enforcement officials. The movement of drugs from Mexico to the United States has been a reality in the bilateral relationship for more than a century, but until recently Mexico was mainly a transit country for drugs originating in South America en route to the largest narcotic consumer nation in the world. Over the last few decades, however, Mexico has been faced with the problem of increased domestic consumption as traffickers began paying for services in kind, rather than in cash. Furthermore, the rise in U.S. demand for chemically produced methamphetamines and other proscribed hallucinogenics has led to a growing network of clandestine laboratories throughout the country. Quickly, Mexico became a producing, transit, *and* consuming country, which exacerbated the problem and the Mexican government's efforts to deal with it. Finally, the successful closing of older Caribbean trafficking routes pushed the cartels to use Mexico as a replacement route at a time when the southern border with Guatemala and Belize was unenforced and planes transporting cocaine could easily land at remote locations, often with the complicity of local law enforcement officials.

Calderón took office on December 1, 2006, having won a razor-thin majority over the second-place candidate from the left-of-center PRD (Partido de la Revolución Democrática [Party of the Democratic Revolution]). His official inaugural ceremony had to be conducted under bizarre, secret circumstances: in the middle of the night and in a small office somewhere in the Chamber of Deputies building. Everything was designed to thwart any attempt by the losing candidate to disrupt the ceremony with the claim that

Calderón had actually lost the election and that he, Andrés Manuel López Obrador, was the legitimate president of Mexico. The military played a key role in organizing this strange inaugural ceremony, which explains to a great extent why Calderón was so beholden to the army and why the military has accepted an active role in combating drug trafficking organizations within Mexico. Without the military's acquiescence and participation, Calderón might well have been prevented from constitutionally taking office. Mexicans were amazed when faced with a strange picture of their new president appearing at a public event in military combat fatigues only a few days after taking office.

There has been much discussion in Mexico seeking to understand why the new president began his administration with a declaration of war against the drug and organized crime cartels. Some argue that it was a way to legitimize his initial tenuous grip on government. Others insist that the incoming president had no choice when faced with the true nature of the cartels' inroads in the northern part of the country and the fact that some parts of Mexico were no longer under the government's control. While not yet in the category of a "failed state," Mexico was in danger of losing control of parts of its territory, requiring a drastic response from the government. Whichever explanation is correct, the situation led Calderón to make this policy the centerpiece of his nascent administration.

Six years later, Mexicans are seriously questioning this strategy of openly attacking organized crime and drug cartels. The 63,700 drug-related homicides and large numbers of other victims during his administration attest to the fact that Calderón underestimated the strength, resources, and will of the criminals, as well as the lucrative nature of the businesses they engage in and are ready to defend at all costs. Unfortunately, the strategy also became the main focus of the relationship with the United States, having overshadowed other aspects of the bilateral agenda.

At the outset of his administration, President Calderón convinced the Bush administration to accept its "shared responsibility" for the growing violence in Mexico and to provide assistance in the fight against drug trafficking and organized crime. The Mérida Initiative was approved by the U.S. Congress and implemented in mid-2008. It included assistance in training, equipment, and intelligence for Mexico and Central America, with an approximate announced value of $1.9 billion over four fiscal years for Mexico and a much smaller amount for the Central American countries.[12] When compared to the $46.6 billion cost assumed by Mexico in human and financial resources from fighting drug cartels, the U.S. contribution amounts to only $1 for every $16 of Mexican federal government expenditures.[13] Mexico does not seek funds through the initiative, as much as it pursues access to U.S. training, sophisticated equipment unavailable elsewhere, and the bilateral exchange of information.

As Felipe Calderón's term ended in December 2012, the main question was whether the strategy of declaring this all-out war worked. If one judges by the degree of violence that the strategy unleashed in Mexico, the answer must be a resounding *no*. In addition, there doesn't seem to have been an appreciable reduction in the amount of illegal drugs consumed by Americans over this period, nor a decrease in the flows of marijuana, cocaine, methamphetamines, and other substances into the United States from South America and Mexico. President Calderón continuously blamed the insatiable demand north of the border and the unchecked flow of arms into Mexico as the key factors leading to the violence in Mexico.[14] However, he failed to admit that lax controls on the Mexican side of the border and rampant corruption are also to blame.

Latin Leaders Call for Reexamination of U.S. Drug Policy

In a desperate attempt to call attention to these issues, the Mexican president and his Central American colleagues in the summer of 2012 called on the Obama administration either to get serious about demand reduction in the United States or "find market solutions" (a euphemism for legalization), which would take the drug business away from the criminals.[15] A growing number of serving and former Latin American heads of state are calling for a reexamination of current international drug policy because they are increasingly frustrated by the fact that Washington pursues its anti-narcotics strategy outside its own borders and does little to reduce internal demand.[16] Voter initiatives approved in Colorado, Washington, and Massachusetts in November 2012 to legalize recreational or medical uses of marijuana now mean that twenty-two states in the union have challenged federal laws against the consumption of at least one prohibited narcotic drug. In the coming years, more such challenges will surely arise, and eventually politicians in Washington will have to address the overall logic of continuing to criminalize drug use and pretend to enforce outdated anti-narcotic laws.

A second issue has been the doubts expressed by many Mexicans with regard to the fight against drug trafficking in general. Why, they ask, should Mexico expend so much money and effort in keeping drugs out of the United States when Americans fail to do much about the demand side of the equation? Would it not be more productive for their government to concentrate on protecting Mexicans against activities such as robbery, kidnapping, extortion, and other crimes than to engage in a losing battle to help Washington keep narcotics away from its consumers? These are questions that the new Mexican administration is facing. Already President Peña Nieto has signaled his intention to adapt the country's security strategy by shifting it away from drug interdiction and toward a concerted effort to protect Mexicans from violence and organized crime.

President Peña Nieto's Policy Changes

Although drug trafficking, organized crime, corruption, and immigration present negative issues in the bilateral relationship, it is important to recognize that many other aspects of the relationship are positive and give both countries the opportunity to cooperate. The time has come for the new Mexican government serving for the 2012–18 *sexenio* (six-year presidential term) to "de-securitize" the bilateral agenda and prioritize other aspects of its relationship with the United States. While it is inevitable that both countries will continue to work on reducing the violence associated with organized crime, the focus should be on those issues that could bring the United States and Mexico closer together—our economies, the stability of our financial systems, North American trade and investment, regional cooperation in Latin America and the Caribbean, as well as problems that affect both countries in a global context.

As we look toward a resolution of the international economic and financial crisis that has characterized the last six years, Mexico needs to undertake a series of urgent domestic reforms that could help pave the way for a more just, prosperous, and peaceful society. Many of these changes have been known and debated for at least the last twenty years. Some are languishing in a legislature that has been unwilling to move the agenda forward for purely political reasons. Others are yet to be designed and presented. All relate to three basic themes:

—bringing about the rule of law and an end to corruption and impunity;
—dismantling the political, social, and private sector monopolies that are a drag on Mexico's competitiveness; and
—modernizing the country's energy sector.[17]

All of these changes can be accomplished with relative ease as long as there is the political will to implement them. Even those reforms that require constitutional amendments are within the realm of possibility if politicians understand that further delay is no longer possible. (For an extensive analysis of the reform process in Mexico, see chapter 3.) In the coming years, Mexico and the United States need to redirect their relationship toward improving Mexico's ability to grow and prosper, while at the same time prioritizing other aspects of cooperation that can make our common homeland a better place to live.

One of the pending items on the bilateral agenda is strengthening the North American Free Trade Agreement. Almost two decades since entering into force, NAFTA has remained an unfinished and less than perfect regime because of the lack of supportive and articulate constituencies in all three countries. Furthermore, trade liberalization has become a domestic political challenge in the United States. While Europe, South America, Asia, and even Africa have spent the last two decades building on various economic zone arrangements, customs unions, and free trade areas, North America has made no effort to use the original treaty as a stepping-stone to further integration and cross-border facilitation. Little has been accomplished in improving NAFTA's framework despite seventeen years of experience. An effort in 2006, during which representatives of the private sector from all three countries met as a tri-national working group, the North American Competitiveness Council (NACC), recommended how to make North America more competitive through further integration, but failed when the governments of Canada, Mexico, and the United States ignored the more than fifty recommendations proffered.[18] The NACC's parent initiative, the Security and Prosperity Partnership, has faded into oblivion, because the United States was mainly interested in the security aspect, while Mexico believed that security could only come with economic prosperity.

The time has come for the three governments and their private sectors to review the functioning of the free trade area and propose further steps to make the region more competitive in the face of increased integration efforts elsewhere in the world. NAFTA has had positive effects in all three countries, and there is no reason why it shouldn't be a work in progress. Now that the United States and a group of Pacific Rim countries have decided to pursue a Trans-Pacific Partnership (TPP), it is especially important that the three NAFTA governments coordinate their negotiating positions. In October 2012 Mexico and Canada were accepted as full parties to the negotiations after a belated decision to join what the United States now considers one of its highest priority foreign policy objectives: increasing its presence and politico-economic ties with the Asia-Pacific region. If and when the TPP becomes a reality, it will constitute—

together with NAFTA and the European Union—one of the most important regional economic cooperation agreements in force.

Another area of cooperation between the two countries results from Mexico's membership in the G-20. Although currently still in a crisis management mode to deal with the global financial emergency, if it is to survive and continue to be relevant, the G-20 must evolve into more of an international "steering committee" where deadlocked global issues can be discussed at the highest political level and solutions found to solve pressing international deadlocks. Some of these are already on the G-20 agenda—climate change, food security, and development—but others are yet to be discussed by the group, for instance, transnational organized crime, trade negotiations, conventional weapons transfers. Mexico and the United States need to consult as closely and as often as possible to ensure that the G-20 process corresponds to our shared interests.

The same holds true in the United Nations, Organization of American States, and other multilateral forums. Although Mexico and the United States might not always see eye-to-eye on the positions each country takes on some of the proposals discussed in these organizations, it behooves both governments to consult on as many of them as possible and seek to harmonize positions as much as possible. This is especially important now that other regional powers like China, India, and Brazil are playing such important roles in determining the global agenda. Sporadic meetings of policy planning staffs and foreign affairs officials need to be institutionalized and lead to regularly scheduled, periodic consultations on bilateral, regional, and international issues of the day.

Revising Mexican Policy toward the Region

Our common region—Latin America and the Caribbean—should be yet another area of common interest. The Obama administration has so far given a very low priority to its regional foreign policy, with the exception of Mexico, Cuba, and to some extent Brazil. Little has been said or done about the proliferation of radical leftist governments in Venezuela, Nicaragua, Ecuador, Bolivia, and Argentina and the resulting divisions within the traditional Latin American family.

I recognize that it is increasingly difficult to speak of "a Latin America." Rather, five different, subregional entities appear to have replaced the nineteenth-century French notion of a *latinized* America. The current reality is separate and distinct political, economic, and ideological groupings, namely,

Brazil and its Southern Cone neighbors; the Andean ALBA nations (Venezuela, Ecuador, Bolivia, Nicaragua, and Cuba); the Central American and Spanish-speaking Caribbean countries, excluding Cuba and Nicaragua; the English-speaking Caribbean; and Mexico.[19] Mexico and the countries of Central America are all quite distinct in their political, economic, and social structures and in the ideological makeup of their current governments. At the outset of his administration, President Calderón proclaimed a new era in Mexico's relationship with Latin America, but the reality never matched the rhetoric.

Mexico's ties with Cuba remained tense and confrontational during the Calderon administration, in spite of the president's declared objective of "repairing" the damaged relationship that he said his predecessor had left him. There were half-hearted attempts at smoothing ill feelings between Havana and Mexico City, but no real progress was made either on the trade and investment side or on the human rights and democracy agenda that Mexico considers a priority. Notwithstanding a quick, last-minute visit to Havana in March 2012, President Calderón closely followed the previous policy of keeping Cuban relations at arm's length. Problems relating to Cuban debt owed to Mexico's development bank and to Cuban migrants in Mexico remain unresolved.

For its part, Havana does not seem to be particularly interested in courting Mexico. Notwithstanding, it is clear that Raúl Castro's gradual changes to the Cuban economy offer Mexico and the United States new opportunities for collaboration and even joint participation in future investments as the island moves toward opening up its economy. This option alone creates an opportunity for both Washington and Mexico City to consult closely on Cuban developments. President Peña Nieto has met with Cuba's Raúl Castro and there now seems to be a genuine desire within both governments to normalize the relationship in the coming months.

Economic relations with Brazil are substantial, but there remain unsolved trade issues in the automotive sector. Furthermore, the Mexican private sector is opposed to the idea of a broader free trade agreement with Brazil. Venezuela is a thorn in the side of many Latin American governments, and Mexico is no exception. President Chavez's decision to nationalize most of Mexican private sector investments in his country led to a tense and confrontational relationship. Many of the above examples are similar to those faced by the U.S. government, so there should be room for mutual consultation and decisions on how to deal with them. It is still too early to tell whether Chavez's passing will result in an improved relationship with Venezuela, but the new government in Caracas will hopefully understand that it stands to benefit from changing the confrontational tactics that characterized the Chavez years.

Mexico should play a greater role in shaping the U.S. agenda toward Latin America and the Caribbean. There is no other country in the region that has one foot in North America and the other south of the Rio Bravo. Working together, Mexico and the United States could devise foreign policy initiatives that would bring other nations in the region closer together. One way of accomplishing this would be for Washington to help Mexico in its budding efforts to establish a development assistance program for the neediest countries of the region.

Contradictory foreign policy initiatives like the CELAC (Comunidad de Estados Latinoamericanos y Caribeños [Community of Latin American and Caribbean States]), which exclude the United States from regional groupings, are counterproductive to establishing a mutually advantageous hemispheric relationship.[20] Instead of creating new regional bodies, Mexico, together with the United States, should work toward strengthening those existing groups that have shown their usefulness and abolishing others that no longer serve much of a purpose.

Finally, Mexico and the United States need to redirect their respective priorities toward one another. Finger pointing and mutual recrimination have never produced desired results, and neither country can claim to be without blame for the current perceptions of a tense and confrontational relationship. The advances made in mutual trust, shared intelligence, and better bilateral mechanisms need to be matched by the political rhetoric. Hopefully, the coincidence of two presidential elections in 2012, with a new Mexican administration and a re-elected Barack Obama, will pave the way for a stronger and more diversified Mexico-U.S. relationship based on shared interest and strategic partnership.

Notes

1. The PRI governed Mexico for seventy-one years until its defeat in 2000 by PAN, a right-of-center political party that had never before won a national election.

2. Carlos Salinas de Gortari, Mexico's president from 1988 to1994, initiated negotiations with Washington for a *Tratado de Libre Comercio* (TLC, known in English as NAFTA). This followed a similar free trade agreement with Canada.

3. In 1994 Mexico became the first country to be admitted to the OECD since New Zealand in 1973 and the first-ever developing economy to join the so-called rich country club.

4. Before his election to the presidency, Vicente Fox was employed by the Coca-Cola Company to manage relations with Mexican bottlers.

5. For a detailed report of how the Bush administration viewed President Fox's proposals on immigration, see "Bush Prepares for Mexico's Fox Visit," September 5, 2001, Presidency of the Republic website (http://fox.presidencia.gob.mx/en/search/?contenido=1758&pagina=1&palabras=foreign+policy).

6. Doris Meissner and others, *Immigration Enforcement in the United States: The Rise of Formidable Machinery* (Washington, D.C.: Migration Policy Institute, January 2013) (www.migrationpolicy.org/pubs/enforcementpillars.pdf).

7. "Managing the United States-Mexico Border: Cooperative Solutions to Common Problems" (www.consejomexicano.org/images/publicaiones/Visin_Frontera_Mxico_Estados_Unidos_Ingls.pdf).

8. "Building a North American Community: Report of the Independent Task Force on the Future of North America" (www.cfr.org/canada/building-north-american-community-report-independent-task-force-future-north-america/p8138).

9. Meissner and others, *Immigration Enforcement*, p. 150, table A-1. Percentages provided by Eduardo Medina Mora, Mexico's ambassador to the United States, in an interview with Diana Negroponte at Brookings Institution, February 21, 2013.

10. Often referred to in Mexico as *ninis*, an abbreviation of *ni estudian, ni trabajan* (those who neither study nor work).

11. This undercover operation by the U.S. Bureau of Alcohol, Tobacco, Firearms and Explosives in 2010 and 2011 allowed hundreds of assault weapons to be carried into Mexico, ostensibly as a way of determining how the smuggling networks functioned. One of these weapons was subsequently traced to the killing of a drug enforcement agent in Mexico, which in turn led to a congressional investigation, the resignation of ATF's director, and an extremely tense relationship between the Obama administration and the Calderón government.

12. Also called Plan Mérida, the strategy was meant to be "an unprecedented partnership between the United States and Mexico to fight organized crime and associated violence while furthering respect for human rights and the rule of law. Based on principles of shared responsibility, mutual trust, and respect for sovereign independence, the two countries' efforts have built confidence that is transforming the bilateral relationship." See www.state.gov/r/pa/plrmo/157797.htm. See also Congressional Reserach Service, *U.S. Mexican Security Cooperation: The Merida Initiative and Beyond*, Washington D.C., January 14, 2013 (www.fas.org/sgp/crs/row/R41349.pdf).

13. Interview with Eduardo Medina Mora, February 21, 2013. From 2006 to 2011 Mexico's budget for direct security-related expenditures ballooned by 295 percent, going from approximately $10 billion to over $46 billion.

14. The term "insatiable demand" was first coined by Secretary of State Hillary Clinton during her first visit to Mexico under the Obama administration in March 2009.

15. See the Joint Declaration by the XIII Summit of Heads of State and Government of the Tuxtla Dialogue, December 5, 2011 (www.presidencia.gob.mx/2011/12/declaracion-conjunta-sobre-crimen-organizado-y-narcotrafico).

16. Former presidents Ernesto Zedillo of Mexico, Fernando Henrique Cardoso of Brazil, and César Gaviria of Colombia have been joined by currently serving heads of state Hugo Pérez of Guatemala and Juan Manuel Santos of Colombia in calling for a comprehensive review of the issue. American public opinion is tilting toward a majority in favor of decriminalizing less harmful drugs such as marijuana.

17. Political parties, state-owned monopolies in oil and electricity, labor unions, telecommunications providers, media conglomerates, and private sector oligopolies are all parts of the Mexican system that need to change if the country is to fulfill its potential.

18. The NACC was an official tri-national working group of the Security and Prosperity Partnership of North America (SPP). It was created at the second summit of the SPP in Cancún, Quintana Roo, Mexico, in March 2006. The SPP is an agreement between the leaders of the United States, Canada, and Mexico to work toward a more integrated North American economy and security region. Composed of thirty corporate representatives from some of North America's largest companies, the NACC was mandated to set priorities for the SPP and to act as a stable driver of the integration process through changes in government in all three countries.

19. Venezuelan president Hugo Chavez founded the Alianza Bolivariana para los Pueblos de Nuestra America (ALBA) in 2004 as a gathering of socialist and social democratic countries committed to regional economic integration based on social welfare. A common anti-U.S. rhetoric also defines the member countries.

20. CELAC, which is composed of thirty-three Latin American member states, was officially launched in Venezuela on December 3, 2011. The regional bloc aims to establish regional unification through political and economic integration. Unlike the Organization of American States, CELAC includes Cuba as a full member and excludes the United States and Canada.

Acronyms

Acronym	Spanish	English
AMAI	Asociación Mexicana de Agencias de Investigación de Mercado y Opinión Pública	Mexican Association of Agencies for Market Research and Public Opinion
ATF		Bureau of Alcohol, Tobacco, Firearms, and Explosives
CARSI		Central American Regional Security Initiative
CBP		U.S. Customs and Border Patrol
CBSI		Caribbean Basin Security Initiative
CELAC	Comunidad de Estados Latino-americanos y Caribeños	Community of Latin American and Caribbean States
CFE	Comisión Federal de Electricidad	Federal Electricity Commission
CISEN	Centro de Investigación y Segurdidad Nacional	Center for Research and National Security
CNDH	Comisión Nacional de Derechos Humanos	National Human Rights Commission
CNTE	Coordinadora Nacional de Trabajadores de la Educación	National Coordinator of Educational Workers
CRS		Congressional Research Service
DTO		Drug trafficking organization
EDII	Espacio Descubre, Interactúa, Imagina	Space Discover, Interact, Imagine
ENE	Estrategia Nacional de Energía	National Energy Strategy
ENLACE	Evaluación Nacional de Logro Académico en Centros Escolares	National Assessment of Academic Achievement in Schools

Acronym	Spanish	English
EZLN	Ejército Zapatista de Liberación Nacional	Zapatista Army of National Liberation
FASP	Fondo de Aportaciones para la Seguridad Pública	Fund for Public Security Provisions
FDN	Frente Democrático Nacional	National Democratic Front
IFE	Instituto Federal Electoral	Federal Electoral Institute
IMCO	Instituto Mexicano para la Competitividad	Mexican Institute for Competitiveness
INCLE		Bureau of International Narcotics and Law Enforcement Affairs
ITAM	Instituto Tecnológico Autónomo de México	Mexican Autonomous Institute of Technology
KMZ	Ku-Maloob-Zaap (campo de petróleo mexicano)	Ku-Maloob-Zaap (Mexican oil field)
PAN	Partido Acción Nacional	National Action Party
PANAL	Nueva Alianza Partido Político Nacional	National New Alliance Political Party
PEMEX	Petróleos Mexicanos	Mexican Petroleum
PGR	Procuraduría General de la República	Federal Attorney General's Office
PISA		Program for International Student Assessment
PRD	Partido de la Revolución Democrática	Party of the Democratic Revolution
PRI	Partido Revolucionario Institucional	Institutional Revolutionary Party
PROBEMS	Programa de Becas de Educación Media Superior	Secondary Education Scholarship Program
RENAME	Registro Nacional de Alumnos, Maestros, y Escuelas	National Registry of Students, Teachers, and Schools
SEDENA	Secretaría de la Defensa Nacional	Ministry of National Defense
SEGOB	Secretaría de Gobernación	Ministry of Government
SEMAR	Secretaría de Marina	Ministry of the Navy
SEP	Secretaría de Educación Pública	Ministry of Public Education
SNTE	Sindicato Nacional de Trabajadores de la Educacíon	National Educational Workers Union
SSP	Secretaría de Seguridad Pública	Ministry of Public Security
STPRM	Sindicato de Trabajadores Petroleros de la República Mexicana	Mexican Oil Workers' Union

Acronym	Spanish	English
SUBSEMUN	Subsidio para la Seguridad Pública en los Municipios	Subsidy for Municipal Public Security
TPP		Trans-Pacific Partnership
TRIFE	Tribunal Electoral de Poder Judicial de la Federación	Electoral Tribunal of the Federal Judiciary
UNAM	Universidad Nacional Autónoma de México	National Autonomous University of Mexico
USAID		U.S. Agency for International Development

About the Authors

ARMANDO CHACÓN is a consultant in the design and evaluation of education programs and policies for governments and not-for-profit organizations and a partner at Newell & Co. (www.newell.mx). He is a columnist for *El Economista* and co-author with Pablo Peña of *How to Change Stories: What Individuals, Firms, and Not-for-Profit Organizations Can Do for Education in Mexico* (Fondo de Cultura Económica, 2012). He was the research director at the Mexican Institute for Competitiveness and an economic adviser for several Mexican federal government agencies.

ARTURO FRANCO has worked with Cementos de Mexico (CEMEX) and the World Bank. Between 2008 and 2011, he was a Global Leadership fellow at the World Economic Forum, where he designed innovative programs for the annual Davos meeting as well as the forum's annual meeting in Latin America. He later joined the Center for International Development at Harvard University as a resident fellow.

EDUARDO GUERRERO is a partner at Lantía Consultores (www.lantiaconsultores.com), a public policy consulting firm based in Mexico City, where he works with policymakers from local and state governments throughout Mexico on security assessment. He has held senior positions at Mexico's Federal Electoral Authority (IFE), the Federal Institute for Transparency and Information Access (IFAI), and the Ministry of Social Development (SEDESOL). He has published numerous articles in *Nexos* magazine (www.nexos.com.mx) and in 2011 published *Security, Drugs and Violence in Mexico: A Survey* for the 7th North American Forum, Washington, D.C.

DIANA VILLIERS NEGROPONTE is a nonresident senior fellow at the Brookings Institution and a member of the Advisory Council at the Mexico Institute of the Woodrow Wilson International Center for Scholars. She practiced international trade law with Paul, Hastings, Janofsky & Walker. She is the author of *Seeking Peace in El Salvador: The Struggle to Reconstruct a Nation at the End of the Cold War* (Palgrave Macmillan, 2011). She writes frequently for the Brookings Institution's Latin America Initiative.

ANDRÉS ROZENTAL has served as Mexico's ambassador to the United Kingdom (1995–97), deputy foreign minister (1988–94), ambassador to Sweden (1983–88), and permanent representative to the United Nations in Geneva (1982–83) and has assumed various responsibilities within Mexico's Foreign Ministry. He holds the lifetime rank of Eminent Ambassador of Mexico. He is president of Rozental & Asociados, which specializes in corporate strategies in Latin America. He is the author of five books on Mexican foreign policy and numerous articles on international affairs. He is a nonresident senior fellow at the Brookings Institution, a trustee of the Migration Policy Institute, and a senior policy adviser at Chatham House in London.

CHRISTOPHER WILSON is an associate at the Mexico Institute of the Woodrow Wilson International Center for Scholars, where he develops the institute's research and programming on regional economic integration and U.S.-Mexico border affairs. He previously served as a Mexico analyst for the U.S. military and as a researcher for Robert Pastor, a professor of international relations and director of the Center for North American Studies at American University. In Mexico, he worked with the international trade consultancy Inteligencia Comercial en Negocios (IQOM). He is the author of *Working Together: Economic Ties between the United States and Mexico* (Woodrow Wilson International Center for Scholars, 2011) and has coauthored op-ed columns for the *Wall Street Journal* and *Dallas Morning News*.

DUNCAN WOOD became the director of the Mexico Institute at the Woodrow Wilson International Center for Scholars in January 2013. Previously, he was a professor and director of the Program in International Relations at the Instituto Tecnológico Autónomo de México (ITAM). He is also a senior associate at CSIS in Washington, D.C., and a researcher in the Centro de Derecho Económico Internacional at ITAM. From 2007 to 2009 he was the technical secretary of the Red Mexicana de Energía, a group of experts focused on energy policy in Mexico, and an evaluator for both the Fulbright–Garcia Robles Commission in Mexico and CONACT, Mexico's science and technology council. He is the author of numerous articles on energy and banking.

Index